1975

Happy Be[...]

[...]

Love

Mother & Dad

Naturalist in the Sudan

Charles Sweeney

Naturalist in the Sudan

Taplinger Publishing Company / New York

First published in the United States in 1974 by
TAPLINGER PUBLISHING CO., INC.
New York, New York

Originally published in Great Britain in 1973
as *Background of Baobabs*

Library of Congress Catalog Card Number: 73-17778

ISBN 0-8008-5466-7

For Kate and Danny
Allah yusallimak

Contents

Return to the jebels   13

And the rains came   24

Dindi and the mother of Tassels   38

Upturned carrots   51

Hyaenas, harvesting ants and hailstones   75

Big nose   94

Animated fir-cones   116

In the world of the bog-bird   140

Darfur journey   170

Leopards at large   196

The haunted jebel   215

Illustrations

between pages 54 and 55

Baobab tree

Duiker
Photo courtesy Peter Ward

Dindi as kitten

Ground hornbill
Photo courtesy Peter Ward

Patas monkey

Saddlebill stork
Photo courtesy Peter Ward

Crowned crane
Photo courtesy Peter Ward

between pages 112 and 113

Macrotermes mound nest

Cotton leaf-roller

Aphids on dura leaf

Odontotermes smeathmani carton over dura

Odontotermes queen surrounded by
big-headed soldiers on guard and workers

Stainer-bugs in scrum around
a single baobab seed

Black stink ants (*Megaponera*)

Idolum diabolicum

between pages 184 *and* 185

Bateleur eagle
Photo courtesy Peter Ward

Sacred ibis
Photo courtesy Peter Ward

Crocodile
Photo courtesy Peter Ward

Hippopotamus
Photo courtesy Peter Ward

Pangolins, Samsim and her son, Sam

Striped hyaena
Photo courtesy Peter Ward

Spotted hyaena
Photo courtesy Peter Ward

Nuba stick-fighters

Bracelet fight in progress at Jebel Kau

LINE DRAWINGS

Spotted eagle-ray   19

A stalk-eyed fly   26

Head of beaked snake   33

Baobab leaf and flower   57

Variations in shape of baobab fruits from
    many trees   60

Greater Kudu   69

Abyssinian roller 100

Large green blue-cheeked bee-eater 101

Sudan lungfish, which can reach a size of
two metres or more 153

Some birds of the Sudd 161

Sausage tree 167

Abdim's stork 181

Hunting-dogs and duikers, Darfur 189

Types of Nuba shields 217

Silver anklet; Nuba fighting bracelets,
Wetu spiked fighting bracelet,
Bahr el Ghazal 224

Nuba charms and cluster of *dom* nut
kernels, Jebel Fungor 227

Some tobacco pipes seen in the region 229

ENDPAPER MAPS

The Nuba Mountains *between pages* 11 *and* 12

Region travelled in Bahr el Ghazal
and Darfur *between pages* 171 *and* 172

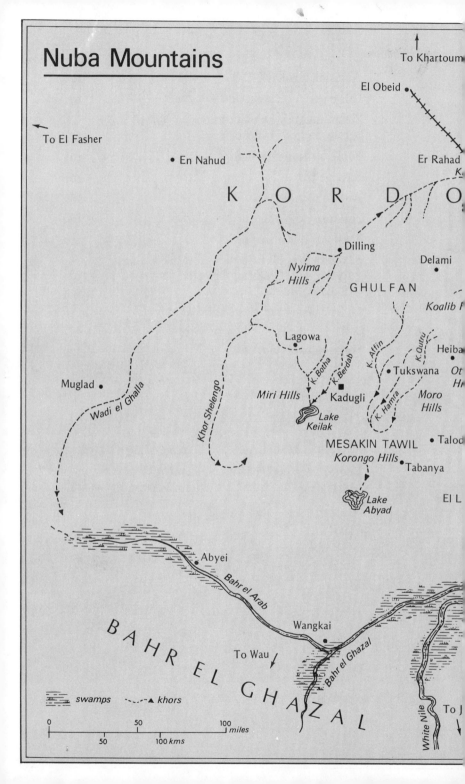

Nuba Mountains

To Khartoum

El Obeid

To El Fasher

En Nahud

Er Rahad

K.

K O R D O

Dilling

Delami

Nyima Hills

GHULFAN

Koalib F

Lagowa

K. Alfin

K. Qutru

Heiba

K. Botha

K. Berdab

Tukswana

Ot

H

Muglad

Wadi el Ghalla

Khor Shelengo

Miri Hills

Kadugli

K. Hamra

Moro Hills

Lake Keilak

MESAKIN TAWIL

Talo

Korongo Hills

Tabanya

El L

Lake Abyad

Abyei

Bahr el Arab

Wangkai

B A H R   E L

To Wau

Bahr el Ghazal

To J

White Nile

G H A Z A L

swamps

khors

| 0 | 50 | 100 miles |
| 50 | 100 kms | |

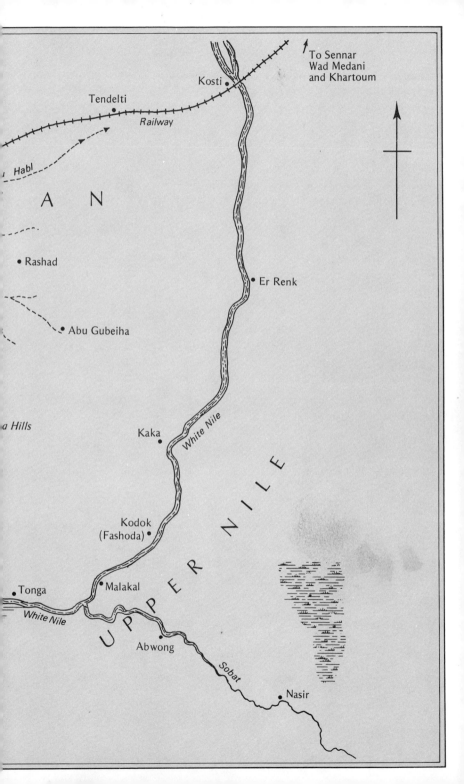

Return to the jebels

Wading into the warm water of Suakin harbour on the Sudan's Red Sea coast my first discovery came when I noticed little underwater explosions in the sand near my feet.

My movements had disturbed a colony of crumb-o'-bread sponges whose grey shapes were studded with conical vents, like miniature volcanoes, some of which forcibly ejected water together with small particles of matter that drifted in suspension in the clear sea. For a time I watched the sponges fascinated by the way they sucked in water through some of their vents, discharging it from others, but then I collected one to take back with me. I found a few bath sponges, too small to be of any commercial value, and some shiny orange and red calcareous sponges.

I was particularly pleased to find the bath sponges, for I did not think my staff at Kadugli, one thousand five hundred kilometres further south in the Nuba Mountains, had believed me when I had told them there were minute animals in the sea which together produced a skeleton, when dried, that was softer and longer-lasting than the finest loofah gourd. The loofah, of course, was familiar to them all being often grown over huts, the plant providing young fruit for eating and old, dried fruits for scrubbing and scouring.

It was not long before I discovered that there were more forms of life in the lagoon than I could possibly hope to collect. The coral rocks, themselves alive and ranging in colour from bright orange to blue with crimson fingers, had their interstices filled with other organisms, and forests growing on their surfaces. Here were living jewels of gently swaying anemones enhanced by the more subtle radiance of twenty kinds of seaweeds, trailing gracious fronds of green, bronze and purple. Like delicate flowers, stalked sea-lilies sinuously undulated their feathery branches in response to the stirring of the sea, a movement as caressing as the most dilatory of breezes, while flitting like tropical birds in this gay garden there swam fishes, mostly wrasses and butterfly-fish, a kaleidoscope of colours in bewildering permutations.

Returning from leave in England some two months before, I had driven overland to Africa via France, Switzerland, Italy to Venice, thence to Trieste, through Yugoslavia and south to Athens; then north again to Turkey, Syria and the Lebanon. In the Lebanon I found that if I continued through Israel I would not be able to enter Egypt; nor would the authorities allow me to proceed alone by the desert route through Saudi Arabia to Mecca's port of Jidda. I might have persuaded or eluded them, but I was not sure how I would then cross the Red Sea to reach the Sudan with my Land Rover. In the end, I found an Egyptian tramp steamer to take me and my car to Port Sudan.

At Port Sudan I took shelter for the night at 'The Flying Angel', the Missions to Seamen Institute, more comfortable and cheaper than the only hotel which was full anyway. The next morning I went to the hotel as arranged to meet Younis and Badr, my assistants, who should have travelled from Kadugli to meet me. I hardly expected to see them since I was two weeks overdue, but an hour later when they came down the road and saw me at the hotel their delight was as great as mine. It had taken them weeks to travel from Kadugli and they had arrived at Port Sudan more than three weeks earlier, but had had no money at all for the last ten days; fortunately they had found a kinsman to support them until I arrived.

At the end of June Port Sudan is no place to linger in, being one of the hottest places in the world. I paid Younis's debts, gathered their few belongings, and drove along the sandy road towards Suakin within two hours of our meeting, welcoming the movement that brought a hot breeze despite the dust carried with it that stuck to our damp skins.

Although I was anxious to return to my base at Kadugli, where I was a Research Entomologist mainly investigating agricultural pests, nevertheless, I thought I could spare two days at Suakin to collect marine specimens to show my staff.

Late that afternoon, as we drove into Suakin, I remembered its ancient history. It was for centuries the most important port of the Sudan, carrying most of the trade of the eastern region besides being the start of the route from the Red Sea to Berber and the valley of the Nile, about the only practical method of entering the country except up the Nile itself. Slaves, gold and silver, ivory, gum arabic, dried dates, grain, oil-seeds, beeswax, dom-nuts, mother of pearl and Trochus shells all passed through Suakin – especially slaves.

Suakin (probably meaning 'seven djinns') was the only town that did not eventually fall into the hands of the dervishes at the close of the nineteenth century, but in the eighteen years of the Mahdiya several battles were fought in the desert around the little seaport.

Finally the siege was lifted, and the dervishes forced to abandon the Red Sea littoral.

At the beginning of this century Suakin still contained a population of over ten thousand people, but its importance rapidly waned. When slavery was officially banned, dealers could no longer use Suakin as a port for slaves, and slaves for Arabia had been the main export.* But the chief reason for Suakin's

* Even today the slave-trade has not been stamped out. In 1967 it was officially estimated that there were still some two million slaves in the world.

final decline was the founding of a new port, Port Sudan, formally opened in 1909 which soon took all the trade from Suakin.

We drove past the crumbling coral wall that had resisted the besieging dervishes and in the centre of El Kef, as the mainland part of Suakin is called, I drew up beside one of the corroded field-guns, a howitzer now used as a convenient lolling post by El Kef's lethargic inhabitants. Two ramshackle *suq* lorries, haphazardly parked at angles to block the sandy roadway between the shabby, weatherbeaten Arab stores, and the drifting barefoot crowd held up our progress to the police-station.

I wanted to enquire where we could camp for the next two nights. Half the stores of El Kef seemed deserted and, as in most Sudanese towns, were lined in crazy rows, their corrugated iron roofs held down by large stones. They resembled an uneven line of playing card houses where the collapse of one would bring all the rest tumbling down.

At the police-station we found a smart Sudanese sergeant who told me I was welcome to use any of the erstwhile government buildings down by the waterfront; they were all deserted, he said, and nobody ever ventured there at night as they were populated by many ghosts.

The port of Suakin is built on a coral islet connected to El Kef by a causeway and viaduct. I had been surprised by the number of people in the mainland settlement, but as we reached the port buildings in the rapidly increasing gloom not a single person was to be seen. When I switched off the Land Rover engine, the eerie silence was broken only by an almost indecipherable sign hanging outside the forsaken shipping agent's office, creaking spasmodically like a disgruntled bullfrog.

The buildings on the harbour front were mostly of two or even three storeys and built of white coral, but there were considerable signs of decay. We made haste to move into one. On the top floor where it was slightly cooler I laid out my bedroll; the floor was rotting in places and there was a mildewed smell to the room, but it was somewhere to sleep.

That night all the seven djinns seemed to be active and I slept but fitfully. It was easy to understand why this part of Suakin was believed to be haunted. The wind moaned round the old building in purgatorial agony and there were creaks and groans, as if the coral foundation was gradually crumbling away. Bats flitted to and fro across my lofty room and rats seemed to play football in the roof.

When at last the great red eye of the sun stared through the cobwebbed, dusty windows my companions were relieved to find themselves still alive.

But now, as I waded about in the harbour, I had no thought of the previous night. Having obtained the sponges and a number of other specimens, I thought I would hire a boat to take me out to the reef that encircled the harbour to find coral samples and perhaps other specimens that I could not obtain close to the shore. Younis soon found a fisherman, Ismail Mohammed, willing to dive for coral.

At the reef Ismail pulled off his dirty *tob*, a garment resembling a mini-nightshirt, and stood clad in loose cotton drawers. For a moment he poised on the stern of the small boat, his stringy brown body disfigured by pale ugly patches of vitiligo, a common skin disease often mistaken for leprosy. Then he dived into the clear sea.

Younis and I watched his thin body grope slantingly downwards until his shadowy form merged with the murky obscurity of the jagged rocks. A flutter of cardinal fishes and wrasses scattered before him, shimmering as vividly in their blues, yellows and reds as butterflies. The dark form of a much larger fish, one of the rock-cods, loomed from tenebrosity into sunlit water and I glimpsed a large staring eye and stupid-looking mouth. Ismail surfaced again clutching a huge mass of red coral, so large that it was only with difficulty we could heave it into the boat. Then he dived again.

Soon I had all that I wanted, but Ismail proved of little use catching any active invertebrates, many of which he feared, and I decided that Younis and I could catch more ourselves by the deserted waterfront where the water was shallower. Ismail poled the two kilometres back to the islet where I paid him. It was midday, but I still had the afternoon and tomorrow to explore.

After lunch of cheese and biscuits I set Badr to wash the coral thoroughly and collect some of the larger organisms hidden in the crevices. I had only a limited amount of preservative for my catch, but I hoped that by washing it repeatedly and then drying it I could carry the coral to Kadugli intact. Once again I set off with Younis to see what else we could find in the relatively shallow sea by the waterfront buildings.

The bottom sand was infested by small flat-fishes, soles that were difficult to avoid for they were almost invisible until they moved. Unavoidably, I trod on one or two. I did them no harm for they squirmed out from below my feet, but I was momentarily alarmed for the other common fish inhabitant of the sand bed was a sting-ray.

This extraordinary fish resembles a skate, but has a whip-like tail that is four or five times the length of its body and equipped with vicious spines. Some of these rays attain a gigantic size and the tail can be used with such effect that flesh is cut to the bone, and occasionally fishermen are killed.

There are, of course, many different kinds of rays, but most inhabit shallow waters, feeding largely on molluscs, crustacea or seabed-dwelling fishes, their flattened forms and large blunt teeth being adaptions for this kind of life. I knew that there were rays present for in the distance I had seen two chasing each other like great flat stones skimming across the surface of the sea, but I had taken little notice of this unusual activity.

It was not until I was about to put my feet down after swimming a short distance through deeper water that I saw the ominous outlines of a dozen or more sting-rays resting almost body to body

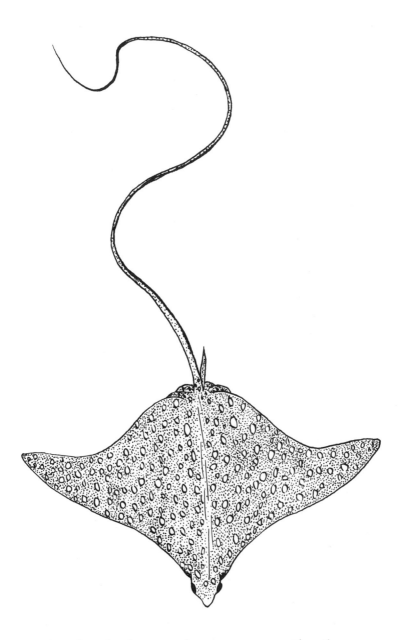

Spotted eagle-ray, may be two metres across with a tail
three or four times as long as its body

below me. They were not very large, perhaps ten or twelve centimetres across, and probably spotted eagle-rays, but I did not stay to investigate. Thereafter, I felt more secure by staying in water I could stand up in and I moved about more cautiously.

I had not forgotten the day some years before when I waded into the sea from the great, deserted sands of Pangani in Tanganyika. Owing to the currents set up by the Pangani River, bathing there could be dangerous at high tide, but then the tide was out. I had to splash a few hundred metres to reach deeper water, but no sooner had I begun to swim than I received a tremendous shock that momentarily paralysed me. It must have been caused by an electric ray, although I did not see anything. Spluttering, I managed to reach shallower water and find my feet; in record time I splashed back to dry land – what a distance it seemed – to collapse exhausted but without serious hurt. I have never liked rays since.

I saw several other sting-rays at Suakin, but I managed to avoid them. I finished collecting that afternoon and spent the next day chiefly indulging my curiosity.

The sea-cucumbers, for example, fascinated me. I spent the greater part of an hour watching one. Like a great leathery caterpillar it crept about on tiny tube-feet on the seabed, the sausage-shaped body about ten or eleven centimetres long, but sometimes stretched so greatly as it moved that it became almost twice this length. The feet appeared to have suckers while the tough brownish skin was studded with minute conical spots. Around the mouth at the more pointed end of the body were small, stubby, branched tentacles, and as it crept along the numerous feelers, arranged in a circle, pushed silt into its mouth allowing it to feed on microscopic organisms in the sand and mud.

At that time I knew little about the cotton-spinner or nigger holothurian, one of the most interesting of twenty or so British sea-cucumbers, but the species I was watching was its close relative. What particularly intrigued me was its method of defence. When I prodded the animal somewhat unkindly with a very spiny rock-whelk, it contracted, reacting in much the same way as some caterpillars. But when I poked it again the result was astonishing. The hind end swelled and then seemed to burst so that the entrails were ejected into the water; from these there rapidly developed a milky fluid that coalesced into numerous sticky white threads several centimetres in length.

These strands became attached to my rock-whelk and hand and would certainly have greatly impeded any normal predator intent on devouring the sea-cucumber. Although it might be thought that such a reckless squandering of internal organs would lead to its speedy demise, and that being devoured by a predator might be preferable, the animal crept away again after a few moments, apparently not incapacitated.

When I returned to England I found out more about sea-cucumbers and, as I had guessed, they almost certainly regenerate their lost viscera, while the white mucus is contained in special cells that, when deposited in water, break open, the contents forming the white threads. There is nothing very unusual in such a form of defence, although this was the first marine creature to use such a method that I had witnessed, and to use the guts for such a purpose was certainly strange. Amongst primitive snakes and some lizards the ejection of evil-smelling fluids from the cloaca is a common although not very efficient method of trying to repel a predator. Some mammals and spiders have a similar habit. But other spiders and some insects (notably, in Africa, the pear-headed soldiers of many Nasutitermitinae, a sub-family of termites) also produce sticky white threads to entangle their attackers, although these strands emanate from glands in the head and cause no injury to their owners.

This was not the only sea-cucumber I found. I saw more of the same kind and several other species. One that lived on the coral had long slender sticky feelers or tentacles, but instead of scooping up its food and stuffing its mouth with silt, the slimy tentacles caught tiny animals swimming past. The prey adhered to the tentacles, and then the sea-cucumber sucked the ends like a child with jammy fingers. Sea-cucumbers are really elongated sea-urchins, the biggest attaining a length of some two metres. Many people, including the Arabs of the Red Sea, eat them. The Chinese make a soup of the dried bodies, while *bêche-de-mer*, or *trepang* as the food is called in Malaya, is popular in many parts of the tropics. Although so slug-like, sea-cucumbers are radially symmetrical animals, like the starfish, the 'arms' running back from the mouth and fused with the body and so scarcely recognisable.

There were so many other creatures to attract my attention that, apart from half an hour to eat a meal, I spent most of the day in the sea. I examined star-fishes of several colours, brittle-stars of delicate shapes, curious sea-urchins, and several kinds of worms.

One tube-worm was common over large areas of the seabed. Hundreds of tubes, some as long as eight centimetres made from sand particles and fragments of shells glued together to decorate a tough silky sheath, like a miniature forest of tree stumps, were spread over the sand in shallow water, but for a long time I could not find the animals that made them. As soon as I approached the worm vanished almost instantaneously into its tube. When I pulled up tubes they were empty, the worm having escaped into the sand, but at last I did manage to see one of the occupants. Gradually, the tips of reddish-coloured tentacles were extruded from the tube until finally these formed a large, plumed fan that moved regally back and forth. The worm breathes by means of these tentacles which also gently waft small particles of food to the mouth.

Many other strange creatures occurred and, although I thought I had finished my collecting, I found there were two more animals I did not want to leave without. One was a giant prawn (*Palaemon*), and the other a cuttlefish, and both gave me great trouble for I had only a makeshift net.

I saw only half a dozen or so of the great prawns, so big that at first I thought they were crayfish. After a considerable time and a good deal of patience, Younis and I managed to capture a specimen that was twenty-three centimetres long, but some were even larger, probably exceeding thirty centimetres in length.

Although I had seen cuttlefish before I had never attempted to catch one by hand. The ones I found were all small, little more than fifteen centimetres long, but it took us half an hour to catch one. They not only swam swiftly but were adept at hiding in crevices or by burying their flattened, triangular bodies in the sand to leave only the top of the sinister head and big eyes exposed. Their camouflage was remarkable, the body being the exact colour of the sand and the exposed part of the head like a small stone or shell. We would only see this remarkable mollusc, whose great relatives are the largest of all invertebrates (one of the several kinds of giant squids is recorded at over twelve metres in length), when in alarm one would shoot out of the sand in a flurry of silt that clouded the water and prevented us from seeing where it settled again.

I had been interested but not surprised to learn from Ismail that fishermen sometimes caught a female cuttlefish in the breeding season and tethered it behind the boat to act as a decoy for the males. In this way dozens of males, attracted by the female, could be caught by hand. This custom is probably an ancient one, and certainly antedates Fabre's experiments with moths and all recent control work based on the sexual attraction of females of insects and other animals.

We had to catch our cuttlefish the hard way, however. Then I found I had no preservative left and so I let it go again. In the late afternoon when I finally dragged myself away from the sea in preparation for continuing my journey south, I had been immersed in that warm, briny water for so long that my skin was as soft and as wrinkled as if I had been pickled in formalin myself.

And the rains came

The late afternoon sun had lost none of its power as we left Suakin to cross the flat desert to the Red Sea Hills. Almost the only vegetation was brittle-brown grass sprouting in dense tufts from the bald red sand like hair from a mangy skin. Except for the speeding Land Rover and its twin streamers of dust hanging in the air with the persistence of vapour trails from an aircraft in a frozen sky, nothing visible moved in this barren world.

But soon we wound our way up Abent Pass to Sinkat and the Summit, high above the plain. Here the rocky hills were still arid but more decently clothed with spiny bushes, various euphorbias and stocky acacias and we disturbed a pair of rock pigeons. I stopped several times to examine plants. One shrubby bush, probably *Salsola*, gave out a faint but unmistakable smell of rotten meat, and we collected some euphorbias, unknown in the Nuba Mountains, to try and cultivate when we reached Kadugli.

At another place there grew dragon's blood trees belonging to the same family as sisal; somewhat resembling a palm with short, thick spreading branches, the tree I examined stood about two point three metres tall. Densely clustered at the ends of the branches the thick, rigid, sword-shaped leaves were each nearly sixty centimetres long. I was particularly interested in this tree* for I

* *Dracaena ombet.*

had not seen it before although I was familiar with other kinds in East Africa, ornamentals that had leaves quite different in appearance from these plain olive ones. The name 'dragon's blood' comes from the bright red resin produced by some kinds of these trees and used as a dye, chiefly for colouring varnishes. One exceptionally large tree★ in the Canaries (Oratava, Teneriffe) is reputed to be the most ancient plant in the world.

We camped some kilometres south of Sinkat at about one thousand metres altitude and several kilometres from the railway that runs from Port Sudan to Atbara. It had been raining softly here and the air was cool and fresh. New grass shoots were already pushing through the soil.

I had been warned that there was no road to Atbara suitable for vehicles and that on no account must I lose sight of the railway; only recently three men, attempting the route, had died in their vehicle (not a Land Rover). When found they had been scarcely two kilometres from the steel lines.

However, the road to Haiya, where the railway branches, one line to Kassala the other to Atbara, our destination on the Nile, was well marked with a good surface. Near Haiya we had to jettison much of the coral, the stench being so overpowering that it made us all feel sick, but I retained enough small pieces for my museum, well smothered in a box of sand.

We lost the railway several times on our journey, once when we found ourselves on an ancient camel track leading towards the interior of the Nubian Desert. In this region the rainfall is at most fifty to sixty millimetres annually, no rain falling in some years with a minimum drought in all years of nine months. Returning we disturbed three Isabella gazelles that fled quickly at our approach, but a Nubian bustard stalked away not bothering to fly from the crawling, bumping Land Rover.

On another occasion the track, indistinct for the past half an hour, simply stopped at a *wadi* so wide and precipitous that not

★ *D. draco.*

even the Land Rover could cross, but after a long detour, we managed to reach the railway again at Musmar, from which station a wide, well-beaten road took us all the rest of the way to Atbara where we arrived well after dark four days since leaving Suakin.

The rest-house was completely full as the Prime Minister and his entourage had arrived earlier, but after some argument with the management, who felt my dishevelled appearance, dusty Land Rover and lean-to tents did not improve the view, we camped in the grounds, my dinner being brought on a tray by an immaculate waiter.

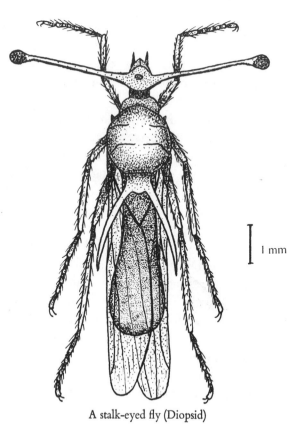

1 mm

A stalk-eyed fly (Diopsid)

From Atbara it was an easy journey following the Nile to Khartoum and then beside the Blue Nile to Wad Medani, the headquarters of the Research Division.

I was held up at Medani but, having first obtained a trailer with food and other supplies to take back with me to Kadugli, and also Mohammed, a driver, I left at the end of July. The rains were exceptionally heavy that year and the going was bad even between Medani and Sennaar, but the deserted land, now filled with thrusting cotton bushes, was a restful green after the desert glare, and every canal thronged with birds. However, soon we wished we were back in the desert.

I had hoped to reach Kosti that day, but when we turned west at Sennaar to follow the railway that ran across the clay plain like a taut umbilical cord a hundred and twelve kilometres long the carburettor gave trouble. Apart from a puncture in Yugoslavia this was the only time my vehicle had dictated a halt for nearly ten thousand kilometres of driving. We spent the night on the plain.

The next morning, in treacly black mud, we progressed twenty kilometres in five hours. The viscous clay built up on the wheels until they bound solidly, and the trailer had to be uncoupled and then winched across some particularly bad patches. Eventually, our way was blocked by a great river of tumbling water, one of the *wadis* normally crossed unnoticed in dry weather. The water was much too wide and deep to attempt to ford. I looked at the railway. The lines approached the *wadi* on an embankment and were carried across on a simple bridge consisting only of twin girders supporting the rails above. There were no sides.

Having measured the viaduct in the pouring rain, I judged that if I drove across the wheels of the Land Rover would just fit with about ten centimetres to spare. The rails were too wide apart for the wheels of my vehicle to straddle them, too close together for the wheels to be inside the two rails, so the wheels would have to be inside one rail and outside the other bringing them very close to the ends of the sleepers. But rather than remain there, perhaps for days, I decided to attempt the crossing.

Like a stiff-legged tortoise the Land Rover limped from sleeper to sleeper. I decided to take off the doors before crossing; then at least if the vehicle bumped off I should have a chance of escape. It took five minutes to reach the centre, Mohammed walking backwards to guide my control of the unseen wheels. Then came disaster. One of the back wheels had crept too near the end of a sleeper; at the next bump forward the Land Rover gave a great lurch, thudded down on the back axle, tilted over towards the drop but miraculously remained balanced.

After the initial lurch I sat quite still. The vehicle rocked slightly, but I dared not attempt to get out.

My companions came up. 'Walk, don't run!' I shouted, as their slight vibration of the bridge communicated itself to the Land Rover. 'Bring the rope, Badr,' I said more calmly. 'Younis and Mohammed, hold the Land Rover, try and stop it falling.' They clung to the side. 'Let's hope a train doesn't come along.'

'*Inshalla!*' muttered Younis and Mohammed in unison.

Once the rope was tied securely to the Land Rover and around a sleeper, I felt it was safe for me to move. After half an hour's struggle with the two jacks, moving the back wheel a few centimetres at a time, we managed to straighten the vehicle. I had to drive over three more such viaducts before we approached Kosti but there was no other serious mishap.

The bridge spanning the Nile at Kosti, which carries both the railway and a single track for vehicles, is a permanent, steel structure, a real bridge, but at this time was isolated at each end by the floodwater for the river had broken its banks and was so high that only another metre or so in depth would have sent the water swirling over instead of under the tall bridge. However, with Younis and Mohammed wading in front I managed to drive the Land Rover onto the bridge. It was a curious sensation to drive surrounded by the river as far as the eye could see, and a relief to feel the marooned bridge below the tyres.

Kosti, on the far side, was lower and there the Nile flowed a mile wide from its normal course; some seven hundred houses had been destroyed, ineffectual earth barricades had been thrown up and debris floated everywhere. The only possible way through the town was our old ally the railway, built on an embankment still, fortunately, not seriously breached.

The storm had not been severe west of Kosti and the going, on the sandy soil, became good for a time. Between Tendelti and Umm Ruwaba we discovered the worst plague of millipedes I had ever seen. There were gaps, but for about thirty kilometres I estimated there was a mean of about ten millipedes for every metre we travelled, their flowing brown bodies surging across the sandy roadway in uncountable hundreds of thousands, all progressing in the same direction from south to north and keeping where possible to the shady places but not averse to crossing the sunlit road when necessary.

Those crossing the road to the north vanished in *sim-sim* fields or the grass, and it was not possible to discover the starting place of the incredible hordes that poured in from the south. The damp sand looked as though it had been raked there were so many tracks left by the passing millipedes, and in several places I noticed that squashed toads or beetles on the roadway were being eaten by the migrating creatures. Most kinds of millipedes are not only primarily vegetarian but largely nocturnal, and are often destructive to crops, but I could find no damage to the *sim-sim* on this occasion. Later I saw several other migrations of millipedes, but never again did I witness such numbers.

With only about a hundred and fifty kilometres to travel before we reached home, our difficulties increased with every kilometre. The track, distinct enough in the dry season, often vanished, obliterated by the almost continual rain and grasses that had grown a metre or even two metres tall. Several times we became temporarily lost. Only by the use of the compass and scouting ahead did we manage to reach Umm Berembeita, a village sixty-odd kilometres from Rashad, a journey that took fourteen hours.

As we entered Umm Berembeita yet another violent storm broke behind us. The village situated on black cotton soil, clay of the worst kind, was completely waterlogged. It took an hour to get the Land Rover and trailer the last kilometre to the rest-house, a thatched roofed, two-room adobe building on the bank of a large *khor,* the Abl Hubl, but there was at least shelter for the night.

The next morning, the great storm upstream having raged all night although little rain had fallen at Umm Berembeita itself, I looked at the *khor* which we had to cross to continue our journey, but the rushing water had risen considerably higher during the night. Last time I had been there the rest-house had been some fifteen metres from the river; now it stood about three metres from the edge of the water, the Abl Hubl having eaten into the high bank.

As I watched the fast rising, reddish-brown flood tumbling by with gurgles as of satisfaction, a wave came down like a tidal bore, bearing on its crest and aftermath, amid a miscellany of debris, a goat twisting and turning in the rushing torrent. Another dead goat floated by and then the brown body of a woman, naked save for a blue cloth fragment round her neck and over her head; an eddy near the far bank caught her for a moment, and then the current took her once more and she swirled out of sight, an arm flung up for an instant as though imploring help. But she was past the aid of any man. A few minutes later the high flood had passed, but the water was still about three metres deep in the middle.

We fixed a stake in the bank to judge when the level rose or fell but, at least for that day, we were stranded.

Later the rain and wind stopped, and the sun redly emerged to draw the water vapour and smells from the saturated land and turn the air to steam.

That day I walked – or rather sloshed and slipped – in the

vicinity of the rest-house. The country was too flooded for me to make much progress, but I hoped I might find something of interest brought forth by the flood. However, I found nothing out of the ordinary that day.

By nightfall the water in the Abl Hubl had dropped only slightly, but such a torrent could not last much longer. Further north-east the upper reaches of the Abl Hubl flowed for months, but here the water normally subsided quickly unless there were further considerable storms upstream. I hoped that we would be able to continue our journey within the following two days.

The next day it was as hot, smelly and steamy as the day before, but it was the second day without rain. I collected a number of insects, including some stalk-eyed flies (Diopsids). These bizarre flies have eyes at the end of five millimetres long, rigid stalks, one on each side of the head, and hundreds were resting together on a leafy bush, flying up in a buzzing cloud when I disturbed them but soon settling again. They are common enough in Africa, especially in moist surroundings, but little is known of their biology and this was a kind I had not seen before.

The floods had disclosed numbers of normally secretive creatures, forcing them out from their retreats, and almost every plant or higher ground had its quota of subterranean or terrestrial spiders and insects. I went to examine an island caused by the flood water. Two burrowing vipers lay coiled in some rocks, but I let them go, pushing them with a stick into the water where they swam away. I moved the remaining rocks more carefully, holding them at the exposed surface and not putting my hand below. I had no wish to be bitten especially while without anti-serum.

A long whip-snake* closely followed by a large skink (in reverse of the usual order for whip-snakes feed largely on lizards) shot away between my legs so quickly that the snake nearly touched me as it passed, but by the time I had swung round to watch it was just an arrowhead wake in the water. The skink, fat

* *Coluber florulentus.*

body waddling with effort, had just reached the water's edge; plunging in it swam off like an overweight rumba-dancer.

Greatly encouraged by all this activity I found another temporary island – this time larger, an ancient termite mound covered with grasses, a bush or two and scattered rocks. It yielded a most interesting snake. I just managed to catch the reptile's tail before it vanished. I pulled gently, then more firmly, but the snake obstinately remained anchored. I did not know what kind of reptile I had grasped, but even the few centimetres of tail that I held was sufficient to indicate that it was one I had not seen before.

I gradually let the reptile move forward so that the grip it had in the hole was loosened, and then I pulled again. This time the snake came free. It was a spotted beaked-snake,★ a non-venomous rarity I was very pleased to obtain alive. With the bird-like beak formed by the upper jaw projecting beyond the lower and curved slightly downwards, and the steel-grey body with lighter whitish spots it is a very distinctive species.

After some time and the removal of more rocks, I found fourteen centipedes,† all the same kind. Never before had I seen so many at once. I put them in a box to keep them alive for study; little was known about the life of this poisonous animal. The largest of my specimens were only about seven centimetres in length, but years later – in Central Africa – I found many twice this size.

This centipede is widespread in Africa and in many places the commonest of the large venomous kinds. It is beautifully coloured; often the body is yellowish-brown with a broad dark green stripe down the back, translucent bluish-green legs, head and antennae, with the hind legs and part of the body orange, but there is considerable variation in colour. The front legs are red and contain the poison-glands that open through the claws, but they are projected forwards and modified to form sickle-shaped

★ *Scaphiophis albopunctatus.*
† *Scolopendra morsitans.*

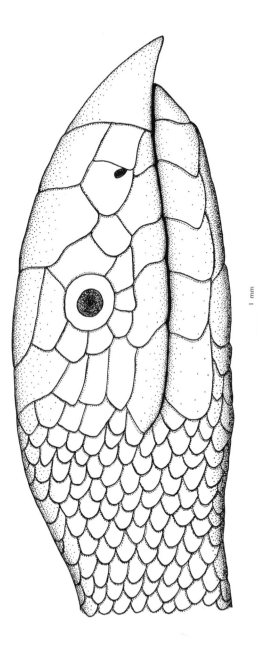

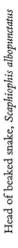

1 mm

Head of beaked snake, *Scaphiophis albopunctatus*

jaws. A centipede's bite rapidly kills small creatures, and causes severe but local and usually temporary symptoms in man, similar to those caused by some snake bites.

It was not for some years that I saw people bitten by this centipede for I was never bitten myself. In each case there was severe local pain that spread along the affected limb, with an accompanying rise in temperature, dizziness and headache. Some swelling and pain lasted for two or three days by which time the symptoms passed.

This handsome but dangerous creature feeds on large invertebrates, especially grasshoppers, cockroaches and their kin, terrestrial beetles and other common insects, but tackles almost any animal to the size of a small lizard or frog. In the Nuba Mountains it lays eggs in April and May, prior to the rains, and the female tends the young for several weeks. It is active throughout the rains, especially at night, but more or less dormant during the driest part of the year, November to February or March, although as it often frequents moister places and is largely nocturnal it is not always greatly affected by the macro-climate.

Apart from a few beetles and wind-spiders or solifuges, many of the latter having taken refuge from the floods on tree trunks, although normally they never climb trees, I found little for the next hour or two, and it was not until the late afternoon that I made my final discovery.

The dense thicket I intended to explore was another temporary island, and as usual I stood still for several minutes looking and listening before I began to search. After a minute a gabar goshawk, unable to bear my silent presence any longer, flew blackly from the thicket flaunting her white barred tail, closely followed by a black flycatcher. At first I detected no other sign of life, but in a moment or two I heard a stealthy movement in the undergrowth as some animal began to force a way through the vegetation away from me.

As quietly as I could, I crawled into the thicket hoping at least to glimpse the creature. By the sounds I was sure it was a small mammal, or possibly a bird, but just after I had burrowed into the damp undergrowth and was trying to free myself from the embrace of the thorny branches, a sound as of a large and angry snake, still invisible but very close, caused me to stop wriggling and lie as one dead.

I could scarcely imagine more awkward circumstances in which to face a marooned and irritable cobra or mamba for I was prone, almost inextricably caught in the thorns and quite unable to protect myself. Scarcely breathing, I listened. There was a long moment of silence, a movement, and then the hissing sound was repeated. This time, however, I recognised it with relief as not that of a snake but the enraged spitting of some kind of cat or viverrid.

Heedless now of scratches, I tore my way forward and almost at once my head emerged in the interior of the covert near the base of a tree. A few leafless stems of climbers criss-crossed the leaf-littered hollow but little light penetrated the riotous growth overhead. Almost invisible in the dappled gloom was a small animal, spotted like a genet but long-legged, with a cat's head bearing comparatively enormous ears. It attempted to escape into thicker vegetation, but I managed to catch hold of the ringed tail.

For a moment it strained away, spitting and snarling in fear, the white spots on the backs of the ears seeming to glow brilliantly, but the sodden leaves on the ground slipped under its feet and the next moment the cub was in my arms. Very bedraggled but full of life, it hissed and struggled but made little attempt to scratch or bite.

With great difficulty I elbowed my way backwards out of the thicket and stood up. While stroking the struggling kitten I examined it carefully, recognising now that it was a serval that I had found. Despite the wet and matted coat, a cut on the foreleg and its starving condition, the little animal seemed quite healthy. Almost certainly to leave it there would have meant its death from starvation and cold. I decided to take it with me.

Back at the rest-house I soon arranged a box of dry fresh grass for the cub to lie in, and gave it some corned beef, all the meat I had. The serval sniffed suspiciously and then retreated to press itself close against the side of the box. But forcing open the animal's mouth I managed to make it swallow a small piece of meat. As soon as this was down, I pushed its nose gently into the rest of the meat. Now the cub hardly hesitated, and finally wolfed all that was there. When I closed the box the serval was contentedly curled up prepared for sleep.

By mid-morning of the third day the water of the Abl Hubl seemed low enough to attempt a crossing. Ominous violet-grey skies to the east made me determined to leave. If we did not cross at once the rain upstream might keep us there for days or even weeks longer.

Three hours later, with the help of about thirty villagers, we were across the river, and despite increasing difficulties and unceasing rain since we left the Abl Hubl we reached Umm Sheheita, a small village of sodden, mouldering huts, disintegrating and entirely deserted for the rainy season. It was not until we reached Tukswana, however, less than twenty-five kilometres from home, that a deep torrent of filthy water in the *khor* there, the final serious obstacle, brought us to a complete halt. Our journey from Wad Medani so far had taken twenty days. I sent Mohammed on foot to fetch a rescue party from Kadugli.

A day and a half later some men, a bull and two donkeys returned with Mohammed, and by the middle of the next day we were safely across the river. We had spent the last two nights miserably camped in thirty centimetres of water; if the men had not arrived I had intended to abandon the Land Rover and walk.

The Land Rover just managed to reach Kadugli under its own power but coughed, spluttered and backfired, pulling so weakly that where there was a gradient or deeper mud it had to be assisted by most of the men. It had been completely submerged twice on this journey and despite immediate oil and petrol changes, when we came to overhaul it at Kadugli we found almost a gallon of dirty water in the petrol tank. However, it had brought us safely home together with our specimens, even some of the coral, and my serval survived the journey without getting its feet wet.

Dindi and the
mother of tassels

After a bath and change of clothing, my first thoughts on arrival at Kadugli were my animals which, of course, I had not seen for several months. There were no new additions to the zoo except for a couple of tortoises, and only Oswald, the ostrich, was absent. All the other animals looked well and healthy.

For the first few weeks I kept the serval kitten in my house. It is often said that servals never become tame, although I cannot understand why and this is certainly not my experience. A more companionable animal than Dindi, as I called him from the curiously sounding Nuba name, *blimi-dindi*,★ would have been hard to find. He lacked the subservience characteristic of the dog tribe (dogs, like all gregarious carnivores, have a hierarchical organisation so that even the most independent dog has an inbuilt submissive instinct), but for a cat he was very sociable and almost always prepared to be guided by me. In fact Dindi's character never changed and he was delightfully affectionate to the moment of his sad death two and a half years later.

The most essential first step was to persuade Dindi to become

★ The usual Arabic name for this cat is *fahad*, but it is sometimes referred to as *gita el lia* or *nimir el wadi*, 'leopard of the wadi'. Another Nuba name is *ra-man-yaro*.

house-trained. From the beginning he used a corner of the room as his midden and at once used a box of sand put there. But it was more difficult to persuade him to go outside for, as a kitten, he was very nervous when out of the house even in my company.

Serval cats are essentially nocturnal although, as is the case with most mammals, environmental conditions may influence their instinctive habits. In the absence of man, their greatest enemy, servals are often active on cool days, but even in almost urban areas they may be seen occasionally in broad daylight.

Dindi was certainly more nervous in the daytime. In the garden he tiptoed cautiously staying close by my side, like a domestic cat out in the snow, and suspiciously sniffing the air, long whiskers and flesh-coloured nose quivering on his white-lipped muzzle. The slightest sound or movement, perhaps only the shadow of a bulbul or the scuttling of a lizard, was enough to make him freeze or even cower to the ground.

While I had been on leave the local goats had been enjoying themselves in my garden. Goats, incidentally, are second only to man as the most destructive pest of Africa, for where numerous they rapidly turn comparatively fertile country into treeless wastes useless to most other animals and eventually to themselves. At least a third of the continent is desert and more and more land becomes arid for various reasons; goats and cattle, by overgrazing, bear a large share of the blame. Now I had returned from leave I was finding it difficult to keep the goats out as in places they had broken down the high thick wall of granite stones and forced the dense euphorbia hedge that surrounded my garden.

The third or fourth time I took Dindi in the garden a goat gave him a severe fright. On this occasion the goat, hidden by bushes, suddenly broke cover and made for a gap in the wall. Dindi tried to sink into the ground, cringing in terror, while I hurled a few stones towards the intruder to hasten it on its way. I could not persuade Dindi to move even after the goat had disappeared so I had to pick him up and return to the house.

At night, however, Dindi was bolder, even venturing a short distance away from me and taking far less notice of stray sounds. Despite his initial nervousness, in a few weeks he was completely house-trained and would go to the door to be let out. He grew rapidly and found some courage, becoming playful even by day.

One evening several months later I took Dindi with me in the Land Rover. We drove a few miles among the Miri road to deserted, open woodland and I turned off the track though the trees for half a mile or so. I wanted to see if Dindi could hunt for himself. Until now he had been fed entirely by me and I had treated him in much the same way I would have looked after a domestic cat. He had meals of milk and mainly tinned meat with occasional biscuits and bones. He loved anything sweet and was fond of several kinds of wild fruits, such as ripe wild figs and the plum-like fruit of the homeid (*Sclerocarya birrea*), but would not touch others although they were edible. Whenever he had the opportunity he would chew any broad-leaved grasses but not, I think, because of any digestive disorder as his scats were usually normal, black or greenish, shaggy, pointed at one end and from three to five centimetres long.

When I stopped the Land Rover and opened the door, Dindi showed no inclination to leave his seat. He loved riding in the car and was, like most cats, disinclined for exercise. I coaxed him, but all he did was to look at me and purr like an electric motor. Eventually I pushed him off the seat. Once out of the car he followed me readily enough.

I walked along slowly, stopping every so often to examine a plant or the ground, Dindi waiting for me, lying down if I lingered too long. I kept watch on the cat, but he showed no desire to wander far away and ignored several small birds that flew around. Yet he was hungry for purposely I had not fed him that day.

Soon we disturbed a flock of guinea-fowl that ran in front of us, one or two laggards flying to keep up with the others. At last

Dindi showed some interest. He craned his long neck and bounded forwards in the direction of the disappearing birds. But only a few paces away he stopped, turning his head to look back at me as though puzzled to find I was so slow. The guinea-fowl vanished and we continued our walk.

A little while later Dindi was attracted by the sounds and movements of a pair of doves feeding nearby. He began to stalk them. I stood still and watched. Again he glanced round to see what I was doing but when I did not move, he turned back after a moment's hesitation to look at the unobservant birds strutting plumply about, pecking now and then at the ground.

Although it seemed to me that the doves could not possibly fail to see Dindi, they took no notice as he crept closer until, about five metres away, the serval suddenly sprang. For all his speed and agility, his prey escaped to flap noisily away over the tree tops. For a moment Dindi's large yellow eyes stared after the vanishing birds; then he sat down and began to lick a front paw. I went up and stroked him and he began his full-throated purr.

On this early outing Dindi may have showed no great prowess as a hunter, but I was determined that he should learn to catch his own food. I was not sure that I would continue to keep such a beautiful and independent animal for much longer, as I could not always take him with me and he tended to mope when I was absent. Fundamentally lazy, unless he was exercised frequently he would become more and more indolent and soon be out of condition. Once I was satisfied he could hunt for himself I could perhaps take him back to the *jebels* he came from and leave him to look after himself.

Whenever I had time I played with Dindi, teaching him to chase a ball, even bring it back to me. This training greatly improved his agility and soon he caught his first live prey, the wriggling tail of a skink! I did not witness his feat but found him with the lizard's tail under his paw, the skink having successfully made off. In a short time I was satisfied that he could hunt having caught rodents and birds on his own. One day in the bush Dindi flushed a pair of button quails (*Turnix sylvaticus*) that flew up under his nose; with one great leap and an outstretched paw he knocked one of the birds to the ground, pouncing on it before it could recover. This was the first time I had seen a button-quail, like a miniature partridge, in the Nuba Mountains. Unlike the ball, he never brought his victims to me but usually ate at least part on the spot.

Dindi was now well over half grown, standing forty-six centimetres at the shoulder and weighing about eight kilos. By this time he was kept in a cage at the zoo where he seemed reasonably happy. Whenever I could I took him out or let him wander freely about the zoo. I could no longer keep him in the house, chiefly because I had other animals there and at home there was nobody responsible enough to leave Dindi with. At least in the zoo he was well fed and there were people to watch, some of whom talked with him, and he could be exercised by Abdulla.

One day, a long way from the nearest vehicle or other track, I found a place with plenty of cover, a rocky terrain far from any village, with any amount of small game: rodents, hares, hyraxes, galagos and game-birds to my certain knowledge. Leaving the Land Rover I clambered over the scattered rocks on the bushy slope of the nearest *jebel*. Dindi was now independent enough to wander from my side, although a call from me would bring him back. I let him wander out of sight and then made my way quickly back to the car.

Feeling sad and rather guilty I turned the Land Rover round and began to drive away. For the first quarter of a mile or so the going was very rough and I could travel only in first gear. Just as the ground became smoother with fewer rocks and trees, I saw Dindi in the driving mirror. Used to following the Land Rover sometimes when I drove it slowly he must have heard the engine and tagged along behind.

I almost relented and picked him up but seeing that he showed no sign of fatigue, I accelerated hoping that he would soon give up. Touching thirty miles per hour (forty-eight kilometres), as fast as I dared travel, I glanced back. The serval was no longer to be seen, but a great cloud of dust blotted out the view behind. I was forced to slow down to negotiate a dry *khor*. As I drove out of the watercourse the dust cloud drifted away and Dindi appeared on the far bank obviously distressed, his coat almost uniformly grey.

It was no good. I had to stop. Dindi came up and flopped down by the Land Rover. A minute later, when he recovered himself, he began to purr. My attempt to abandon him in such a disloyal fashion was clearly a failure, and I was heartily sorry that I had ever thought of it.

Caressing his head as he laid it on my lap, I drove slowly back to the road and so home. I never tried to lose him again.

Apart from the difficulty of returning Dindi to the wild without heartbreak, there was another strong reason against this course. Serval cats still survived and were sometimes even quite common in the wilder parts of the Nuba Mountains, but so great a toll was taken by hunters that they had been almost exterminated in some districts. Where present, the cats tended to live in hill country, particularly wooded valleys or well vegetated, rocky *jebel* slopes where water was near, but they avoided thicker forest or open plains except for the banks of watercourses.

The young, usually produced at the beginning of the dry season in September/November, one to three per litter, could be hidden amongst tumbled rocks, small caves or, occasionally, on stream banks in a secret lair – a small grass form pressed out by the parent's body in dense thorn.

The other common cat of the Nuba Mountains, apart from the wild cat and the leopard, is the caracal or African lynx, called *umm rashat* (the mother of tassels) by the Arabs, the name 'caracal' being a French corruption of a Turkish word meaning 'black-eared'. More locally the Baggara often called the caracal *arabish bang* or just *bang*, a name given to a number of predatory mammals.

About the size of a serval, the caracal is a sturdier, more powerful animal with more massive limbs and habits similar to those of the leopard. For example, it may hoist the carcass of its prey into the fork of a tree or hide it amongst boulders, and the call is often mistaken for the coughing grunt of a leopard until one becomes familiar with both cats. But it purrs readily like a serval and, in spite of its heavier build and ungraceful walk (the back legs are slightly longer than the front ones), it is almost as agile and just as fast as the serval, capable of running down even animals such as the red-fronted gazelle.

I was not able to study the caracal to the same extent as the other cats of the Nuba Mountains, for I kept only one in captivity for a short time and it seemed to be common only in the Tucma, Habila, Otoro, Delami region; from Lagowa east to Dilling and in Rashad District, areas I visited only occasionally. Most of the Baggara and many Nuba seemed to have no knowledge of the caracal. All the same it was by no means scarce in the places named. Perhaps its status has not changed; I hope so, although even by the time I left the region in 1956 there were ominous signs of 'progress'.

For example, an open-air cinema and the first petrol pump had just come to Kadugli, and in that year a more efficient, more automated cotton gin was brought to replace the ancient roller ginnery that like an old paddleboat puffed and clanked its way through the cotton season, spewing out the white gold in foamy waves. Although I did not like these innovations, they did not directly affect the wild life and were good things in themselves, helping to raise the standard of living or provide amenities for the people. But they were, I think, the first signs of a revolution that without care and planning would mean doom for most of the remaining animals.

The first caracal I saw was an emaciated amber-eyed kitten in the hands of some Arabs near Rashad. The cry of this pathetic creature reminded me of a chick cheeping. The infant was very red, much brighter in colour than the adult for the white hairs that usually give the full-grown animal's pelt a grizzled appearance do not appear in the kitten for some months after birth. I was interested to see that it was fairly densely spotted on the sides and the belly, with spots much darker than those of older caracals.

In the remoter places the caracal seemed to be more active in the daytime than at night. I disturbed one feeding on a large buzzard (*Buteo*) at mid-morning when I was exploring in the Nyima *jebels* west of Dilling. The cat made off without a sound, but it was fairly obvious what had happened. The buzzard was still warm and only the head had been crushed; beside it lay a dead lizard, *Agama colonorum*. The buzzard must have caught the lizard and settled to feed, only to be struck down by the caracal before it could take flight. In the Nuba Mountains caracals feed mainly on birds and rodents, including hares, and at least sometimes devour snakes. I waited for an hour or more, but the caracal did not return.

Like the leopard, both the caracal and serval are hunted by the Nuba and to a lesser extent by Arabs for their skins and teeth which are highly valued for adornment, but some Nuba clans eat the flesh of all these cats and parts of the body are sometimes used in witchcraft and medicine.

On one occasion when on trek some miles east of Delami I heard the excited yapping of dogs not far away in the uninhabited bush. Taking my old twelve-bore shotgun, for it was possible that the disturbance was due to a rabid dog or jackal, I left my camp to see what was going on.

I arrived just in time to see an unpleasant sight. The motley pack of pi-dogs had treed a caracal that was crouched, almost invisibly, on the branch of a small tree about four metres from the ground. Four or five hunters, following the dogs, had also just arrived and through the trees I saw the caracal knocked to the ground by a volley of stones. Before I could intervene, two of the tribesmen beat the cat to death with heavy sticks, the others kicking the excited dogs away.

By not allowing the dogs to attack the fallen cat and by using sticks instead of their spears, the hunters obtained an almost unblemished skin, more valuable than one with spear or gunshot damage. The hunters told me that they always hunted serval cats and caracals in this way at night, and that they obtained almost a dozen skins each year in this manner.

Caracal skins were not as valuable as serval skins, although the ear tassels and teeth were highly valued, but an unblemished serval skin would fetch about £E1.750 m/ms (£1·75) from a trader, a lot of money for a village hunter.

Traps were also used to catch these cats and other animals, but even the simplest trap (and some were very ingenious and complicated) required a lot of time to set and visit, so that they were used but seldom, especially as the larger animals were uncommon. Traps for smaller animals – ground squirrels, guinea-fowl and so on – were simpler to construct, frequently used, and often successful.

The usual serval cat or caracal trap was the same as that used for leopards or even antelopes. It was constructed from rope made of tebeldi bark or *zaff* (*Zizyphus*) arranged in a hidden noose put in a suitable position on a trail used by animals. If the noose is touched a bent, very springy sapling is triggered to fly into the upright position pulling the noose taut and either breaking the cat's neck or strangling it sooner or later. Many traps misfire, needing to be carefully and expertly set to work properly.

I did not want Dindi killed by hunters or trappers, and I felt he might have much less chance of escape than a cat raised in the wild. He was so used to humans that, if I had released him, he might well have gone too close to any people he met and perhaps been killed.

By these arguments I convinced myself that it would have been the height of cruelty to return Dindi to the bush; yet being unable to give him all the exercise and companionship he needed, I tried to find him some congenial company. There was little chance of finding another serval cat myself. If I had offered a large enough reward no doubt I could have found hunters willing to bring one in alive, but I did not want to encourage people to catch animals. As a temporary measure I kept Dindi with the two wild-cat kittens I had reared and which were now full-grown.

The wild-cat (*Felis lybica*), called locally *kadis el wadi* in Arabic or *mooderi* by the Nuba, is stouter and more robust than the domestic cats of the Nuba Mountains, thin, scraggy, long-legged, furtive animals often black and white although tabbies or even marmalade cats occur and I saw one that must have had a Siamese ancestor. Wild-cats have short coats of grey or yellowish fur, lighter below, with often indistinct blackish markings on the back and invariably black striped legs and a ringed, black-tipped tail, the blackish rings becoming more distinct towards the end of the tail. As they breed freely with domestic cats, which were often as feral, all kinds of colours and markings could appear.

Wild-cats were common but being nocturnal and wary were seldom seen. Those I saw were far from savage, unlike the Scottish wild-cat (*F. silvestris grampia*), for example, even the adult soon becoming tame enough to feed from one's hand. All the same, I was not at all sure if Dindi and the two wild-cats would tolerate each other.

I need not have worried. From the first Dindi accepted the two wild-cats, Harami (thief) and Haikal (skeleton), and they suffered Dindi, but although they never squabbled and all three slept together, otherwise Dindi more or less ignored the wild-cats. I never saw Dindi playing with the others, but Harami and Haikal often had mock fights or romped together. Dindi was very playful at times, especially in the evening when it was cool, but he preferred human company.

Dindi ignored most of the other animals as well, including the monkeys, but often used to stalk the antelopes or birds. None showed any serious fear of Dindi, but most tactfully walked away to a safe distance when he was about, as though he had a nasty smell.

Occasionally when an absent-minded gazelle or a hungry duiker would wander too close Dindi would spring at it, striking with his paw as he leapt, causing the antelope to shy away and run a few yards, but he made no attempt to follow up his initial assault. Nor did he ever draw blood; it was just play.

All the same he often eyed the smaller birds that were free to wander in the zoo compound. Despite his training and the fact that he was well fed, I was afraid his instinct might prove too much for him one day, and I might not be in time to stop him. In the event, he never did attack any zoo bird, partly because I was usually with him and always somewhere near at hand when he was released for exercise, but also because I had a very reliable ally.

Amongst the mixed flock of birds the undisputed leader was a large spurwing goose (*Plectropterus gambensis*), aided in turn by his consort. This great gander looked even larger when, with wings flapping and with hissing red beak, he became enraged. His black back shone with a bronzy sea-green gloss and the bony spur on each white shoulder, like the canine tooth of a leopard, was nearly three centimetres long, a winged dagger he could use with skill.

The spurwings regarded themselves as the protectors of all the other birds smaller than themselves, and soon put to flight the playful baboons and followed the pythons at a watchful distance ready to do battle if necessary when the reptiles were let out of their enclosure to drag their great lengths around the compound. Thus whenever Dindi came close to the flock of birds that tended to huddle together near the spurwings in times of apparent danger, the spurwings threatened him. Once when the gander flew at him Dindi, after one startled look, took refuge in one of the trees in the zoo.

I never discovered how fast Dindi or any other serval could run when fully extended although for about three hundred metres Dindi had been right behind when I had accelerated to nearly fifty kilometres per hour on the day I had tried to abandon him in the bush. One day I chased a servaline that was on the roadway scarcely six metres in front. Thick bush crowded the sunken, sandy track and the cat bounded away along the road.

The Land Rover was travelling at about forty kilometres per hour; although I pushed the accelerator to the floor, the cat gained rapidly and vanished around another corner about five hundred metres from the first, and by the time I reached the second corner it was out of sight. It could have been running at no less than fifty kilometres per hour, and sixty or perhaps sixty-five kilometres per hour I consider to be the top speed of one of these long-legged cats.

One day, some two years later, I was playing with Dindi, by then a powerful animal whose agility never failed to amaze me. He could leap over two metres into the air and turn as he did so to strike down a ball as it fell. On this occasion we were having a rough and tumble, I catching his tail or rolling him over, he avoiding me or striking out with his front paws in mock attack. Suddenly the movement of his paw and of my bare arm coincided and he drew blood, two long but shallow scratches across my forearm.

The wound was nothing, but Dindi refused to play any more, turning away when I tried to coax him. Instead he walked off and lay on the grass. I sat down not far away. A moment later he came up and very gently began to lick the wound he had made on my arm, and then lay down beside me.

It could have been only a few weeks later that I noticed Dindi licking his own front leg. Examining his leg I found a small wound just above his ankle. It did not seem very serious, but it was deep, rather like the hole left after squeezing out the larva of a tumbu fly, although this was not the cause. I bathed the wound in an antiseptic solution. The next day I looked at it again, but there was no sign of inflammation.

For some days I treated Dindi's leg daily, but though the wound seemed to get no worse it did not heal. I was away then for almost a week. On my return I looked again at his leg, expecting to find it healed or almost healed. To my dismay the wound was much worse; still not particularly inflamed but much larger with a white ligament exposed.

I took Dindi to the house and kept him there for obviously he found it quite painful to walk on this leg. There I dressed and bandaged it but in a short time Dindi had the bandage off and was licking the sore place continuously. When I went to him he purred loudly and began to lick me.

Over the next few days I found it impossible to stop him licking the wound, now a gaping hole of three or four centimetres and as deep as the bone. I was in despair. I managed to obtain some sulphanilamide powder from a visiting veterinary assistant, dressed the wound and put Dindi by my bedside where through the night I could try to prevent him from licking. The next day he seemed better although at no time had he seemed in pain or to lose his appetite, and always he purred as loudly and licked my hand whenever I appeared.

A night or two later before dawn I woke to hear him stirring on his bed of blankets; I put out my hand and he licked it once or twice, purring softly. I leant out of bed to look at him, but he seemed to be sleeping. A few minutes later he was dead.

Upturned carrots

'Hamad *Effendi*, how many trees have been recorded this week?'

'I think one hundred and twenty-two, Doktor.'

'What's the exact figure?'

Hamad thumbed through the sheaf of grubby papers he was holding and scratched his head. For some reason the sheets, scrawled with untidy figures and words in Arabic, were in assorted shapes and sizes. I sighed.

'Never mind, Hamad. Give them to me; I'll look at them.'

I had five teams of men, each in a different part of the Nuba Mountains and throughout the year I visited each area in turn, checking on the written records, examining many of the trees myself and sorting out the various problems that arose.

The main purpose of the work was to discover as much as possible about the baobab tree and the insects associated with it, particularly stainer-bugs, bright reddish, six millimetres long insects that bred mainly on the baobabs when not attacking the cotton crop. The men recorded the flowering and fruiting periods of the trees and the changes in populations of stainer-bugs. In Hamad's area each of a hundred and fifty trees had been painted with a number and each was supposed to be visited weekly.

That evening at my camp I went through the records Hamad

had given me, and the next morning I called the men together. As usual there were a number of queries that took some time to sort out, but I was concerned chiefly about the unrecorded trees.

'There are nine trees only partly recorded. Why is this?' I asked.

I discovered, as I had expected, that bees had chased the men away. Honey-bees were one of the chief problems in this work. In some areas most of the baobabs possessed at least one hive, the occupants of which usually regarded the whole of the under canopy of a tree as their territory. In *Jebels by Moonlight* I related how we were driven away from our camp by bees, but on several other occasions I had similar encounters. In various parts of Africa between 1948 and 1967 I had personal knowledge of seven deaths directly caused by honey-bees, and there was hearsay evidence of others.

Few people cared to trifle with bees, therefore. Yet occasionally amongst the Nuba (as in some other tribes of Africa) a man seems to be as immune to stings as the ratel.

A smoking branch and a reliance on magic are the only protection of the naked honey-hunter and, of course, most hives are only pillaged at night. But one day I saw an elderly Nuba robbing a large hive in a baobab tree.

Watching from a distance, for the bees were buzzing angrily all around the tree, I saw the man plunge his arm several times into the nest to remove pieces of dripping wax that he placed in a half gourd. Finally, he climbed to the ground down a ladder of pegs hammered into the tree trunk, the bees still swarming thickly about him. He moved away from the tree, shedding most of the bees, and I spoke to him, but he knew little Arabic.

His skin was punctured by numerous stings, the tiny barbs even hanging from his cheeks. He robbed bees' nests for a living, I understood, finding several each week during the honey season. Nonchalantly, he patted and shook his only clothing, a pair of loose, short cotton pantaloons, squashing several bees that had crawled inside, while a couple more flew out, droning sadly.

The tribesman seemed quite indifferent to his stings; he had no anticipation of pain and in the event probably felt none, having implicit belief in his magic.

Hamad's men had no such faith. The sight of a hive was enough to panic them and I do not blame them since, despite their caution, most of them had been stung at one time or another.

I asked Hamad, 'What about the other twenty-eight trees not yet recorded?'

'There are some troubles, Doktor. Some of the trees have a small animal that is poisonous.'

I was anxious to see this creature that, so they said, occurred in some numbers, was spiny and the size of a small mouse.

We made our way through tall grasses and shrubby trees until we reached the group of three baobabs in question. A dense mass of a very prickly, purple-flowered *Solanum* (a plant of the potato family) grew waist high below the trees. Zubeir, the man responsible for these records, would not come any closer. Looking about, and painfully scratched on my bare legs by the recurved thorns of the *Solanum*, at first I could see only a few stainer-bugs. Then I found another insect that I suspected was the cause of Zubeir's horror. I picked it up. 'Is this it?' I asked, holding the insect out.

Zubeir would not touch the creature which was a rather monstrous long-horned grasshopper called *Anepisceptus horridus*. Really quite a handsome insect, the female was shiny black, the male browner with yellow rings around the obese abdomen, it was at the same time repulsive with a fat, oily look, spines that bristled on the enlarged thoracic shield on the back and a goggle-eyed head sunk on its chest.

Quite unlike a typical grasshopper, it was not only flightless and unable to jump, but was also rotund, ambling along with its soft bloated abdomen scraping the ground. This grasshopper and similar relatives are to be found over much of Africa, all the kinds being vegetable feeders, and all with the reputation of being poisonous if handled.

While it was true that from a gland on each side of the thorax the creature could excrete a copious fluid caustic enough to blister a sensitive skin, I was sure that the fluid would have no effect on Zubeir's horny feet or hands. I told him so, but knowing he would not carry out his duties properly I gave him the trees of another man, who had no fear of the grasshopper, and solved this small problem.

Collecting all the information I required to collate was never as simple as it appeared. Apart from staff difficulties and sickness, flooding and bees, and the occasional difficulty (as with the grasshopper), hardly a week passed without some other crisis. My assistants were 'plagued' by snakes, leopards and lions, scorpions and centipedes, falling fruits and branches, lightning and winds, and vague fears of devils or supernatural animals.

Despite these excitements, recording proceeded surprisingly smoothly. Nor should it be thought that every baobab contained aggressive creatures. Apart from the bees, only one in several hundred trees was inhabited by any 'dangerous' animal. In fact, although there was always much to interest me, I was disappointed at the paucity of larger animals. For me, the only disagreeable part was that, near villages, the giant trees, especially if partly hollowed, were often used as latrines.

In the deserts of Darfur and Kordofan as well as in the Nuba Mountains, I discovered many of these trees to be hollow, some holding as much as three hundred gallons of water. In the more arid regions some trees were well-known by the nomadic Arabs as being the only sources of water for many miles and regular halting places for camel trains.

Often the shell was sixty centimetres or more thick, hairy with fibres inside that resembled giant fungal hyphae. Even at the height of the dry season, however, it is almost impossible to destroy or

Baobab tree

Duiker

Dindi, the serval, as a kitten

Ground hornbill

Patas monkey

Saddlebill stork

Crowned crane

hollow a baobab by burning, so most of the artificially hollowed trees, some of which were known in the early, savage history of the country, must have been hacked out by men, as insects might gnaw out the inside of a potato.

The vitality of such tree husks is often astonishing. Perhaps completely hollowed out with much of the bark stripped away, one of these obese giants may still live for years producing leaves and even fruits. More often a hollow baobab does not contain water for frequently there is a large hole at the base like the entrance to a cave. Such a hole may be two metres or more in height and in a normal-sized tree there is sometimes room for fifty or more people to stand without undue discomfort. The inside of one tree that I measured was about seventy-five square metres, another was over a hundred square metres in area with the cavity extending more than six metres up the trunk.

Near Teisi I found a 'house' in a baobab with a wooden door and square window, while the floor had been closely paved with large flat stones. It was some distance from the nearest habitation, unoccupied, and we never discovered the owner.

Twice elsewhere, at later dates, I saw homes where a large baobab in the garden had had a privy installed, one even having a complete flush system. A few years ago while travelling in the northern Transvaal I came upon a roadside baobab equipped with seats inside and out for the convenience of travellers, while near Leydsdorp over a hundred years ago there used to be a hollow baobab known as the Murchison Club used as a bar for prospectors; creeper-clad and deserted for many years, the tree may still exist.

Many Africans believe that baobabs appear overnight, by magic, and possess souls or are inhabited by the spirits of their ancestors. Some even think that the trees walk about at night but have to stay in one place by day, a belief I can well understand.

One curiosity of the baobab, remarked upon by many travellers, is the apparent absence of seedlings and young trees, something that probably helps to account for the African belief in the spontaneous generation of fully-grown trees. After some months of work on the association of insects with the trees the same thought occurred to me. Why had I never seen a really young one? The smallest I had found by then was taller than a man. I searched locally without success and came to the conclusion that goats, those ultra-destructive creatures, had eaten them all. Eventually, high on a *jebel*, I discovered a tiny baobab; after that I found a dozen or more seedlings scattered in places well away from the goat pastures.

When I came from the north to meet the solitary advance guards of the baobabs from the Nuba Mountains it was easy to imagine that they were great warriors bent on invading and crossing the vast arid tracts between them and the sea; as massive and immovable as lighthouses, darkly immobile by day, but plodding onwards towards their goal by night. Across the jagged hilltops, over the ravines, march the trees, garrisoning the villages on their way. Sometimes the giants cluster together, stubby fingers touching, as though solemnly conferring, planning their nocturnal route. It was almost a surprise to find them in the same place the next morning. At other times when by day the wind blows strongly through the hills to howl along the valleys, the trees shake their massive heads, as if dancing in frustration at being rooted and at the slowness of their progress to the distant coast.

Of the many curious trees in Africa, the baobab is perhaps the most bizarre. I first encountered them in the coastal regions of East Africa, but it was not until I went to the Sudan and began to investigate this great tree and its fauna, work I continued for many years in various parts of Africa, that I became fascinated by these elephants of the vegetable world, witnessed their birth and death, and learnt more about them than any other tree.

In Dar Nuba the baobabs mostly come into leaf in April/May, the leaves falling in September through to November; flowering is mostly in May/June, the flowering period sometimes lasting several weeks on individual trees, while the fruits appear from

July to January, persisting in some cases to the following September. Trees begin to fruit from about eight to ten years old, but do not produce maximum fruits, often a thousand or more, until twice this age or more.

The leaves are similar to those of a horse chestnut, each set of five leaflets on a long petiole or stalk, the dense greenery, the bulky trunk and swollen branches giving black shade over a large area. The white, waxy, gardenia-like flower, pendulous on a long stalk, is large, sometimes fifteen centimetres across but

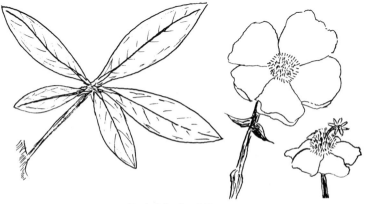

Baobab leaf and flower

often smaller, the stamens fused into a globular pinkish-grey mass. The flowers are faintly sweet-scented at first, but last at most only a few days and sometimes brown in a few hours, with a carrion smell as they decay.

At the height of the dry season the trees are leafless, as stark and rugged as though sculptured from the rocks among which they mostly grow. Most *jebel* slopes and crests support the trees, but they occur on any well-drained sandy or gravelly soils and the real giants are found on the plains. On occasions baobabs are found precariously rooted at the top of *khor* banks, sometimes as virtual islands, the huge roots the captors of soil and lesser plants. Many take grotesque shapes due to the pressure of the elements; sometimes the larger branches – that can be six metres in circumference – break or bend to form enormous arches covered with *Cissus, Capparis,* convolvulus or other creepers. The bark, grey, shining and smooth, sometimes pinkish or even coppery, is usually convoluted, fissured or furrowed in parts with large ledges or cavities caused by bark folds that become the resting places for seeds – miniature gardens of lichens, grasses, orchids, *Sansevieria* and many others.

Although the wood of the baobab is too soft and spongy for use as timber, to the African peasant the tree is of enormous value. Floor mats can be made from the fibrous heart, ropes for many purposes from the stringy inner bark, so many baobabs by settlements stand stripped of bark halfway up the trunk. Sometimes smaller trees stand entirely naked, but they seldom die, the bark eventually growing again. In the bark is a high percentage of mucilage sometimes used for tanning, and the bark cloth was once widely used as clothing, although it is rarely seen today. The bark became a source of paper in the First World War, baobabs in Mozambique were stripped and the bark made into paper in South Africa.

In parts of the Nuba Mountains a special use is made of the thin, springy branches. Amongst the Moro, as in most other clans, the emphasis on stoic courage applies not only to boys and men but to girls and women. Just as the males have to prove their ability to suffer pain without complaint, those excelling at sports and grade-tests being the most honoured, so do the females, and a girl has to prove her courage before she is allowed to marry.

Thus, early in life, a girl's lower incisors are knocked out; she has to undergo cicatrisation without showing fear or pain, and other initiation trials. But instead of fighting each other with heavy staves and serrated shields as amongst the men (although girls of some other clans do fight with sticks), the girls have whip-fighting contests called *lepido* when whippy baobab branches are the weapons. They lay about each other with such vigour that blood and injuries are frequent, the stringy baobab switches making cutting, durable whips since the longitudinal fibres are so strong. The bravest fighters attain an adult grade, but those showing cowardice or lack of skill may have to wait a year or more before the next whip-fight and the chance of being upgraded.

The edible leaves of the baobab, too, have many uses. Young leaves are eaten raw, used in soups or fresh leaves are boiled to make a kind of spinach especially in times of food shortages. They are a source of glue (although the pollen is better) and used in medicine as an astringent or to reduce perspiration in fevers.

It was chiefly the fruits (called *gongoleis* by the Arabs) that interested me, however, for it is their seeds on which the stainer-bugs live; stainer-bugs attack cotton bolls and were the insects that were the main object of my research in the Nuba Mountains.

The fruit is extraordinary. Hanging down on a long stringy stem the woody pod varies in colour from green to a greyish, reddish or yellowish-brown, and when ripe in size from about eight to thirty-five centimetres long (the largest I found) and three point five to nearly seventeen centimetres in diameter. The hard pod is sometimes smooth on the outside, but more often has a dense, felty pubescence, like the pelt of some mice. The shape is astonishingly variable—nearly round, almost oval, elongate with parallel sides that narrow to base and apex, sickle-shaped, almost triangular and so on.

When ripe the pod plummets to the ground, sometimes breaking on impact but more frequently remaining intact until the shell rots or is broken open by man or other animals. To be hit by one of these pods would be painful, but it would be unlikely to kill you unlike the heavier, more solid fruits of the sausage tree (*Kigelia*) and the *doleib* palm (*Borassus*), both common trees whose falling fruits could be lethal.

Inside the baobab fruit pod lie a variable number of hard dark brown seeds embedded in a white, dry, acidulous pithy matrix, sometimes of the texture of polyporus or foam rubber, at other

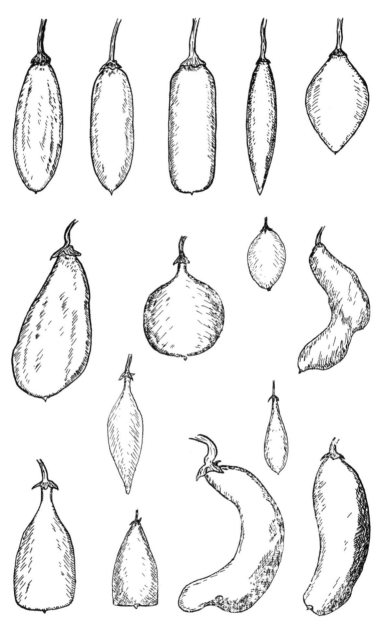

Variations in shape of baobab fruits from many trees

times (usually in older fruits) rather like flour. Pleasant to suck, being acidic and refreshing, the large seeds are sometimes roasted or ground to make a drink, or else eaten mixed with maizc, millet or sorghum to make a gruel.

The fruit is used in many other ways. The seeds are a source of oil (called fony or reniala) which is golden in colour, pleasant tasting and smelling, and non-drying. The pulp matrix is often eaten as a kind of porridge; made into a lemonade; used for seasoning food; substituted for cream of tartar or baking powder; used to curdle milk; as a rubber coagulant; as a diaphoretic for dysentery or fevers; when burnt, as an insect repellent, and when added to stagnant water is said to make it safe to drink. The hard woody shells make very handy and quite durable containers or water scoops.

Livingstone referred to baobabs as upturned carrots, an apt description for the trunk tapers from a broad base, its bark is often pinkish hued, while the branches resemble the fibrous roots of a carrot. Several other descriptive names have been given to this grotesque tree – elephant-bark tree, because of the often fissured or wrinkled grey bark; gouty-stem tree, from the swollen trunk and limbs; sour gourd, monkey-bread, cream of tartar or lemonade tree, names referring to the tart acidity of the edible matrix in which the seeds are embedded, a pulp containing tartaric acid, glucose, pectin and mucilage.

But the name baobab by which this tree is most commonly called in English is really a native name from Senegal, where the tree was discovered by Adanson, a French explorer, in the eighteenth century. Other African names number at least a hundred; in the Sudan and other Arabic-speaking countries *tebeldi* is the common name.*

* The Nuba call the *tebeldi*, *mansallo* at Kadugli; *tuberli* around Dilling; *oro* in Tegele; *kishawiyi* in the El Liri Hills. At Jebel Daier they call it *fak*, while the Dinka name is *dungwol*; the Shilluk, *gag*, and the Nuer, *kusha*. The botanical name, *Adansonia digitata*, honours the explorer; the second, or trivial name, derived from *digitus*, refers to the shape of the leaf.

Probably the largest tree in Africa and perhaps attaining a great age, the baobab holds no world records in these respects. There is little real evidence concerning the potential age of baobabs, and the tree forms no distinct annual rings (despite the counts said to have been made by some people). Nor is there any majestic crashing to earth when these mighty trees die; in most cases they simply go into gradual decline and slow decay until there is left no more than a pile of fibrous strands and strips of papery bark. In five years I recorded the collapse of only four trees in Kadugli District, although elsewhere I saw a few others felled by wind and decay.

There were still seven trees that Hamad and his men had not visited. One of these had collapsed; the bases of the largest branches were as large as the trunks of ancient oaks. At three other trees snakes had been seen and the men refused to go near. Near another baobab, a tree that stood on its own, a leopard had been seen. A sixth was hollow and said to contain some sort of supernatural being, while the seventh, also hollow, had 'certain signs' that indicated it was dangerous. I never discovered what these signs were.

I went to each of these trees in turn. At the first we disturbed several brown parrots feeding on broken baobab fruits on the ground.

After the brown parrots flew away, I searched for a long time, but there was no sign of a snake. At the next tree I was luckier. It was an odd-shaped, twin-trunked tree with several hollows in the bole and larger branches. I investigated these holes, poking a stick into them. The trunk contained nothing, but as I perched on a low branch and inserted my stick a snake shot out so quickly that I slid over sideways to find myself upside down but still holding tenaciously to the branch with my legs which were locked round it.

The snake, a fair size, had touched me as it passed and dropped to the ground. By its size and darkness I knew it was probably one of three venomous kinds – a cobra, mamba or boomslang – but it had moved so quickly that I had scarcely seen it. The men scattered, not having been very close to the tree from the beginning. Now they were nowhere to be seen. Nor was the snake visible any longer for it was hidden somewhere in the grasses.

My position was somewhat awkward for my head was about two metres from the ground and below me was a tangle of unpleasant-looking thorns. In slipping sideways I had grazed my bare legs and I knew I could not hold on for long; nor could I right myself again for the thick branch to which I was clinging was quite smooth and I could obtain no grip with my hands. All I could do by myself was to drop into the thorns below. I bellowed loudly for help.

At first there was no response and I thought I was quite alone everybody else being well out of hearing by now, but at last Younis appeared with some others a good distance behind him. Treading cautiously, he hacked his way into the barbed undergrowth and, standing below, held up his arms. I was just able to reach his hands; holding them I was able to release my legs and swing to the ground, but we both fell amongst the thorns.

I was determined to catch this snake if we could find it, but after an hour's search I was compelled to give up on that occasion. Some days later, however, I returned to the baobab equipped with a kind of basket made from netting. I climbed up to my former perch, placed the mouth of the basket over the hole and poked my stick through the wire into the hole. After waggling the stick a few times the snake shot out as it had before. But this time it found itself trapped in the netting. Quickly I squeezed the wire of the opening together and the reptile was captive. It was a one-and-a-half-metres-long Egyptian cobra and I took it back to my zoo.

The Egyptian cobra was the commonest cobra of the Nuba Mountains, although the spitting or black-necked cobra was nearly as numerous. The majority of individuals I saw in the Nuba Mountains were wholly dark, almost black, with a purplish sheen, the underparts only a little paler, greyish-black, but there was considerable variation in colour in the Sudan generally. In the extreme east of the Nuba Mountains, where I was unable to stop running over one in the Land Rover, and on the plain around Jebel Mageinis and near Kodok (Fashoda) where I caught three or four at different times, the colour was reddish-brown. Elsewhere I found a few with distinct banding on the body, while in western Darfur I found a brownish-yellow, banded form of the same snake.

Amongst the specimens I kept alive at various times I was surprised to find a considerable variation in food preferences. While Egyptian cobras are recorded as eating almost any small animal, such as various rodents, young birds, birds' eggs, frogs, toads, other snakes, lizards and even small fishes, in captivity one of mine would eat only frogs and small toads and lived for about eighteen months on this diet alone before I released it.

Another refused all food but survived for eight months without eating. A third fed on other snakes and a few frogs but ignored rats, birds' eggs and other food offered. A fourth much preferred birds, while others would eat virtually anything if not too large or too small. As is the case with a good many other animals, each snake was probably conditioned to eat only animals commonest in the area it came from.

Another oddity about them was the fact that all my captives were very fond of water and on a hot day often submerged in their pools like so many pythons. Yet, it is often said the Egyptian cobra is a snake of dry or arid conditions where the relative humidity is low. Of course, it is tolerant of such conditions for a time, and is often found in arid areas, but there seems no doubt that it lives by preference near water and, given the opportunity, not only drinks a good deal but also desires to submerge itself in water.

The largest black-necked cobra I ever kept measured one point nine metres, but the Egyptian cobra attains a much greater length.

In 1955 I had very considerable difficulty in getting the better of one monster discovered in the Government garden at Kadugli (in these gardens vegetables, limes and other fruits were grown under primitive gravity irrigation from a well) which, after catching alive, I was forced to destroy. It was preserved whole and measured (without any stretching) 2,540 millimetres, one of the largest, if not the largest, ever recorded. Of course, most were much smaller and few exceeded about 2,100 millimetres.

The third tree was infested by a snake that proved simpler to deal with. Mustapha, responsible for this tree, told me as we walked through the bush that he had seen a small black snake which he called *abu laqqaz*, a name meaning the 'father of stabbing or prodding'. I knew this was one of the names given to a small burrowing viper in reference to the snake's habit of carrying the head raised and pointed downwards as though ready to dive back into the earth. It was usually only on the ground surface after heavy rain, but several people were bitten every year and it was potentially lethal.

More sinister Arabic names for burrowing vipers are *abu ashara daquiqa*, the 'father of ten minutes', in reference to the supposed virulence of the venom and the time a man may expect to live after being bitten (an exaggeration, of course, and many people who have been bitten have recovered), and *abu daffan*, the 'father of burying'.

We approached the tree and, searching around, I soon disclosed two 'fathers of ten minutes'. Despite their irascible twisting they were easy to catch. Lifting some rocks I disturbed another small snake; it was about thirty-five centimetres long, a warm brown colour with a speckling of white spots on the back and sides. I had never seen this before and later I found another one near Kadugli. On leave in England I found out at the Natural History Museum that this was the Somali snake, *Micrelaps boettgeri*, the first recorded from the region. In fact, the museum had only five specimens, four of which were from Somalia.

I was pleased to have found a snake I did not recognise, and the men were pleased that I had caught the snakes whether I could identify them or not. 'But,' they said darkly, 'there are many other snakes and dangerous animals here.' In the end they agreed to carry on if they could work in pairs and not alone.

We went towards the baobab near which the leopard had been seen. The bush was certainly thick enough to afford cover for any amount of game, although in fact there was little. We disturbed a kudu, the largest animal found in the Nuba Mountains proper, that crashed away in panic flight, but otherwise I saw nothing larger than a tortoise.

This was the common hinged tortoise, *Kinixys belliana*, very widely distributed in Africa and, like all common, widely distributed animals, very variable in physical characteristics. In fact, when I eventually gave the carapace of one of these tortoises from the Nuba Mountains to the Natural History Museum in London, it was reported as being the first record of the subspecies *schoensis* from the Sudan, but I am doubtful whether it is really distinct and not synonymous with *belliana*, the typical race.

It was not to be expected that the leopard would still be there; not that I could have done anything about it if it was, but a whole party of men would certainly have scared it away. I searched about for the spoor or other traces of the animal, but found nothing except duiker tracks. I doubted that the leopard had really been seen for there were often false alarms regarding the big cats, and any largish animal heard but not seen was believed to be a leopard. On the other hand there were leopards in the area and the man was certain he had seen it. Once again I suggested that two men should do the work and this seemed to satisfy them.

A few hundred metres away was the next baobab, the one with 'certain signs', so we walked towards it. Trying to discover what these signs were and why the tree was 'dangerous' occupied the short journey, but nothing the men said made sense to me. Even Younis, who was with me, failed to explain.

I examined the surroundings. The *gardud* soil (from the Arabic, *garad*, to scrape, and the name given to soils formed by the weathering of the rocks that cover a large part of the Nuba Mountains) was very stony but thickly wooded. A short distance away on a sandy *khor* the tall, slender leafy stems of *ganna* or bamboo swayed, alive in a breeze that we, eight or nine metres below the feathery tops, could not feel. Here and there were small, spiny trees with greenish, highly scented bark so thin and papery that it flaked in strips like paint applied to a greasy surface. Earlier in the season the small, red flowers appeared before the leaves uncurled but now amid the thin foliage the trees bore tiny greenish berries with a purplish bloom.

The trees were *Commiphora africana*, called *gafal* or *luban* in Arabic, the aromatic bark of which contain a resin, a form of bdellium, a balsam resembling myrrh (also obtained from *Commiphora*), highly valued by the ancients and still used in modern medicine. Many Sudanese employ the resin for various purposes, particularly as a perfume, or internally in the belief that it has aphrodisiac properties.

It occurred to me that perhaps this balsam tree had something to do with Mustapha's reluctance to visit the baobab, but no, the other trees had nothing to do with the difficulty, only the baobab itself.

Under the canopy of the baobab grew some small, rough-barked trees (*Lannea*); over one grew *Capparis tormentosa*, a bush climber with velvety leaves, and bearing solitary, fragile, sweet-scented flowers, white with delicate pink stamens. In this extra shade most of the stainer-bug population of the baobab had gathered, massed together in resting pools of blood red.

The baobab was hollow, but the only visible opening was some four or five metres up the trunk. Closely examining the trunk for insects, my ear almost to the bark, I became aware of a curious sound. I pressed my ear to the tree; it sounded as if it were alive, as though there were innumerable little clock wheels revolving inside. I had discovered the reason for Mustapha's awe but not the cause.

With Younis's help I clambered onto a massive lower branch, walked along it and peered into the hole in the trunk. There was an almost tangible fetid odour, and the furtive sounds became louder as though some monstrous organism were stirring in the bowels of the trunk, but I could see nothing. The musty smell and the sounds were enough, however; it was obvious that the tree was filled with bats.

To make sure that only bats were within I made the men gather a bundle of dry sticks that they soaked in petrol from the Land Rover. When this was handed up to me I lowered the bundle into the hole on the end of a piece of string. I dropped a match in. There was a whoosh and cloud of smoke, fumes and flames rushed out of the hole opening almost singeing my eyebrows and beard.

Cautiously I put my head in the hole; the sticks were blazing furiously and by their light I could see that the cavity took up almost the whole of the main trunk, now filled with many hundreds of bats in such a twittering frenzy of activity that their massed movements soon dowsed the flare.

With an improvised net I fished out several. They were leaf-nosed bats, *Hipposideros caffer*, a small, common grey insectivorous bat with long pointed ears, widely distributed in Africa. I never found such an enormous colony again, however.

The discovery of the bats seemed to allay Mustapha's fears. He would not admit that their unknown presence had had any influence on him, however, and was of the opinion that the 'evil signs' were still there. Nevertheless, with tactful persuasion and embarrassed by the cheerful scoffing of Younis (who was highly regarded as a *faki*, or religious, and therefore with considerable influence in such a matter) he bravely quelled his misgivings and agreed that he could carry out his duties in future.

We had spent all day in sorting out these difficulties, and it

Greater Kudu: (*left*) head of female, (*centre*) male, (*right*) head of male

was now late afternoon. There was one last tree said to contain some sort of supernatural being. I thought that probably bats were again responsible.

The youth concerned was a very black-skinned Sudanese of mixed Negro and Arab blood called Magdoub, a Moslem like most of the others. The baobab, when we finally reached it after twenty minutes across squelching terrain, was larger than average and amidst rocks thickly interspersed with trees and bushes. To reach the tree there was only a narrow trodden path. In the bole was an oval-shaped hole almost hidden by tall grasses.

'What did you see?' I asked Magdoub.

'I did not see anything, Doktor. I heard only strange noises.'

Apparently Magdoub had visited this tree, the last on his list, late in the afternoon two days before. As he had reached the baobab he had heard what he said was a sort of moan (*walwela*) and he fled. '*Wallahi*, there is an evil spirit here,' he concluded.

Under the tree canopy was a sandy place still moist after recent rain. I found not only the spoor of a hyaena but also drops of blood. Somewhat cautiously I bent down to peer into the opening in the tree, holding my long sheath knife that I carried not as a weapon but for many odd jobs. I did not think it at all likely that a hyaena was inside the tree, for they normally had their lairs amongst the rocks, but having no other weapon I kept the knife handy in case.

Gradually, my eyes became used to the gloom. The trunk was partly hollowed and there must have been another hole higher up for there was a source of light besides the opening at ground level. The tree appeared to be empty; I went inside and stood upright. Then I heard a plaintive mewing sound, a single syllabled cry resembling that of some shrikes, repeated at very short intervals.

Whatever animal was making the noise was certainly no adult, but I still could not see it until I moved carefully forwards, and there in front of me were two pathetic, puling bundles that began to drag themselves about on seemingly broken hind legs. They were infant striped hyaenas.

There was no sign of the parent which I think must have died somewhere in the bush in the last day or two. Not only did the blood on the ground indicate that it was wounded, perhaps by a spear or gun, but the two young hyaenas were starving. I took them back to my zoo.

AUTHOR'S NOTE

Distribution, numbers, size and growth of baobabs

1 *Distribution*. In the Sudan and Ethiopia the African baobab is found in suitable places below about a thousand metres from about latitude 15°N to the Bahr el Arab with few trees south of the river. It is absent from the true deserts of the north, although said to occur in the western Sahara at about latitude 18°N (where, in the El Hadr depression, hollow trees were a source of water in the fourteenth century), and absent from the swamps and rain-forests of the south.

It reappears in Kenya and Tanzania, especially in the coastal areas, and is often common in Zambia, Rhodesia, Malawi and Mozambique in drier regions, being found as far south as the northern Transvaal. It is also commonly encountered in Senegal and the drier parts of other countries in West Africa, while Arab traders introduced it to parts of India and Ceylon.

In Madagascar there is a similar species, *A. madagascarensis,* while *A. gregorii* is the baobab of tropical Australia. Attempts have been made to distinguish separate species or races of African baobabs but with little success; today all baobabs in Africa are regarded as the same kind despite variations, especially in their fruits.

2 *Numbers and size of baobabs.* In Kadugli District I estimated there were more than ten thousand of these trees, and perhaps a hundred thousand or more in the Jebels generally. I took measurements of over a thousand baobabs in the Nuba Mountains. The tallest I found (esti-

mated by the vertical stick and shadow method) was about twenty-four metres but most were eighteen metres or less. For its enormous girth the baobab is not a tall tree; in fact, often the girth is greater than the height of the trunk.

The mean girth of eight hundred and forty-five trees of five different areas, measured at about a metre from the ground, was seven point five metres, about one in fifteen trees being over twelve metres in circumference. Several had bifurcating trunks close to ground level; one with four huge trunks giving a total girth of about thirty-four metres. Sometimes, exposed on the soil surface, I found roots extending seventy metres.

Remaining trees were chosen for their large size. The two largest were twenty-four point eight metres (about seven point nine metres diameter) and twenty-seven point four metres (about eight point eight metres diameter) in girth. Elsewhere in the Sudan, Central, East and South Africa, I measured other large baobabs but none exceeded the circumference of the twenty-seven-metre tree in the Nuba Mountains. Reputedly in Tanzania, there is a tree of a hundred and thirty feet (nearly forty metres) in circumference but I have not seen it.

Although probably the largest tree in Africa, the baobab holds no world record. The giant redwood *(Sequoia gigantea)* has a strong claim to the title 'largest tree' since there are living specimens over ninety metres tall and nine metres in diameter, but some peppermint gums in Australia are said to reach a hundred and twenty metres tall, and almost undoubtedly the largest single tree in the world is a *Ficus benghalensis* in the Botanic Gardens in Calcutta which is one thousand two hundred and fifty-one feet (three hundred and eighty-one point three metres) in circumference and over thirty metres tall.

The baobab belongs to the *Bombax* family *(Bombacaceae)*, principally found in the American tropics, a family of about a hundred and forty different species. Some are of considerable commercial importance, such as the kapok or silk-cotton tree *(Ceiba pentandra)*, the balsa wood tree *(Ochroma lagopus)* and the durian *(Durio zibethinus)*, the fruit of which has the most delicious taste but smells and looks like egg custard made with bad eggs and sour milk. The kapok has been successfully introduced to parts of Africa but the durian is rarely found. However, an occasional tree thrives and several times I have been able to sample the fruit harvest while holding my nose.

3 *Growth.* It is not surprising that very few people have noticed young baobabs for they are insignificant even when quite tall and I never found them to be common. All the same the stem is distinctly bulbous where it emerges from the soil and tends to taper towards the apex even in the smallest seedlings. I grew some young plants and took measurements.

The rate of growth was not constant in all the seedlings, of course, but the mean increase of ten tiny seedlings was about twelve centimetres in girth and almost one point two metres in height at the end of two years. I was forced to transplant two of the trees and two others were destroyed, but after four years the remaining six seedlings had increased in circumference by a further six to eight centimetres and in height by twenty-five to thirty-two centimetres, all having produced more branches and become bushier.

I also planted a number of seeds, nearly all of which germinated. Eight seeds were planted on 1st July, 1952. By October, 1955, there were five robust young saplings surviving, and the girths at this time varied from twelve point five to twenty centimetres.

From these and other data I considered that in ten years the circumference of a tree might be between forty-five and sixty centimetres, in fifty years perhaps one point two to two point four metres. This would mean that many of the largest trees in the region, those of more than about ten metres or more in circumference, were several centuries old, in some cases conceivably a thousand years. A number of mature trees were carefully measured three to four years after their first measurements, but showed no appreciable increase in girth. This seemed to confirm that increase in size is very slow once a tree reaches a good size.

Perhaps, after all, the baobab is a valid contender for the title of the world's oldest tree, but there is strong competition. A peepul tree, *Ficus religiosa,* in Ceylon is reputed to be one of the oldest trees known and a part of this tree, said to have been brought from India nearly three hundred years BC, still survives. But a dragon's blood tree *(Dracaena draco)* in Teneriffe is a close contender, too, while some people believe that a cypress in Mexico is six thousand years old, and it is estimated from the annual rings of felled giant redwoods that these trees reach an age of four thousand years or more. A bristlecone pine *(Pinus aristate)* in Nevada, USA, at an estimated four thousand years seems to be the official record holder.

Hyaenas, harvesting
ants and hailstones

Amongst mammals the hyaenas probably have the worst reputation of all. Most people of all races regard them with revulsion as craven, ghoulish, mis-shapen creatures of disgusting habits, images far from the truth.

In Africa they are strongly associated with witchcraft and magic, a relation fostered by their mournful, almost ventriloquial, cries and the insane cackling of the spotted hyaena, together with their nocturnal, often skulking, habits. Many are the stories of their great size and stealthy cunning, of their seizing animals and people, of their supposed hermaphrodism★ and of were-hyaenas. But often in the folk-tales throughout Africa the hyaena is depicted as the brainless one, probably in an attempt to counteract superstitious fears of these familiars of witches.

In the Sudan there are many tales of Mfina, the hyaena, and Abu Halima, the jackal, in which the jackal always outwits the larger animal, and in *The Scurrying Bush* I retold a fable relating how the bushbaby tricked the hyaena. But the hyaena is not

★ Many Europeans also believe hyaenas to be hermaphrodites for the sex organs are far from obvious; the testes do not descend into the scrotum in the male; there are large labial swellings in the female, while both sexes have large anal pouch glands. It is thus difficult to decide the sex from a casual examination.

always bested in such folk-tales, as the following story from the Nuba Mountains tells of the striped hyaena.

The animals could not decide which was the strongest. One day Mfina called them all together to judge the issue. After they were all assembled Mfina said, 'Here is a big round stone. Let us see which animals can break this stone, for whichever animal can do this he would be the strongest and most feared of all.'

The stone was large, smooth and solid and all the animals agreed that indeed it would be a great feat to shatter it. Most thought it impossible, but one after the other they tried their strength. El Far, the rat, and Sabera, the squirrel, tried to break the stone with their teeth; El Arneb, the hare, and Umm Tigdim, the duiker, kicked it; Nimir, the leopard, and Fahad, the serval, clawed and chewed at it; Tigl, the baboon, tried throwing it about, while Umm Girfer, the pangolin, attempted to squeeze the stone between her scales, but none had any success.

At last it came to Mfina's turn, all the other animals being exhausted. However, El Hamil, the mongoose, said, 'Let the insects try first to see if they can break the stone.'

So the insects tried, but they all failed; the only ones that might have succeeded were the termites, but they took so long about it that the other animals became tired of waiting.

Finally, there was left only the hyaena. Mfina took the stone in his great jaws, exerted all his strength, and lo! The stone flew into many fragments.

At this all the animals were greatly frightened and ran away, and ever since have avoided the hyaena.

The largest common carnivores of the Nuba Mountains are the leopard and the striped hyaena (*Hyaena hyaena dubbah*), called *mfine karang* by the Arabs to distinguish it from *mfine balto*, the spotted hyaena (*Crocuta*). During the *kharif* (rains) from about May or June until well into the dry season, the striped hyaena may be seen frequently, but after December the animals are rare and retreat to the west and south where more food and water are available.

The spotted hyaena, although widespread and very common in some parts of the Sudan (the Ethiopian border, for example, and parts of Darfur) is an unusual visitor to the Nuba Mountains proper. The only other African hyaena, the brown (*H. brunnea*), is restricted to southern Africa where the striped hyaena does not occur, but the aardwolf (*Proteles*), a secretive, weak-jawed, insectivorous relative of the hyaenas, occurs, although I did not see it in the Nuba Mountains only in northern Kordofan.

I had the greatest difficulty in rearing my two striped hyaena cubs after I took them from inside the baobab, although their eyes were open and they were, I estimated, about a month old. Unlike most of the other young mammals I had kept, I could not persuade them to drink cow or goat's milk. Finally, I had to feed them forcibly with skimmed milk from a dropper, but even later they had little interest in any milk.

After a few days one of them died despite all my efforts to save it, but the other survived. Several weeks later, still clinging to life, the survivor had grown scarcely at all. However, once it began to eat minced meat it began to thrive and grow apace.

The gestation of the striped hyaena is a little more than three months and usually a litter will contain one or two young, but occasionally three or even four. Unlike those of the spotted hyaena the young are not black but resemble the coloration of the parents. When born, the cubs are blind, helpless, piteous objects quite unable to walk for the first two weeks or so, and they do not seem to be completely weaned until they are four or five months old.

At first my cubs were able to drag themselves about using only their front legs, and always went round in a circle, the back legs being scarcely capable of movement and dragged behind, but as they grew, of course, they became more functional. It was as though the hindquarters had been partially paralysed and even the adult never seems to recover completely.

It was only to be expected that these cubs should come to

accept a human foster parent since I have never found an infant mammal that would not. But I thought that adult hyaenas were quite untrustworthy, until I came to keep them. Despite this, I knew that in Ancient Egypt as early as the fifth dynasty (2750 BC) the striped hyaena was kept and sometimes bred by man, the animals being forcibly fed on ducks, geese or other birds to fatten them for the table. Today some Arabs and Africans still eat the striped hyaena.

One day word came to me that a grown hyaena had been caught alive by tribesmen in a village forty-five kilometres from Kadugli. This was astonishing news for it was extremely rare for any adult animal to be taken alive, and should such an accident occur the beast was normally quickly killed. True, pets were quite common, particularly amongst the Arabs, but these were almost always caught when young and were usually inoffensive creatures. Unfortunately I was too busy to collect the animal myself, but I had some men working not far from the village. I sent Younis with the lorry, instructing him how to deal with the hyaena. Two days later the lorry returned.

Despite their stint in the bush and having had to cope unexpectedly with the hyaena, the men looked remarkably cheerful if unwashed, disreputable and tired. The hyaena lay on sacking in the back of the lorry, trussed up so completely that it was scarcely able to move a muscle. I was glad to see that Younis had followed my instructions and used strips of cloth not rope and that the animal seemed quite unhurt. The tribesmen had suggested that the best way of incapacitating it was to break its legs.

There had been no time to prepare any sort of enclosure for the animal, so I decided to take it up to my house and keep it in the garden for a time.

Once there, the men removed the hyaena and laid it under a tree as I instructed. I fastened a stout collar round the hyaena's neck to which I clipped a horse chain. The other end of the chain I fastened round the tree.

While the hyaena was still helpless I examined it carefully for injuries, but beyond a slight head wound and a superficial gash on one front leg I could find no damage. It was a mystery to me how it had been caught in the first place and I never found out, but I think it must have been trapped by accident in a cattle enclosure or perhaps a hut, and then possibly knocked unconscious with a stick or stone. I put antiseptic on the wounds and decided to cut its bonds.

First of all I cut the cloth round its jaws and then I released the back legs. The hyaena made no movement. I then freed the front legs taking good care to hold a flat board as a shield between my arm and its head. Although the hyaena made no attempt to bite, I had a great respect for the immensely powerful jaws and teeth. Now it was free apart from the stout collar and chain.

For a few moments it lay without moving while we stood out of range and watched. I began to think that perhaps it was internally injured after all. When I moved up to it again, however, the hyaena struggled to its feet. I moved back. The animal watched but only bared its teeth slightly uttering a strange moaning. The onlookers were chattering loudly and when I moved gently towards the hyaena once more with my hand outstretched, the animal made to escape, lolloping off in the opposite direction only to be brought to an abrupt halt by the chain.

It was obviously completely terrified, backing away and moaning whenever I tried to coax it, snarling and snapping, showing its great teeth, and making mock charges that made me skip back out of reach. I noticed, however, that it very quickly realised the limit of the chain and soon began to stop short of this limit.

There was nothing I could do with it at this time. After the experiences the animal had had it would have been remarkable if I had been able to approach it closely. I sent everybody away, placed a bowl of water within the animal's reach, and retired into the house to watch. I told my servants to stay right out of sight of the hyaena for the rest of the day.

Later I went to my office, returning again towards evening. The hyaena, which we named Tik (the local Nuba name; *'ngo* is another Nuba name, while the Nuer use the expressive name *yah*), had, I was pleased to note, drunk most of the water in the bowl. There was no sound and nobody about when I took a hunk of meat to Tik. He let me approach a little more closely than before but would not take the meat. After talking quietly to him for a long time I went away, leaving the meat.

The next morning the meat had gone. For the next two or three weeks I kept everybody away from Tik and talked to him at least once a day. At first he refused to eat or drink when I was there, and would show his teeth and sometimes pretend to charge. I stood my ground, making no sudden movements, and took no notice of his aggression. In fact, mostly I ignored him altogether, just letting him become used to my voice and presence. Towards the end of this time I began to walk him about the garden. He still snarled at me in a half-hearted manner but made no attempt to attack even when my back was turned. By tugging gently on the chain I persuaded him to walk along. Even when used to me, he still would not let me touch him.

Tik soon settled down in his new enclosure at the zoo and even became used to people staring and commenting about him. After a time he allowed me to touch him, and soon learnt to come when he was called, holding up his great head to be stroked and rubbed, showing great delight and moaning with pleasure. Tik also let Abdulla, the keeper, fondle him.

When I was alone with him Tik would play like a dog, pretending to bite but never doing so in earnest, and I would often put my hand in his mouth while he gently chewed. He was never really happy out of his enclosure, however, unless alone with me at night, for he was still nervous of humans and especially of loud voices.

In front view Tik was a handsome animal with his long-eared, Alsatian-like head; powerful forequarters, the throat, muzzle and feet a deep glossy black; and great front legs with massive paws half as big again as those of the back feet. But seen from the side he was much less impressive, the back sloping away to his weak hindquarters and small hind legs. When alarmed or angry, however, his long crest or mane that reached almost to his bushy tail was raised giving him a most formidable appearance.

Striped hyaenas vary considerably in size, markings and colour. Tik measured a little more than a hundred centimetres from nose to tail base, and his tail was another thirty-four centimetres long. He stood sixty-eight centimetres at the shoulder and weighed about thirty-six kilos. But another male striped hyaena, called Fisi, that I kept at another time was a good five centimetres taller and tawnier than Tik who was a rather dirty whitish-grey ground colour. Although dog-like, hyaenas are most closely related to the cat family from which they are believed to have been separated some time in the tertiary era about thirty million years ago.

Hyaenas are well adapted to their scavenging life; the large front paws hold down a carcass so that they can tear at it with their strong teeth set in powerful, arched jaws that enable them to crunch the biggest bones; the neck is exceptionally muscular, and the fur, which is coarse and wiry, is not easily matted with blood or other fluids. Striped hyaenas normally hunt in ones and twos, probably never in packs. Of course, many may be attracted to a feast and I have seen as many as ten or a dozen at one carcass. The larger, more powerful, spotted hyaenas are often seen in packs.

Contrary to the usual belief, hyaenas are by no means exclusively carrion eaters, although this is often their main food. Both kinds will attack any young or helpless animal, goats, sheep and domestic fowls, guinea-fowls and other birds, and even locusts and other large insects. I once chased a striped hyaena in my Land Rover for a short distance when it ran at just under fifty kilometres per hour; it is thus capable of chasing and catching many antelopes, for it has considerable endurance, but I have never seen striped hyaenas hunting in the manner of spotted hyaenas. From experience, I know that the striped hyaena will chew bark and roots, or dig up bulbs when hungry. There is evidence to suggest that in ancient Egypt hyaenas were also sometimes used for hunting, like dogs.

A strong belief in the Nuba Mountains (and elsewhere) is that the striped hyaena will attack a man sleeping in the open, or even a lone man walking at night. Several such reports came to me, but I had no first hand experience of attacks on humans, and I believe that most, if not all, such reported attacks were of other animals, spotted hyaenas, hunting-dogs or leopards perhaps. All the same for such a nervous animal the striped hyaena is often extremely bold. Several times I have met them at night when they showed little fear (I related one such instance in *Jebels by Moonlight*), and they often enter villages at night. On several occasions I noted their tracks along the sandy main street in Kadugli, and one passed regularly through my garden between September and November, 1954, at about the same time each night.

While it seems very unlikely that striped hyaenas ever attack people except perhaps in very unusual circumstances, there is no doubt that the spotted hyaenas will (see also Chapter 8). In my travels around Africa I came across several Africans who had been injured by this beast. Spotted hyaenas have been known to enter huts to seize children or old women. They not only kill the young of other animals, especially antelopes, but will hunt adults, pulling down stragglers from herds of animals as large as zebra or wildebeest, and running down solitary hartebeest or even kudu. Where they are common they are undoubtedly a hunting predator of as great or greater importance than the big cats. They can run surprisingly quickly, being capable of over sixty kilometres per hour despite their ungainly appearance, and are thus faster than most antelope.

Packs of spotted hyaenas are loose communities apparently established for hunting purposes and are considerably less permanent than those of, say, the baboon. Exceptionally, solitary hyaenas are seen. Like the hunting-dog, spotted hyaenas tend to be on the move most of the time except where game is plentiful and fairly static, as in some reserves. In East Africa I saw packs of as many as thirty to forty individuals, but in the Sudan (they are rarely seen in the Nuba Mountains, although I recorded them in El Liri forest, around Subu some forty-five kilometres west of Talodi and near Lake Keilak) the most numerous pack I saw was made up of only eight or nine individuals.

Although hyaenas are regarded with disapproval, and certainly the spotted hyaena is not the most attractive looking of animals, they are really no worse and no better than any other predator. Lions, despite their grace and strength and their emotional appeal as 'big pussies' are just as ready to eat cadavers, and after such a meal they stink just as much as hyaenas. Nor is the lion's much vaunted family life all that it is usually said to be: cubs often die of starvation or are abandoned, and lions squabble over a kill to a greater extent than hyaenas. Hyaenas at least take better care of their young, and are certainly not as lazy. Few other mammals will respond as quickly to kind treatment as either of these hyaenas, and both are more certain tempered than any other large carnivore.

To any objective beholder Tik was undoubtedly a beautiful animal, and very clean now that he did not have to find his own food. He ate about two and a half kilos of meat and bones a day, usually goat's or bull's meat left over at the local butchery at the end of the day, but even so he was one of the most expensive animals I kept at the zoo. His enclosure was half open at the top, for he was unable to jump or climb a four-foot-high fence, but I was forced to cover over part of his quarters with wire netting to protect him from visitors.

Although Tik was tame and affectionate and quite harmless, for the hyaena's sake I did not allow Abdulla or anyone else into the enclosure to clean it. Instead, we used a long pole with a board nailed to the end to drag the debris to the fence where it could be removed easily. Tik often made Abdulla's work twice as long by pretending to fight this pole; indeed he bit it in half several times. When finally I left the Sudan, Tik was presented to Khartoum Zoo.

During this time I was making a survey of insects on baobab trees. Besides the ubiquitous stainer-bugs, my main study, I recorded more than a hundred different kinds of insects associated with baobabs. Some of these, like a little brown flea-beetle (*Podagrica*), lived on the leaves; others, such as the garishly coloured spiny larvae of a small green and brown moth (*Earias*) lived on the flowers. A few more lived in or on the bark or roots, and quite a number inhabited the ripe seeds, while others, like the bugs, *Odontopus*, competed with the stainers for food.

Still others, such as an assassin-bug, *Phonoctonus lutescens*, devoured the insects that lived in the trees. This assassin-bug was particularly interesting to me as it fed almost exclusively on the stainer-bugs, mimicking them to a surprising degree. Not only was the assassin-bug coloured in the same manner, but the colours were arranged in a similar way even to the extent of the two black bars on the wings and a black line on the thorax. Instead of the long, thin and flexible mouth tube of the stainer-bug by means of which it sucked the juices from plant tissues, the assassin-bug had a short, stout, pointed tube.

Mingling with the crowded stainer-bugs one of the assassin-bugs looked very similar but could be distinguished by the larger size and distinct neck. I watched many assassin-bugs feeding and made a particular study of their habits. They were certainly well named. With its long front legs one would suddenly grasp a passing stainer, often using its middle legs to help to subdue the prey, until like a dagger, the assassin-bug then sank its pointed mouth tube into the struggling stainer to inject it with paralysing saliva.

Often the predator turned the stainer on its back first so that the softer belly was stabbed and, dagger-like mouth still piercing the prey, the assassin-bug would begin to suck it dry, a process that might take several minutes. Finally, the almost empty skin of the stainer was discarded and the assassin-bug, sated for the time being, moved slowly away. Even the young, wingless assassins attacked the stainer-bugs, usually choosing those of a similar size, but sometimes a young one might attack an adult stainer two or three times as big as itself. A stainer very rarely escaped from even the smallest assassin, although the struggle was then often prolonged.

I found very many different kinds of assassin-bugs (*Reduviidae*) in my travels. They are amongst the leopards of the insect world. Some, like *Phonoctonus*, were large, capable of piercing one's skin to cause a painful prick that often irritated for some days; others were minute and preyed on tiny, fragile insects. The numerous species had different methods of concealment and attack; some resembled their prey to a surprising degree; others were sticky so that particles of soil or vegetable matter adhered to their backs to make them invisible until they moved. Still others hid under flakes of bark or lurked in flowers or foliage to catch unwary bees or flies.

Some of the insects that I found were unknown to science. For example, a few beetles and termites, and some of the strange little creatures known as web-spinners (*Embioptera*). Probably as closely related to termites as to any other living group of insects, web-spinners have very secluded habits and are hardly known even to most entomologists. Yet they are easily found and occur often in vast numbers. They live in family societies like termites and ants, concealing themselves under webbing spun over crevices on trees, rocks, soil grass roots and many other places, even within the nests of ants or termites. Only the males are winged (not in all species) and, although the young and females live as vegetable scavengers, in some kinds the males are believed to be partly carnivorous.

Leptembia sweeneyi is a large, pale species that I found on several occasions in the southern part of the Nuba Mountains in the rains, when the males are often attracted to light. The colonies of another kind are found in silken galleries on baobab trunks. On one occasion several hundred females and young were present, but usually they occurred in smaller families. One curious fact about these insignificant but interesting insects that resemble small termites with a greatly enlarged segment containing silk spinning glands to each front foot, is their ability to run as quickly backwards as forwards along their runways.

The discovery and collection of unknown creatures did not interest me as much as the fascinating way many animals lived. Thousands of 'new' species of animals are discovered every year. But next to nothing is known of the lives and habits of thousands of even common kinds that have been labelled.

I have always retained a particular interest in the social insects, especially the ants and termites. In my youth I kept and studied almost all of the thirty-five or so kinds of ants indigenous to Britain, but despite such fascinating species as the red *Formica sanguinea* that makes slaves of the black *F. fusca*, it was only when I came to the tropics that I really appreciated the great diversity of habits and forms of these insects and of the more primitive termites, absent in Britain, that show such a remarkable evolutionary convergence with ants.

Already in my first two years in the Nuba Mountains I had collected and watched with wonder many of the local termites and ants. One of the termites that intrigued me I recognised as a *Pseudacanthotermes*, but I did not know the species. I collected some in 1952 and presented them to the British Museum (Natural History), but they were not further identified until 1962 when they were described as a new species, *P. harrisensis*. On the baobabs were several common ants and termites. Large oval-eyed, reddish ants (*Tetraponera*) with long thin bodies scurried about singly with urgent speed, ready if alarmed to vanish with almost magical celerity behind a leaf or under loose bark. A moment later the large-eyed head would poke forth again as though to see that all was clear. The white larva of this ant, which usually nests in hollow twigs, bears a remarkable if much reduced resemblance to a baby in swaddling clothes.

In contrast to the red ants was a short, squat flattened black kind (*Meranoplus magrettii*) with spines at the corners of the thorax. It crawled over the bark with tortoise progress and curled up to feign death if touched. Sometimes, in moister areas, a much more pugnacious ant (*Odontomachus*) lived, often nesting at or near a tree base. Equipped with a virulent sting this was one of several kinds to cause complaints from my men. It had the curious habit, when face to face with a foe or some unwelcome object such as a finger, of opening the long, almost straight mandibles to make a line at right angles to its flat, square head, and then snapping the jaws together again with such force that it would be projected backwards sometimes several times its own length. In this manner the ant could escape from immediate danger.

Occasionally, I found the very hard, domed mounds of harvester termites (*Trinervitermes*), in places so numerous that it was impossible to drive a Land Rover between them. These colonies were always very populous, tens of thousands of termites to each mound, the nest containing many granaries full of cut grass gathered when plentiful to provide food for the winter. Several times on a still, moist night I can remember listening to the termites in their millions as, frantically active, they cut and collected grasses for their underground chambers. The sound produced by each little insect as it dragged a blade of grass longer than itself towards the nest was inaudible, but the millions working together made a scratching rustle that I could hear even in my tent. In such places, the termites' activities result in a complete stripping of young grass thus leaving little pasture for graminivorous animals.

Another noticeable harvester is an ant, *Messor barbarus*, an insect famous in literature from the time of Solomon. In one of its several racial forms it is found from the Caspian Sea and Persia to Tanganyika and in South Africa, and is widespread in the Mediterranean countries. There seems little doubt that the harvesting habit in both ants and termites is an adaptation to more arid conditions, for true harvesters are more numerous in semi-desert regions where food is scarce for prolonged periods. Such harvesting insects sometimes extend their range into wetter regions but are then found in the drier parts of these regions.

The first time I appreciated the effect and numbers of harvesting ants was from the air when I was flying somewhere over North Africa; for a few seconds I saw the ground dotted with bare circular patches as though the grassland was suffering from ringworm. At first I thought I must have seen a curious village, but then I realised that I had been looking at clearings made round each nest of a harvesting ant, clearings so numerous that almost half the immense plain had been denuded. Later, I saw a similar sight in the Sudan when flying in an Auster over Kordofan; mile after mile of circular or oval sites denuded of grass, each patch several metres in diameter, and so distinct from the air that they were much easier to count than huts in a village.

In the Nuba Mountains this harvesting ant (*M. barbarus*) was rarely as noticeable although common enough. Several nests occurred within a few hundred metres' radius of my house, and there was one large and populous colony scarcely a stone's throw outside my garden wall.

For a year or two I paid little attention to this nest, but one day I noticed an unusual amount of activity. It was towards the end of the rains and the harvesting of grass seeds was at its peak, when I saw continuous columns of ants moving to and from the nest, an elevated crater about twenty-three centimetres high and nearly a hundred centimetres from rim to rim with several entrances. This round city, containing many thousands of ants, stood in the centre of an almost circular bare patch of soil some six metres in diameter, and there were three main roadways radiating from it.

The main highway, trodden smooth, was more than fifty centimetres wide where it left the bare surround of the city and entered dense grasses; it continued for another six or seven metres, the trail gradually narrowing until it became scarcely three centimetres wide and then indistinguishable. From this point, although here and there the road was still visible, only the columns of ants indicated the routes as they dispersed into the grasses that waved like giant redwoods above their heads.

The main highway ended at three entrance and exit holes at the nest, but the two other tracks leading to the colony were narrower, less well-defined, and each ended at a single entrance to the nest. At different times of the year, depending on the activity of the colony, the number of exits from the nest varied and at the height of the dry season the city gates were often completely closed.

On this occasion almost all the ants, shining black and of two main sizes, the smaller workers about four to five millimetres long, the larger workers nine to eleven millimetres with massive square heads of a dark reddish hue, were on the main highway. I noticed that most of the ants were moving in one direction, away from the nest, and I traced their course out through the grasses until I found a confused *mêlée* of ants. At first I thought all the ants came from the big colony, but there were desperate fights in progress and I soon realised that some of the battling creatures were from another, much smaller, colony of harvesting ants close by.

Struggling groups of ants fought fiercely together, not only attacking each other but trying to pull the grass seeds away from one another. Although I had not witnessed the start of the battle, it seemed obvious that foraging columns from the two different nests had met, engaged in battle, and that each side was trying now to capture as much booty as possible. As foolish as men, the ants squabbled when in fact there was a sufficiency for all in the vast grass forest.

The battle was certainly violent. I saw several ants with their abdomens nipped off still staggering about while many more were minus a limb or antenna. Gruesomely, one decapitated worker, still upright, moved its legs in slow, hesitant motion to carry the headless trunk aimlessly about. Some of the mutilated ants acted as though in pain, hobbling round quickly in a tight circle, blundering into obstacles, heedless of other workers.

I watched one ant snatch up a fallen seed and scurry off towards the smaller nest only to be waylaid by three others, members of the rival army, one of which, a massive-headed worker, bit the carrier severing the abdomen and one leg. The two others tried to wrest the seed from the wounded carrier, the three moving first one way and then another, but the mutilated ant that had found the seed would not let go. At last they moved back towards the large nest, dragging both the seed and the wounded ant, and I lost sight of them.

The harvesting ant collects so much seed that where the nests occur amongst cultivated graminaceous crops, as they often do, the farmer may lose a noticeable proportion of his harvest. It has been calculated, for example, that about ninety litres per hectare is taken by the ants from wheatfields in parts of North Africa. It is interesting to note that the ants have even been the subject of legislation in Jewish law, for in the Mishnah, the collection of oral precepts forming the basis of the Talmud, the rabbis decided that, at harvest time, any grain dropped by the (human) harvesters, any ungarnered stalks, and those standing at the corners of a field, belonged to the poor. So it was decided also that any grain dropped by the ants, or brought out to be sunned on top of the nest, likewise belonged to the poor, while that harvested by the ants and stored in their underground granaries belonged to the owner of the field. However, there seems to have been a minority opinion that all the grain gathered by the ants should belong to the poor. Either way the ants were robbed.

The subterranean granaries of a populous colony are sometimes very numerous, and the total amount of seed in an average nest may measure over a litre. When finally, a year or more later, I dug out the large nest near my garden I obtained nearly a litre and a half (one thousand, four hundred and fifty centilitres) of vegetable matter from the seventy flat cell-like granaries of varying sizes that belonged to the colony; although a certain amount of trash was included there was still more than a litre of seeds.

The ants are fond of eating the radicle or sprout of the seed, and since the seed often begins to germinate in the damp, underground granaries, the insects frequently bite off the radicle. This not only prevents further germination but helps to convert the starch of the grain to sugar, making the stored seed much sweeter when it is finally eaten. It was believed by ancient writers that the ants were very wise thus to purposively increase the sweetness and storability of their food, a belief that has been fostered by many modern authors, but I think it is more likely that the young root sprout is simply a tempting morsel and the results are fortuitous for ants often eat the immature root of growing seedlings.

Nevertheless, the ants do have a method of preventing germination that seems to be deliberate, done with a knowledge of cause and effect. Often damp seeds are taken out of the granary to spread in the sun on the nest surface. This usually dries them sufficiently to kill them or at least to delay germination; the heat also has the effect of causing the hard husk or shell of many ripe seeds to split or crack so that they are more readily eaten. The ant larvae are fed by the workers on a kind of ant 'bread' made up of the premasticated contents of such seeds.

The unwanted debris of the nest, particularly the husks of seeds, chaff and the hard parts of insects (for the ants not only live on vegetable food but will attack most kinds of insects) are thrown out of the colony in one place on the side of the nest. This midden is often large, although much of it may be blown or washed away from time to time and sometimes, as I have seen, termites and other insects may reap a rich harvest from the ants' rubbish. There is often much of interest to the entomologist, too, for such middens sometimes give a clue to the smaller insects of the area and I have found the remains of several interesting kinds that otherwise I would not have known to exist. Even more would a botanist, interested in collecting the seeds of the region, find great reward by opening up the granaries, perhaps saving himself months of work.

I watched the two warring colonies for more than an hour. There was no doubt that the larger colony proved victorious for many of the ants left the field of battle to return to the big nest with grass seed booty, but I saw none manage to reach the smaller nest. Whether this was a single incident, or the conflict had been continuous over a number of days, or if since the founding of the two colonies warring raids had been intermittent, I do not know. But other entomologists, observing these ants on the Mediterranean, have recorded battles that have lasted for weeks.

My observations were put to an end by one of the most violent storms of the season; soaked, I reached my house. I had only just entered when a noise as though a hundred machine-guns had begun to fire deafened me. I tried to shout at Ahmed who stood at my shoulder, but it was impossible for him to hear. In any heavy storm the corrugated iron roof of the house drummed loudly under the beating rain, but this noise was incredible. Looking out, I saw it was hail, a most unusual occurrence – so unusual, in fact, that most of the inhabitants had never seen hailstones before. Some of these were the largest I had seen myself for, after ten minutes or so, the hail passed, and I picked up several stones as large as a small lemon, and not one of the thickly littered white stones was much smaller than a python's egg. Once the villagers overcame their initial distrust of such magic, many gathered up the cold white stones to store them in their huts.

It was with great wonder my servants examined the hailstones, astonished to find them so cold. Artificial ice from a refrigerator was fairly commonplace, but they had never imagined ice could drop from the sky. At least one Nuba was killed that day, as well as donkeys and goats, all hit by hailstones.

Only a few days later a grass fire spread right up to my garden wall but fortunately the grass was still too moist to burn really fiercely although it swept over the two ants' nests. I had not visited the ants since the day of the hailstorm, but the day after the fire I went to see if they had survived. At the larger nest there was already activity, but there was no sign of life at the smaller colony. I dug this up in due course. I found several half-filled granaries, numerous dead ants within the nest, but the city was dead, not a living ant there. Whether the colony had died because of the stronger neighbouring ants, or whether the fire had completed their work, was uncertain, but the fact remained that the city no longer existed.

Big nose

Travelling in the wet season produces expected difficulties in Africa. One hazard in the Sudan was perhaps unusual, but fortunately not very common. After heavy rain some sandy tracks dried out, becoming apparently firm but still saturated and fluid below the surface crust, a condition known locally as *umm jemaleih* and akin to skating on thin ice. At one moment it was possible to be driving on a seemingly perfect surface, at the next brought to an abrupt halt, the vehicle sinking sometimes to bonnet depth as though in blancmange. Few driving hazards are more disconcerting.

But the dry season also had its perils for the traveller. Bush fires were commonplace, being caused by lightning late in the season, honey-bee hunters, charcoal-burners, or the villagers burning weed growth as a preliminary to planting when the rains returned. Others were started by travellers, it being the habit of Islamic wayfarers to leave a camp fire burning.

Most devastating of all, however, was the *Sibr el Nar* (the Festival of Fire) that occurred usually in December when the *kujur* (priest) led the villagers to start fires in the hills with the object of driving away any evil spirits that were lurking about preparatory to causing harm during the coming year. Fortunately, in the Nuba Mountains proper, the country was mostly too broken for a fire to sweep devouringly across the land.

It was a different matter on the flat, tall grass plains or open woodland to the south and west where fires could be a major danger to the traveller. Even those few fortunate enough to travel by motor-vehicle (almost invariably a lorry) were not always able to escape, especially as most lorries had unshielded propeller shafts around which dry grasses tended to wind themselves to become hot and burst into flames. Several government Commer lorries were destroyed in this manner and at least one driver burnt to death.

Only once did I find myself in any serious danger from a bush fire. I was on trek in January making my way back to Kadugli through country to the south-east of the Nuba Mountains. We pitched camp after a long, tiring day. There had been no rain for three months and for some hours I had driven across open thorn savanna where the tall grasses stood in straw-yellow, brittle ranks on desiccated clay soil so cracked and fissured that it resembled a badly fitting jigsaw puzzle. Climbing into bed soon after seven, I fell asleep immediately.

About six hours later I was awakened by the tent canvas, an awning that unrolled from the Land Rover roof to be fastened by guy-ropes to the ground, collapsing on top of my bed. I pushed my way out from under the material in time to hear the sound of some heavy animal blundering away. It took me a few seconds to realise that the night was strangely illuminated by a reddish glow in the sky.

Standing on top of the Land Rover, for I could see nothing but grass and tree tops from the ground, I gazed towards the north where the sky was brightest. It was like looking at the light reflected from a great city. The wind blew strongly, warm and fire-scented against my face, and I could hear the faint crackling of the flames as soft ashes began to float down from the sky. There was no doubt that the fire was approaching rapidly.

Despite the disturbance the men were still asleep under their own canvas on the other side of the Land Rover. Jumping to the ground I roused them. We had to leave at once. Even during the few moments I had watched, the fire, fanned by the wind, was much nearer, coming from the north on a very broad front; only to the south, the way we had come the day before, did there seem any chance of escape. There was no sanctuary nearby for the grass savanna, studded with low, already sere trees, stretched to all horizons. Had it not been for the animal that had uprooted the guy-rope (most likely a hartebeest) probably we would all have slept until it was too late to escape. As it was the fire nearly caught us.

We bundled everything into the Land Rover as quickly as possible. I was astonished how quickly the fire approached. Like an advancing army pursuing a routed enemy the flames surged forward in great leaps behind a barrage of sparks and hot cinders setting light to parts of the rapidly narrowing belt of grass still between us and the main fire front so that dozens of little advanced fires started until engulfed by the main blaze. Tree tops burst into sheets of flame to shoot skywards above the rest with the effect of individual shell bursts, while the vegetation below hissed, crackled, popped and exploded to add more terror to the heat, and the unburnt grass shivered and rippled as if anxious to flee before the inferno.

My three men scrambled aboard, slapping at sparks scorching their clothes or the canvas hood of the Land Rover. I pressed the self-starter, but perhaps in my anxiety to be gone I fumbled; the engine, that until now had invariably started almost immediately, refused to fire. I tried again, keeping my thumb hard down, but the only response was an ill-mannered whine.

Fortunately, the starting handle was easily accessible. Shielding his face, Younis jumped out with it, but in his excitement found difficulty in engaging the end. Controlling a mounting panic I joined him and together we managed to push it home. I dashed back to the cab. Younis swung the handle furiously and to our relief the engine came to life. The heat was now intense, the nearest flames seemed to tower above us scarcely thirty metres away. Just as I engaged the gear I glanced at a fresh flame that had just come to life in line with my side window. Between it and us there was what seemed to be a small dark boulder rolling steadily over the ground. Once again I leapt out, picked up the tortoise, hurled it to Younis, and was back in the car and driving away before the others realised what had happened.

After the first acceleration that left the fog of smoke and fumes behind, I drove more slowly trying to keep due south. The dark, the smoke and the long grass made driving hazardous and I soon lost the path of flattened grasses made previously by the Land Rover. We hit a hidden termite mound or rock that nearly turned us over, but I did not stop to investigate any possible damage (later I found the track-rod had been bent).

It must have been about a quarter of an hour later that we found our way blocked by fire ahead. I stopped the Land Rover and from the roof looked about us. Apparently, I had driven more west than south and we seemed to be ringed by flames in depth. It seemed that the only way of escape was to drive directly into the fire where it seemed less fierce in the hope that our momentum would carry us through before we caught fire or the petrol exploded.

Any hope of escape now seemed slender, but I drove slowly as close to the ring of fire as I dared looking for a gap in the flames, or at least a point where they seemed less fierce. Unexpectedly, glimpsing an unburnt area, still to the south, I accelerated, and we hurtled over the ground. For a few moments I could see nothing and expected at every second to thud into a tree, but then the smoke cleared and we found we were out of the encircling flames. In front lay the cool, peaceful savanna; looking back I saw the fire soon close the narrow, unburnt gap through which we had escaped.

Continuing south, for we were still not out of danger as the fire still moved after us on a very wide front, eventually we came to a wide dry *khor*, possibly the Shelengo, found a way across, and stopped on the far bank. The width of the *khor* and its bare, muddy bed was, I thought, sufficient barrier to the flames, at least at this point. No doubt the fire, when it arrived, would cross somewhere, but, if so, we could then either continue our southward retreat or return across the *khor* where the fire should have died down.

I was surprised to find that it was only half-past two, three hours before dawn. Any further desire to sleep had gone, however, and while Ahmed made tea, I arranged a seat on top of the Land Rover cab from which I could watch the progress of the fire. By the time I had drunk two or three cups of tea the wall of flame, seemingly infinite, was only a few hundred metres away.

So far we had seen few animals, but now a small flock of high-stepping ostriches, a cock and several hens or young birds, illuminated from behind by the awesome glow, arrived on the opposite bank of the *khor*. For a moment they ran along the bank, then the cock bird half ran and half jumped, crossed over the *khor* to be followed by the others in single file. The huge birds crossed almost within touching distance but, ignoring us, quickly disappeared into the grass. Almost immediately a panic-striken hare tumbled over the north bank into the *khor*, picking itself up in an instant to race down the dry river bed below the Land Rover before vanishing like the ostriches on the south bank.

Hot ashes began to fall on us again, and the flames began to leap like some monstrous, many-limbed beast trying to cross the *khor* where the ostriches had passed. Fortunately, the greener vegetation of the *khor* bank had a sobering effect on the wild flames and, although parts of the far bank became incandescent, the advance was halted. In a few minutes the fire died down as the fuel was exhausted to leave only isolated areas fiercely burning. To the west and east, however, the *khor* was bridged by the flames, probably begun by drifting embers, and soon the grass to the left and right of us began to blaze fiercely in several places, the conflagration beginning to spread slowly sideways towards us.

It was time to move again, but instead of running further southwards before the fire I decided to return across the khor and continue our northward journey over the scorched and reeking land. We had to pick our way carefully for there were still red embers and smouldering wood, but we found a small area on the north bank where we could breakfast. Everything in the Land Rover was smeared or covered with drifting ashes, and the breakfast of fried eggs that Ahmed produced was no exception. I ate it as dawn came and the fire consumed our night's sanctuary on the south bank.

The sun was up by the time we set out once more northwards, but now instead of dense, waving grass all was smoking desolation studded with leafless, charred trees. At least once a year most trees on the plains are subjected to fire, with the result that all dominant savanna species become strongly fire resistant, and it was an experience to see blackened, apparently dead woodland burst into renewed life after the first rain.

We made good progress across the fire-denuded plain, but I stopped to watch the birds at one place where a tongue of unburnt bush ablaze around the edge projected into the blackened area.

I often watched the birds that came to bush fires or that followed locust or termite swarms, recording some thirty species in the Sudan, but I never saw as many kinds at one time as I did that day. Swifts dashed daringly through the smoke, soaring up in the clear sky to glide down before twisting and turning they disappeared into the smoke again, their speeding, sickle-shaped forms mocking the bounding flames that seemed about to pluck them from the air.

The swifts were not in numbers – I counted only nine – and amongst them flew two or three small, dark short-winged birds about the size of a sparrow that tantalisingly never emerged long enough from the smoke to be identified. Several Abyssinian rollers, light and dark blue birds with chestnut backs very like the European roller but with long graceful tails resembling slender tuning forks, took advantage of a larger tree the fire had yet to reach, perching there before swooping down, seemingly into the flames, to snatch one of the numerous grasshoppers or other insects driven out by the heat.

Abyssinian roller

I noticed two or three black, fish-tailed drongos, a small party of noisy, grey-back shrikes, black, white and grey long-tailed birds, and some red-breasted wheatears. Several lapwings were scattered over the plain at a further distance. But amongst the smaller birds were two beautiful kinds that I was surprised to see. One was the rufous-crowned roller, a bird that I did not record from the Nuba Mountains and which I had seen only once previously. Only a single one was hawking the insects, but it took no notice of me and I moved to within a few metres to obtain a perfect view through my binoculars as it perched on the same low branch each time after a foray.

Larger in body that the Abyssinian roller but with a shorter, square tail, the violet-purple of the tail and wings, pink underparts, and head with a large white eye-stripe and black bill gave the rufous-crowned roller an even more striking and colourful appearance than its commoner relative.

Large green blue-cheeked bee-eater

The other bird, the large green blue-cheeked bee-eater, of which there was a flock of seven or eight, I had seen briefly on several occasions before but only along densely wooded *khors* or swamps, never at a bush-fire. It was delightful to be able to observe so clearly these brilliant flashing green birds with their long curved bills, elongated central tail feathers trailing behind, as they flew like delicately carved jade magically brought to life.

While circling the burning area we disturbed a grasshopper hawk, almost running it down it was so reluctant to leave its prey, but it flew up almost under the Land Rover wheels to soar high and wait for our passing before descending again to continue its meal. Not far away over the charred plain were the plump silhouettes of three ground hornbills, the largest of the hornbills almost a metre long with a wing expanse of one and a half metres or so, birds often misnamed 'turkey' or 'turkey-buzzard' amongst Europeans in Africa.

I drove slowly towards the hornbills. As with all large birds on open ground they have a minimum 'approach distance', allowing you so close but no nearer without taking alarm. Few large ground birds will permit anybody closer than about twenty to twenty-five metres in my experience, although the distance varies with species and circumstances. In a vehicle, however, it is often possible to go a bit closer by circling in a narrowing spiral.

However, on this occasion, although the hornbills were busy feeding on the charred body of a puff-adder, they soon waddled away on their stout legs, black feathered bodies held erect, but glancing backwards over their shoulders now and again to show the huge, black bill and the short, high truncate casque at the base. The male, distinguished by his red throat, led the retreat followed by the two blue-throated females. When I tried to close the gap, accelerating slightly, the three birds lumbered into the air almost simultaneously, great wings showing the white feathers as they beat heavily towards the horizon at tree-top height.

I thought about following them, but they rapidly became mere specks in the distance and showed no sign of landing again, so I continued on my way. Several times previously I had studied this curious hornbill and its habits, but I had not yet kept one in captivity.

Shortly after seeing the hornbills we came to the limit of the burnt area and the going became slow and tedious again. During the afternoon, however, we struck a Baggara cattle trail that, although unused for many years, enabled us to make faster progress. We soon lost this path, but the acacia woodland was fairly open again with many game trails, and we continued our north-westerly journey. I had not been here before, but I could tell from the nature of the topography that we could not be far from Lake Keilak. Once more we came to a burnt area that stretched as far as the eye could see. Rather than cross this and probably be forced to camp amid the blackened ashes, I decided to spend the night in the unburnt woods.

Sheltered by the trees I ate my supper while looking out across the fire-swept plain. In the dusk I noticed a pair of ground hornbills still foraging only a short distance away close to a small flock of guinea-fowl. Younis wanted to go and see if he could shoot one or two guinea-fowl but, as I saw that the hornbills had now flown off into a denser patch of bush, an island including some evergreen trees where the ground was broken by several dips and depressions, I would not let him. I thought that after dark I would go and see if I could find the hornbills for I was sure they were roosting in the evergreens and I did not want any disturbance.

When I set off towards midnight there was no moon and the night was very black and misty, the stars obscured by thin, high clouds. Despite the darkness I found my way easily enough to the place where the hornbills had disappeared, only a few hundred metres away, by walking along the edge of the burnt area.

The clump of greener trees where I was sure the hornbills were roosting stood out as a darker amorphous shape against the lighter sky at the edge of a shallow, dry *khor* surrounded by bushes and thigh-tall grasses that had once been lush. Nevertheless, the copse was not difficult to penetrate, although in the rainy season it must have been an impenetrable tangle. As quietly as possible I crept into the thicket, occasionally flashing my torch into the trees to try and spot the birds, but the foliage was thick in places largely due to overhanging creepers. Although I made little sound the night was so silent, except for the faint rustle of vegetation that occurs on the stillest night, that my own deliberate movements seemed loud to my ears. There was not even the rasp of a cricket to be heard. Then there was an explosion of sound so sudden and startling that my heart leaped; the whole copse seemed to be alive and struggling to escape in every direction. A wing beat in my face as a large bird launched itself from above, and instinctively I clutched at it, but the bird escaped. Frantically, I swung the torch beam about, but, apart from a brief glimpse of speckled feathers, the light showed only deserted trees and shrubs.

In the distance I could still hear rustling, but otherwise the noisy flight of alarmed birds had passed. I realised that I had blundered among and awakened the flock of guinea-fowl I had seen earlier that must have gone to roost in the trees, and I was sure that the hornbills had departed with them. Cursing the guinea-fowl, I was about to move on when my ear caught the sound of movement near my feet. Swinging the torch-beam the light disclosed the black form of a crouching hornbill caught in a bush, one wing outspread with the feathers in disarray. Perhaps it was the bird that had brushed my face and, off-balance, had landed in the shrub. Leaning forward, I picked it up.

Delighted with my unexpected capture, I took the big bird back to my camp. It proved to be unhurt and I put it carefully into a grass-lined box to transport it home.

My hornbill soon adapted himself to his new life. He was free to walk about the zoo compound after I had clipped a few feathers in one wing to prevent his flying over the fence, and I was surprised how quickly he made himself at home. At first he was nervous and kept clear of some of the bigger caged animals, avoiding all humans, but he quickly joined company with the other birds that roamed the compound. It was not long before he undoubtedly recognised me and Abdulla, the keeper, and after only a few weeks he would come waddling over immediately on sighting one of us, uttering a croaky call the while, as if he were clearing his throat.

He was christened *minkar kebir*, which means 'big nose', but I usually called him Nosy. Hornbills are certainly amongst the world's most intelligent birds and Nosy's name suited him for not only was his great beak his most obvious feature, but he was also very inquisitive. Once I was accepted as a 'friend' he became very affectionate and would often come up to squat down nearby. I soon realised that he expected to be scratched and stroked, much as a dog will ask for the same attention. After being scratched on one side, Nosy would shift his position to bring his other side to my notice, while his beak would half open in enjoyment.

Nosy's final seal of approval came perhaps three months after his capture. His main food consisted of offal obtained from the local butcher, supplemented by an occasional dead rodent, snake or other animal that I might find, and a few insects or lizards that he sometimes caught himself. On this day I was watching him feed when he detached a particularly noisome intestine with the tip of his bill and presented it to me, by dropping it in my lap as I crouched down beside him.

The ground hornbill's beak, so massive, clumsy looking and so out of proportion that it appears laughable to most human beings, is really a marvellously precise tool. Attached to a small head that has enormous eyes equipped with long eyelashes and encircled by naked skin, the bill is so light that it weighs no more than a few of the bird's feathers, yet it is rigid and strong enough to peck a snake to death, so powerful that it can tear the flesh of a tortoise out of its shell, and can be used so delicately that with the tip the bird can pick up an ant and hold it.

To see Nosy picking over pieces of carton from a termites' nest showed the astonishing versatility and control he had over his unwieldy looking bill. The carton I gave him was often in heavy, large pieces yet, using his bill as a lever, he never had any difficulty turning the carton over. Then with great dexterity he picked up sometimes as many as a dozen termites as they scurried for cover again, holding each termite, or sometimes two or three, with the tip of his bill before throwing it into the air and opening his mouth to catch it as it fell.

Even for such a large bird the ground hornbill's appetite is great and little comes amiss. Not only will it attack and eat all kinds of insects, spiders, snails and other invertebrates, but the birds will devour any vertebrate it can overpower, carrion, and many fruits and seeds.

I have watched ground hornbills feeding some dozen times in various parts of Africa, and on one occasion one of four birds discovered a snake. There had been a fire through the area some days before, but there were islands of bushes and grasses untouched by the flames. The hornbills were scattered when the one found the snake, a fairly large reptile, and attacked it in the usual fashion, spreading its wings and dancing and jumping about. It was difficult for me, even with binoculars, to see exactly what was happening for, although the grass was burnt, there was still a stubble left and the large bird's antics caused the dry ash to fly up creating a black snowstorm.

The three other birds moved rapidly towards the dancing one, running with long strides over the ground. Every so often the bird with the snake darted his long bill forward to peck as he continued his buoyant dance, his wings flapping to hold him poised so that only the tips of his toes seemed to touch the ground. One of the running birds, and perhaps the others as well, uttered a deep call sounding like 'hough-hough, hough', the first two notes following on top of one another, the third uttered after a pause, but before they reached the snake it managed to escape into an unburnt patch of grass. After a minute's futile searching the hornbills wandered off.

The ground hornbill's remarkable voice is often heard; despite its deepness the penetrating boom carries a long way. People often describe the call as like the grunt of a lion, and perhaps it does have the same strange ventriloquial power, but to me it more closely resembles the boom of some African drums or even the deep sound that can be made by blowing into the neck of a big bottle. There is quite a difference in the voices of the two species, the

Abyssinian ground hornbill (*Bucorvus abyssinicus*) found only north of the equator, and the southern ground hornbill (*B. leadbeateri*), for I have listened often to them both, but I cannot describe the distinction.

On another occasion I saw two ground hornbills behaving in a very curious manner, running from grass patch to grass patch as though chasing something or like dogs following a scent. The only other animal nearby was a lapwing behaving in a demented manner but which the hornbills ignored. I could see no connection between the lapwing and the bigger birds and, as lapwings tend to become hysterical on small provocation, its presence seemed to be accidental. I thought perhaps the hornbills were harrying and trying to catch a small rodent or similar small animal.

Unable to contain my curiosity I moved towards the two hornbills causing them to stride away, and for some minutes I searched the ground; except for partially burnt, sparsely stemmed grass there was no cover, but the lapwing was still flying round, crying piteously, and its interest I thought must be more than casual after all. A moment later I found this to be the case for three small lapwing chicks ran to scatter in different directions and to freeze again in a second. It was late in the year for such chicks, but it was undoubtedly the lapwing brood that the hornbills were after.

To see such a cumbersome-looking bird as a ground hornbill take to flight, even though on enormous wings, makes one wonder how it manages to fly at all. Yet, once in the air, it is a powerful if slow flyer, although it seldom flies very far to escape the attentions of man. At times, however, I have seen them fly so high that they have been scarcely visible. It is possible as is the case with some other heavy, ground-dwelling birds that the large, inflatable air sac at the throat aids flight by altering the centre of gravity to enable the bird to rise; but the functions of this sac are not fully understood and it may also help to keep the bird cool by exposing such a large area of naked skin to the air.

Unlike other African hornbills, neither of the two species of ground hornbill closes its nest by plastering up the hole. It sometimes nests high above the ground in holes in trees or even cliffs, but probably more often chooses old stumps, hollow logs or rotten trees. The nest is made of sticks, often lined with leaves, and there are one to three dirty white, stained eggs that take about three months to incubate. It is said, although I cannot confirm this, that female and male take it in turns to incubate the eggs, but there is no doubt that the female often leaves the eggs during the day and may hunt a long way from the nest. In southern Kordofan breeding takes place in the early rains and I have seen the young in September and October.

Naturally, a bird as large and conspicuous as this ungainly hornbill is the subject of much superstition and legend. In some parts of East and South Africa, the Bantu will never kill one, the birds being regarded with reverent respect except by some tribes during a prolonged drought. Even then the drought has to be exceptional and the bird is killed with reluctance.

The belief that the ground hornbill is associated with the fall of rain is widespread but possibly originated amongst the Zulu. In extreme cases, all his other magic having failed, a rain-maker may demand the death of one of these birds. The hornbill is killed and cast into a stream or lake in the belief that the smell of the bird will make the water 'sick' and cause rain to fall to wash it clean again. In East Africa the hornbill is said to control the rain, and during a drought only the death of a bird will release the rain.

I did not hear of these Bantu superstitions amongst the Nilotic or Hamitic peoples of the Sudan, but they too regard the ground hornbill with respect. On one occasion the driver of a lorry, working temporarily for me, refused to continue his journey until the next day after seeing one of these birds cross the track in front of him, and the belief is widely held that it would have caused disaster to do so.

Nosy lived for a long time in my zoo compound. His wing

feathers grew, but although he could fly again he did not desert me. All the same I felt it was time he should return to his own kind, since I had no intention of trying to catch him a companion.

Soon, during the late rains, a peak period of insect activity, I went to look at an area of crops near Lagowa where insect pests were reported to be causing serious damage. I took Nosy with me, made a detour on my way, and released him not far from the place where I had first caught him. I scratched his head, neck and back for the last time in farewell, and put him down with a muttered *'Ibshir bil kheir!'* (May your way prosper!)

Nosy stood up, shook his feathers and looked about; he waddled a step or two and then came back, squatting down and cocking an eye up at me, asking for more caresses. Firmly, I hoisted myself into the Land Rover and drove away, but I stopped in a short time to watch. At first I thought Nosy was going to follow for he began to walk towards us, but next I saw him going slowly off in another direction; he ran to chase an insect and was lost to sight.

Starting the engine again, we began to bump back across country towards the track to Lagowa. A kilometre or so from where we had deserted Nosy I noticed two other hornbills. I wondered if they were Nosy's companions of last year.

Near Lagowa I found cotton fields almost totally destroyed by the cotton leaf-roller (*Sylepta derogata*). The adult is a pretty moth with a wing span of twenty-five to twenty-seven millimetres, all four wings being similarly marked with thin, dark, zigzag lines on a cream background. It flies at night, the female laying its tiny yellowish-green eggs on cotton leaves. The newly-hatched, translucent larvae, scarcely more than pinhead size, are gregarious at first, but separate when older, each to live inside a rolled up leaf.

That season I had watched several rolling their leaves; the larva, grown to a small elongate caterpillar, still green but with blackish markings and spots, crawls round the plant, finally selects a leaf and cuts it partially across near the base without completely detaching it from the plant. Then, holding the edge of the leaf, the caterpillar turns it over and over until the rolled leaf is trumpet-shaped. The insect then secures the leaf in this position by means of silk produced from its own silk-glands. Finally, the caterpillar pupates within such a roll before developing into the adult moth, having first destroyed several leaves by feeding upon and rolling them.

The life-cycle from egg to adult takes between a month and six weeks, but I never recorded more than two generations a year. Like many other insects, the cotton leaf-roller survives the dry season in a resting stage during which it is completely inactive until the next rains.

Some other insects spend the dry season as a pupa, often inside a hard, homemade case and further protected against the climate and predators by being buried in the soil, inside plant tissues or other concealed places. Different kinds endure the dry season as minute eggs; still others live as adults, dormant and inactive in some hiding place. But a number, like the cotton leaf-roller, survive in the larval form. Towards the end of the season many fully-grown caterpillars of the leaf-roller do not pupate until the following year. Most of the larvae I found in the Lagowa cotton fields would take refuge in the soil, or amongst trash, remain in that condition for several months, and only turn into adults, mate and lay their eggs the following August.

Despite their protective leaf-roll, predators and parasites (chiefly tiny Braconid, Chalcid and Elasmid wasps) take an immense toll so that often the leaf-roller population never builds up to become particularly destructive. In the Nuba Mountains, however, the natural control sometimes breaks down as in the area near Lagowa. I saw many fields with every cotton plant infested by the roller and so defoliated that they would produce no pickable cotton at all, a tragedy for the local farmers.

Another leaf-roller had also caused very serious damage to the *simsim* (sesame) crop. Sesame is an erect annual about a metre tall, and one of the most ancient crops of northern Africa. There are a number of varieties with differently coloured seeds, white being the most favoured, although the brown grow best in this region, and the oil from the crushed seeds is exported for making margarine, cooking fats, tinning fish, etc. But a good deal is used locally, sometimes the uncrushed seed being roasted and made into small cakes or sweetmeats.

I spent some hours examining the *simsim* crop. *Antigastra catalaunalis* is only an insignificant pale brownish moth with reddish veins on the wings, being scarcely ten millimetres long, but I estimated that it had destroyed about eighty per cent of the crop. The green larvae not only roll leaves and eat them, but also bore into the seeds, often webbing together the topmost shoots of the plant. I learnt a great deal about the habits and life-history of this little moth and some of the other troublesome insects on the various crops of the region which was very useful on later occasions.

In contrast to the cotton and *simsim*, the *dura* (sorghum) crop seemed to be good I was pleased to find, *dura* being the staple food crop. The sorghum aphis was abundant in places, but it had been very largely destroyed by predators, including lacewing larvae and ladybirds, before it had caused much damage. Termites had devoured a few plants, first covering the stalks with their thin earthen carton made from soil particles mixed with saliva that baked hard in the sun.

Often this earthen covering stood for weeks after the plant inside had been carried away by the termites, a hollow mound conforming to every node and branch of the original until washed away by heavy rain or finally crumbling to dust.

After spending two or three days studying the insects in the crops, I left the region and camped for the night on my journey back to Kadugli. The sandy soil of my camp site was still saturated, although it had not rained that day. Nearby, I found a foraging column of the black stink ant, *Megaponera foetens*, an ant I had first seen in Tanganyika. Having made camp early, it was still light enough for me to take some not very successful pictures of the hurrying black army, which had been raiding a nearby termites' nest and was now marching home in a column a metre and a half long and five to eight ants abreast, each ant carrying one or two termite nymphs stolen from nurseries deep in the termites' mound.

The next morning I found a large termites' nest (*Odontotermes*) and decided to dig out the termites to discover the queen. The soil, being sandy, was not difficult to dig, and Younis, Badr and I soon disclosed the nurseries of the nymphs and then the egg chambers deep inside. Finally, we came upon the queen cell about a metre below ground level and not below the surface mound as I had expected.

The cell itself was made of dense, loamy soil particles glued together with secretions from the termites, and the floor, seventeen by seven centimetres, had been smoothed flat. From this floor rose a perfectly rounded dome, smooth on the inside but roughly hewn and jagged on the outside. Penetrating the walls and floor were small holes, the only exits or entrances, through which the worker termites could reach the queen.

The queen termite, once gravid, so expands with eggs that she stretches to many times her virgin size; from perhaps twelve millimetres before fertilisation she becomes ten times as long as thousands of eggs develop. This great swelling is only possible because the skin joining together the sclerotised or hard segments of her abdomen stretches. In the photograph, the dark bars to be seen on the back are the segments, scarcely separate in the unfertilised female, and all the white is stretched skin. The head and thorax, seen to the left, remain the same size as before.

The queen termite becomes no more than an egg-laying machine; the vast, soft sac that her formerly neatly proportioned abdomen has become makes it impossible for her to walk again, the six tiny legs on her thorax being quite inadequate to do more

Macrotermes mound nest

Cotton leaf-roller

Aphids on dura leaf. Note predaceous larvae

Odontotermes smeathmani carton over dura

Odontotermes queen surrounded by big-headed soldiers on guard and workers. The 'king' is below the fourth blackish 'line' on the back of the queen

Stainer-bugs in scrum around a single baobab seed

Black stink ants (*Megaponera*) marching back to nest carrying termites after raid (*above*)

Idolum diabolicum, a brightly coloured mantid in defensive attitude (*below*)

than wave uselessly should she be in danger. But despite her physical helplessness, enclosed in her rock-hard cell deep in the ground and surrounded by thousands of workers and soldiers ready to die for her, she is invulnerable except to a determined, powerful predator. No parasite, although both parasites and tiny predators often invade termites' nests, some even tolerated by the inhabitants, ever seems to reach the queen.

Carefully, I broke open the queen cell; the domed roof separated from the floor, disclosing a queen nearly a hundred millimetres long. Even so, this was not the largest I had found. Not long before I had discovered a queen of *Macrotermes bellicosus* (species of *Macrotermes* are the largest termites of Africa) that measured one hundred and fifty-two millimetres long.

Putting down the opened cell a little way from the nest, I brushed off many of the workers and soldiers surrounding the hapless queen so that I could photograph her, but three or four dozen remained.

Unlike ants, the males of which normally perish within days or weeks of the mating flight, most male and female termites pair for life. Details vary in different kinds of termites, but I had watched the *Odontotermes* I was now studying on many occasions.

The colonising or mating flight takes place always after rain during daylight when the weather is dull or wet, usually in late June or early July. Incredibly, after weeks of preparation within the nest and often several false starts (eager reproductives are restrained by the sterile workers), every colony over a large area responds to just the right meteorological stimuli to begin to re-lease their winged males and females at almost the same moment. In often unbelievable numbers they take to the air, sometimes so thickly that they create a low-lying mist. Standing in the midst of such a swarm their softly fluttering wings and bodies have brushed my face, landed in my hair and beard, and it has been difficult not to swallow some.

The flight is short-lived, an individual seldom being airborne as long as half an hour, most coming to earth in a few minutes, but as more and more males and females are released by the workers, swarming may continue for the rest of the day and start again the next day.

As soon as a female drops to the ground, she sheds her wings, each of which is provided with a line of weakness, the humeral suture, near the base, so well developed that one or more wings sometimes drop off in flight to send the insect spiralling softly to the ground.

On the ground, the female finds a vantage point, a twig on the soil, a stone, a grass stem or the like, where she raises the tip of her abdomen in the air at the same time vibrating rapidly like a hen bird. The odour she produces and helps to waft about with her oscillating body attracts the dealated males frenetically scurrying about nearby. As soon as a male touches her, the female stops pulsating and makes off rapidly to find shelter, the male following, his head as though glued to the tip of her abdomen. For a time several males may follow one female, often in train.

It is not usually long before the female discovers a suitable crevice (although first she may reject apparently ideal places) to disappear from sight closely followed by her spouse. Here, if undisturbed, the termites mate, the female becomes the 'queen' and begins to lay eggs which hatch into nymphs that become the first workers of the colony. Periodically, she is fertilised by the male; the colony grows, soldier forms are born and, probably in the third season if conditions have been favourable, virgin males and females equipped with wings are produced, replicas of the original founders of the colony. The queen may live many years and during her lifetime produce tens of thousands of eggs.

As I took pictures of the queen I had unearthed, I saw that the king was still at her side where he had been trying to hide below the bloated body of his mate. He can be seen in the photograph below the fourth visible segment (dark line) from the head or left end of the queen. I was surprised how quickly the soldier termites, the large headed forms in the picture, took up their positions facing outwards around the queen to guard her. This was even more apparent later, when they formed an almost perfect circle.

The soldiers' efforts availed them nothing, however, for they together with their progenitors were soon pickled in spirit, despite the reluctance I felt at ending their lives. They had lived longer than most all the same; of the queen's and king's myriad brothers and sisters few would have survived the pack of predators that descends upon every termite swarm. Other insects and many birds destroy them while in flight; amphibia, reptiles, rodents, birds and men gobble them up on the ground. People often make ingenious traps for the swarms as they emerge from the nest. Even after pairing and successfully finding shelter, those few that survive are still not safe since ants, burrowing reptiles and other animals may find them, and fungal growths kill many.

Animated fir-cones

In the driveway outside my office were two Baggara Arabs with a large sack. I groaned to myself and went out to see what they had caught.

One of the problems, and there were many, with my zoo was trying to discourage people from catching animals and then bringing them to sell to me. I was not an animal collector and did not sell animals to other zoos or museums. I was a naturalist curious to learn and, as I have explained before, I did not really want to keep a public zoo. Fortunately, I managed to dissuade most people from deliberately setting out to catch animals, but at the same time I had to buy or was given many that I did not want, particularly easily caught animals, such as tortoises, that in most cases I released again.

When I saw what the two men had in their sack, however, I was delighted for they had brought me a female pangolin and her large son. Pangolins were common enough in the Nuba Mountains and I had seen them several times, but I had not been able to catch one. In *Jebels by Moonlight* I mentioned one attempt to dig up a pangolin's burrow. My second attempt was as fruitless. We had marked several burrows that appeared to be occupied and one day I set out with a gang of men to try and dig one up.

All the burrows were in sandy areas but at the first, after easy digging to start with, the ground proved to be very rocky. The pangolin had dug into soft soil below two enormous boulders impossible to move short of using dynamite. Disappointedly, I was forced to abandon this attempt and try another burrow some miles away. Here digging proved easier and after several hours we opened the whole burrow, but it was unoccupied. I had to give up that day.

Some days later I tried again. Digging was hard work; the burrows, all made by the pangolins themselves, had openings about twenty to twenty-five centimetres in diameter, the tunnels sloping downwards quite steeply although the direction, angle and bends depended largely on the type of ground. The burrows varied from about three to five metres in length and usually ended about a metre below the level of the burrow entrance. As most burrows were dug in rising ground this meant that a much greater depth of soil had to be shifted to reach the end of the tunnel. All the burrows I found were situated so that there was little danger of flooding.

Failing again to excavate a pangolin after several days, I gave up. It took too much time, and the effort of rounding up and transporting a digging gang was not the least of the difficulties. I made one further effort when it was suggested to me by one of my burlier helpers, obviously too big for the job, that perhaps some-one could crawl into the hole with a rope, tie it to the pangolin, to enable us to pull it out. I had heard that this was done sometimes and thought it worth a try. But who would crawl into the hole? No grown man could do so. Eventually a skinny boy reluctantly volunteered, prodded by his elders.

Holding the end of a rope between his strong teeth, the youth put his head into the hole but withdrew it almost at once, saying something indistinctly to the onlookers.

'What does he say?' I asked.

'He says there could be a python in there.'

This was a distinct possibility, and I did not blame the boy for refusing to continue even in the face of his elders' encouragement, but another boy offered to try. Removing his only article of clothing, a piece of string round his waist, the child lay flat and wriggled eel-like into the burrow entrance until only his feet were visible. It was a tight fit. For a few moments he made no visible movement, then slowly his feet disappeared. We waited for five very long minutes. Putting my head near the hole I shone my torch along the burrow, but there was no sign of the boy. I began to regret ever letting him into the burrow, and I had a horrifying vision of his suffocated body lying out of sight. In great alarm I pulled on the rope. To my relief there was a tug in return and soon I was able to see the boy's pink soles jerkily moving backwards up the tunnel.

As soon as his feet left the tunnel he was dragged out and pulled upright. Sand grains adhered to his sweaty body from head to foot. Brushing the dirt from his woolly hair with his hands, the boy explained that he had seen the pangolin in the light of the torch he had taken with him, but that he had been unable to touch it because of the rocks in the way that prevented him from squeezing past. By this time it was late and the men would not dig, but we returned at sunrise with the idea of digging the animal out. However, the same boy wriggled back down the burrow to return and report that the pangolin was no longer there, which was no more than I had expected. Nevertheless, I gave the lad a large *bakhshish* and he ran off none the worse for his adventures.

After all these efforts I was therefore particularly pleased to see the Arabs with the two apparently quite healthy and unharmed pangolins. It took the whole day before they were mine, however, for lengthy negotiations were required. The men wanted £E50, a vast sum. After trying to convince them I could not afford such an amount and failing, I left Younis and my Effendi to argue with them. The Arabs said that they had intended to take the animals to Khartoum but had been told to come to me; it was explained to them that nobody there would give them anything like £E50 and that in any case the animals would be dead long before they reached Khartoum. By evening they were convinced or were so wearied by the argument, that they accepted £E5 which was probably as much as they really had anticipated in the first place.

There are four kinds of pangolins in Africa (and three more in southern Asia), two large, ground-dwelling species and two much smaller arboreal ones, the tree or black-bellied pangolin and the small-scaled pangolin, both forest forms found mainly from West Africa to Uganda. The two ground pangolins are similar in appearance and habits, but the giant pangolin is larger on average, is a forest rather than a savanna dweller, and is not known in the Sudan.

The Sudanese pangolin, Temminck's pangolin or scaly anteater as it is sometimes called, is found over a large part of south, east and west Sudan, its range extending to South West Africa, Orange Free State and Mozambique in the south, and Kenya, Tanzania, etc., to the east but is more rarely seen than even the aardvark. In and about the Nuba Mountains it was quite common in suitable places, but many local people appeared to have no knowledge of it, especially in the Kadugli area. It prefers sandy or *gardud* soils and burrows were sometimes found in the hills, but I never found a burrow on cotton soils or clays. Near Lake Keilak pangolins dig their tunnels in the sandy areas but sometimes forage on the clays, even to the water's edge, where occasionally I found their peculiar spoor. I believe they sometimes entered the water, although I never saw one swim there.

When the Arabs left I took the two pangolins to inspect them more closely. Called *umm girfer* locally, Temminck's pangolin resembles a yellowish-brown or greyish-brown animated fir-cone growing to a total length of nearly one and a half metres. My female, which I called Samsim, because of her habit of sniffing, was smaller than this while her son, Sam, was two-thirds her size, but the largest of the six or seven of these animals that I subsequently kept in various countries, and of a few others I was able to measure, was seventy centimetres plus a tail of about fifty centimetres, or one point two metres in all; when resting on all fours the height of the back was about thirty-five centimetres and he weighed twenty-one kilogrammes. Samsim was not quite so big.

Until I obtained Samsim and Sam I had briefly examined only one juvenile. Now I could see what a truly extraordinary mammal I had in my possession. The head was long and slender, unscaled but with sparsely hairy, leathery skin rather like a turtle's but not as thick. The nostrils were permanently moist, narrow and readily closed at will. At first I thought both Samsim and Sam were suffering from some eye disease for the tiny eyes were surrounded by heavy, swollen lids that lacked eyelashes, but I soon discovered that this was as nature intended. The ears were no more than short grooves.

The back, tail and upper parts of the limbs were equipped with overlapping, horny, finely striated scales (really modified hairs greatly enlarged and flattened) that, like hair, grew and were renewed. The belly and insides of the legs, for both animals were not in the least shy and made no attempt to roll up even as I handled them, were covered with quite thick, rather loose skin that tended to wrinkle considerably when the pangolin moved. The tapering tail was flattened, more or less concave below but rounded above, Samsim having a median row of six scales on the tail, but Sam having only four.★ The hind limbs resembled scaly elephant's legs, longer and stouter than the front legs, and were armed with five short claws, the soles being moist and spongy, but the five claws on each front leg were long and curved, for digging.

As I soon discovered, pangolins have no difficulty in climbing a vertical fence or even small trees given a hold for their powerful

★ Temminck's pangolin, *Manis temmincki,* has a median row of four to seven scales on the tail, while the giant pangolin, *M. gigantea,* has eleven to fifteen, this being one of the chief physical differences between them.

claws (which are never used in defence despite their formidable length and strength), but it is doubtful if they ever climb in the wild state since they avoid obstacles. One captive of mine climbed almost to the top of a tree. Pangolins are slow and clumsy climbers but even a high fall does no harm as the scales are so resilient. They also swim occasionally but possibly never by intent. Swimming is something few animals can avoid at times in the rains, and the pangolin uses its front feet for propulsion in the water, the large claws acting as paddles. But even in a slow current progress is minimal and the creature is easily submerged in choppy water.

Even had I never seen or heard of a pangolin before, it was quite obvious from Samsim's and Sam's appearance that they were highly specialised mammals, but to see them in action was even more impressive.

At first, knowing that the aardvark or antbear would eat minced meat, raw eggs and other food in captivity, I cut up some beef as finely as possible. I did not know how long the Arabs had had the pangolins but they had not been fed for several days. However, neither would touch the beef and I tried them with various other foods to no avail. Then it occurred to me that they were probably thirsty, for many animals will not touch food when thirsty, so I presented them with a saucer of milk.

Sam showed some interest in this and putting out his long tongue he drank some, but it was not until I put Samsim's snout in the saucer and she had blown a lot of bubbles that she decided milk was drinkable.

A pangolin's rounded tongue is a most remarkable instrument. About thirty centimetres long it is prehensile, flattened towards the tip and lies in a sheath-like extension of the oesophagus. It is slimy along its length, the slime being supplied by enlarged maxillary glands on either side of the throat. As the tongue rapidly flickers out of the toothless mouth so the termites and ants on which the animal feeds adhere to it and are drawn in to be left on the sides of the oesophagus tube when the tongue is extruded again.

There is no pause for swallowing as in most mammals, the insects being picked up with great speed and dexterity, each tongue load pushing the previous loads down towards the stomach. The droppings are tiny rounded or irregular pellets that consist of the chitinous remains of their prey.

But Samsim and Sam used their tongues much more slowly for drinking, dipping the organ in the milk, curling up the end to retain as much liquid as possible before withdrawing the tongue. After five or six dips with the tongue, however, Sam seemed satisfied, while Samsim only twice extruded her tongue; they could not have obtained very much of the milk. Once I found that they often drank water it was always provided.

Putting Samsim and Sam back into a specially strengthened cage, which had been made available by the release of a mongoose, I set out to find them some natural food. Ants and termites may be abundant, but it is not always easy to find quantities at short notice at the beginning of the dry season. It took me an hour to collect a jarful of harvester ants (*Messor barbarus*), the first ant I saw in numbers. But the pangolins took no interest in them, totally ignoring the swarms of worker ants that thronged about them; when the ants began to run all over Samsim she simply moved away. Obviously, it was not going to be as simple as I thought to support the new arrivals.

That same night I collected more than half a dozen kinds of ants, all common in the neighbourhood, but to my dismay the pangolins also ignored these offerings. However, the next day I discovered a very large nest of honey-ants (*Camponotus maculatus*) and although Samsim ignored the workers and pupae, she eagerly ate larvae and eggs. With her amazingly dexterous tongue she picked out the white larvae and egg clusters with ease, somehow avoiding the swarming workers, but the food was soon devoured and Sam had eaten nothing. At last, by the end of the day, I found an ant that Sam would eat, a small, subterranean cocktail-ant (*Cremastogaster*) that both pangolins devoured greedily.

A week passed by which time I knew that either I would have to release the pangolins or find some other way of feeding them. I was exhausted having to spend several hours a day trying to find food for them. I had collected more than thirty kinds of ants and of these the pangolins would eat only two, both difficult to find, and occasionally the young of others. I had also found that they would not eat one of the commonest termites, a snouted-termite (*Trinervitermes geminatus*) whose small, hard mound nests were a common feature of many grassland areas, nor would they take any interest in portions of the nests of more than half the other kinds of termites we were able to find fairly easily. I was able to keep the pangolins alive, but to do so meant employing several men, as well as keeping me busy. Not only did the pangolins refuse most ants and termites,* but they ignored all other forms of insect life that I offered them.

A pangolin's stomach is very small for the size of the animal, as I discovered much later when I dissected one that had been killed by hunters, and there are various alimentary modifications as would be expected in such a specialised animal. The stomach is more or less divided into two parts, a larger section and a smaller pyloric part which seems to act in a similar manner to the gizzard of a gallinaceous bird to grind up the hard, chitinous parts of its insect food. Pangolins are said to swallow small stones as an aid to digestion, but I found no such pebbles, only fine grains of sand none bigger than two millimetres or so in diameter. The stomach is capable of containing between a litre and a litre and a half of ants or termites, and being a big and very muscular animal, although with a low metabolism, a pangolin requires to feed at least once a night. The digestion is rapid and in the feral state it probably eats more than once in twenty-four hours. Yet it can live without food for several days, perhaps even for a week or two.

* Pangolins that I kept in Nyasaland would eat worker driver-ants, those of several *Camponotus* spp. and *Trinervitermes* nymphs, similar spp. to those refused by Sudanese pangolins.

I decided to try and solve my problem by letting the animals roam freely for an hour or two each night so that they could find their own food.

On the first occasion we loaded Samsim and Sam into the Land Rover and I drove to an open area where there were plenty of snouted termite nests. Here I set the pangolins at liberty and waited to see what they would do; Younis and a couple of others came with me in case I lost the animals, but I need not have worried. Samsim's utmost speed was under five kilometres per hour and rarely exceeded one to two kilometres per hour, and they made no attempt to evade us. In fact, we were completely disregarded as were the lights we trained on the animals from time to time. Far from being timid, I have never known a pangolin do more than roll up for a few moments and snort when discovered by humans, thereafter unrolling if left alone, myopically staring, before continuing on its snuffling journey as before.

There has been more information published about the Indian pangolin than the African species, and in many books some of the habits of the former are credited to the latter, while the giant pangolin (once regarded as the same species) has been confused with Temminck's pangolin, although they differ in some aspects of their behaviour and habits. Thus it is often stated that Temminck's pangolin (also called ground pangolin, Cape pangolin, even sometimes 'armadillo' in South Africa) carries her young on her tail like the Indian pangolin, which is not the case, at least once the young is fairly large.

Samsim and Sam soon demonstrated this. As soon as they were set free to wander at will, Sam immediately clambered on his mother's back clinging to her shoulders with his long front claws, straddling his back legs over her back and curling the tip of his tail tightly below the base of her tail (see illustrations between pages 184 and 185). As he was a good size and weight, and I would have thought much too big to be carried, he slowed Samsim down considerably and soon tired her. In this position she was unable to shake him off (not that she tried) and even if she curled up he still clung on. Most Sudanese believe the animals are mating when they see a mother carrying her offspring, and thus say copulation continues for weeks. The Arabs from whom I obtained Samsim and Sam believed this as Sam was a male, a fact readily ascertained as pangolins have a long pendant penis although the testes are hidden internally. I believe that pangolins normally mate in the burrow.

When Sam climbed on his mother's back at first I let them be, and Samsim began to carry her son about with her usual deliberate and tank-like purposiveness that reminded me of a tortoise; a shuffling gait with most of the weight taken by the hind limbs on their tough, elastic feet, the forepart of the body swaying from side to side, the front claws touching the ground only occasionally.

There were plenty of snouted-termite mounds close by, but Samsim shuffled past them. It was five minutes or more before she found an attraction, a crack in the ground. She snuffled at this for a moment, Sam's head peering down immediately above hers; then she pushed her tongue in the crack, flickering it in and out so rapidly that it was only by kneeling down beside her that I could see the tiny white termite nymphs adhering to it. Almost immediately Sam stuck out his tongue and began to feed in the same crack. I might have been another pangolin for all the notice they took of me. However, there could have been few termites available for Samsim soon moved off, Sam still holding tightly to her like the Old Man of the Sea to Sinbad.

They came to a termite nest, a small mound of *Odontotermes smeathmani*, a common species, but although I knew they would eat this termite, Samsim only paused for a moment before moving on. I lifted her back, but she still ignored the nest. Then I broke the mound open, disclosing large numbers of the inhabitants, whereupon both pangolins began to eat. Samsim had made no attempt to open the nest for herself which surprised me. I thought this might be due to having Sam on her back, and as Sam's weight probably prevented Samsim from foraging normally on subsequent occasions I separated them.

When wakeful, Sam rarely descended from his mother's back voluntarily. Once or twice he clambered down when feeding on termites brought to the cage, for he almost always took longer at a meal than Samsim, and occasionally when sleeping he left his mother's back to curl up by himself.

Some years later I obtained another mother, and her baby, also a male, but less than half his mother's size. The youngster rode on his mother's back like Sam but in this case laid his tail to curl the tip to the right and not to the left of the base of the parent's tail. Perhaps some pangolins are 'left-tailed', some 'right-tailed'; it was noticeable that Sam was invariably 'left-tailed', but the other infant always 'right-tailed'. But I once had an adult pangolin that sometimes used his left front claw for digging, sometimes his right and occasionally both feet at once. Samsim and Sam never used more than one claw at a time.

A pangolin never seems to have more than one young at a time. The smallest baby I have found could have been only a few days old, for her scales were still flexible and light in colour. Unfortunately, the parent had been killed, and although I did my best to rear the baby it died. But during the few days I managed to keep it alive it would sometimes cling to my fingers so tightly that it was difficult to remove. A baby of this size would not be able to ride on the back of the mother as an older infant would. It is not long before a baby pangolin is able to walk, and it probably accompanies its mother within a few weeks of birth and possibly may ride on the tail at this age. It is sometimes stated that the mother protects her infant by rolling up with the baby clasped inside her soft stomach, but, while this may be the case with some pangolins, I have never seen Temminck's pangolin protect her young in this manner.

Samsim, relieved of the burden of Sam, was able to move about a little more energetically. She never once attacked a snouted-termite mound and it may have been because of the strong, pungent smell that these termites have. Nor did she ever attempt to dig into one of the larger mounds of the giant termite (*Macrotermes*), possibly deterred by the hardness of the mound walls and perhaps because she could sense that the termites were nowhere near the surface. It took a sharp hoe to open one of these nests in the dry season and often the mounds seemed deserted until moist soil was reached. However, Samsim would eagerly catch any of these termites when she found the fragile earthen tunnels they made away from their nests.

Sam undoubtedly missed his transport. On the first night I took him out alone he did not move but swung the forepart of his body from side to side. After a while he sat up in the usual pangolin manner, balancing himself on the tripod of his hind feet and tail, to peer myopically around and sniff. At this moment Samsim was five or six metres away and Sam could not possibly have seen her, but he must have caught her scent for he shuffled as fast as he could in her direction, caught up with her and climbed rapidly on her back. Separating them again, I put Sam back in his box until Samsim had eaten her fill.

After some days Sam gave up his searching for his mother and began to move about slowly. He came to a broken termitary (one I had opened for him) and began to feed. Thereafter he always fended for himself, successfully finding a meal on most nights.

With all the pangolins I have kept, but most noticeably with Samsim and Sam, it was exceptional for any to dig for long, if at all. They normally wandered about until they found ants or termites to their liking that were exposed or only shallowly hidden, and all the pangolins showed preferences, only feeding on some kinds. One, I remember, did break open an *Odontotermes* mound that was fairly soft due to recent rain; then for several days, as I took it to the same locality, it returned to the same termite nest, digging out only the soft soil where the termites had sealed up the nest until, in the end, half the mound had been excavated. I think that termite mounds found with a gaping hole in the side or half destroyed have been attacked by aardvarks, or by pangolins when the nest was newly made or soft with rain.

Yet a pangolin is capable of strong, rapid digging and even the hardest soil does not resist for long. Although normally a pangolin chooses more friable or sandy soil to dig its burrow, sometimes the subsoil is rocky and compacted, yet the animal usually persists and tunnels through astonishingly hard ground. At the same time half completed burrows are not uncommon.

In all the months I kept Samsim she never once did more than make a few almost casual digging movements to obtain food. Her ability to detect her prey was remarkable; apparently by scent she located the invisible termites or ants, and she seemed to be able to distinguish between 'edible' and 'non-edible' kinds. Only rarely did she pause at a non-edible kind, or where there were only a few of an edible kind. Sometimes she stopped where I could see absolutely no sign of any ant or termite, inserted her tongue in a crevice and extracted numbers of the insects. Her ability to do this, presumably because of her greater experience, was much higher than that of Sam who generally found his food in obvious places.

Another trick of Samsim's, which may or may not be common amongst her kind, but which Sam never learnt, I discovered some weeks after she came into my possession.

One night I took her to a new locality and it happened that nomadic Baggara Arabs and their cattle had camped there recently. Samsim was released as usual. I did not give her much attention to begin with, I had seen her in action so often, and there being a clear, bright moon I switched off the spotlight. Samsim disappeared. After a few moments I took my torch to find her before she wandered too far away. I discovered her lying on her back, something I had never seen her do before. However, she rolled over as I came up and shuffled off. I watched her closely. She came to one of the numerous cow-pats left by the cattle and dried on top, and stopped. To my astonishment, she lifted the dung and holding it in her front paws, rolled over on her back again.

This action, of course, reversed the cow-pat, which rested on Samsim's chest disclosing the damp underside where termites scurried in moist activity. Raising her head slightly, Samsim's tongue flickered to catch almost all the scurrying termites before they could hide again. In moments she dropped the cow-pat and ambled off.

In twenty minutes or so Samsim was replete; during this time she devoured the termites from under nine or ten cow-pats, each time clasping the dung in her front paws, rolling on her back to reverse it before using her tongue to catch the insects. She spent some time on a particularly large cow-pat that swarmed with termites, first catching the visible ones, then breaking the dung into pieces on her chest to disclose those that had hidden themselves again in the crevices. Sometimes she rolled completely over on her back; at other times, with smaller pieces of dung, she rolled on her side only to hold the cow-pat for a brief moment before dropping it.

Now that I had seen Samsim at work in this manner she was much easier to feed. All we had to do was to find a place where cattle had spent some time, and I could reduce her feeding time by an hour or more. However, Sam's mealtimes were still long drawn out, for, although he would devour termites from under dung, he never obtained as many. He simply scratched the cow-pats on the ground where they lay, occasionally turning the drier pats over by accident, but he never adopted Samsim's very efficient method.

Samsim not only employed this reversal procedure to cow-pats; she would do the same with any large droppings and pieces of bark or wood if they contained termites. She left more recent, still wet dung alone (this rarely contained termites in any case), only selecting that with a dry crust. On one occasion, without touching the cow-pats, I marked each one I thought contained termites. Then I let Samsim loose. She disregarded about a third of those I had marked, but included several I had left unmarked. When I turned over the marked ones she had left there were no termites there, but all those she had chosen contained the insects. She was almost infallible.

Both pangolins must have accidentally eaten the other inhabitants of dung occasionally, but despite my often close attention I never saw them do so. Their diet was restricted to only certain kinds of ants and termites. Samsim once held a cow-pat still moist enough to contain numerous small, white dipterous larvae as well as termites, but when she had finished there was not a termite to be seen yet the larvae still remained, apparently as numerous as before. Many beetles also often inhabited cow-pats, but somehow the pangolin's tongue avoided them.

The fate of captive pangolins in zoos has never been happy, for they rarely live long. Probably the Indian pangolin (*M. crassicaudata*) which has lived for about two years holds the record, but few pangolins survive for more than a few weeks. Feeding is always a problem in non-tropical zoos. I was lucky for their natural food was available, but the longest time I ever kept a pangolin before releasing it was about eighteen months. The potential longevity must be at least ten years.

Pangolins are much hunted in most parts of Africa, largely for the scales and other parts much in demand by witchdoctors. The scales are also sold as charms or fashioned into rings and other ornaments, while most people find the flesh makes very good eating. Pangolins are a chief's prize in many parts of southern Africa. Many classical and mediaeval writers refer to giant ants as large as jackals or even tigers, and there is a persistent tale of great-clawed, gold-digging ants inhabiting regions of north India where the soil is often auriferous in the Himalayan foothills. Solinus, Pliny, Herodotus and others all mention such gold-burrowing ants, and of all the possible fossorial animals these might be, pangolins are the most likely but, alas, none of my animals ever dug me any gold.

Soon after Samsim and Sam had settled down and I was able to satisfy myself that they could be looked after in my absence, I was able to take some leave and I set out with Younis, Badr and Ahmed again to travel to the Bahr el Arab, following the same route via Muglad.

At Abyei I was disappointed for the second time for the dilapidated pontoon ferry was still inoperable, half awash with black water, so there was no way of crossing the river. It had been my intention to explore the western 'Bog', the country between the Bahr el Arab and the River Lol, home of the Malwal Dinka. Instead, I spent some days investigating the swamps upstream from Abyei.

There can be few regions in Africa, or indeed the world, where the bird life is as prolific as in parts of the vast swamps of the southern Sudan, and nowhere have I found birds as unconcerned at my presence as in and around the great man-free marshes that expand after the rains for unknown distances from the Bahr el Arab and the lesser streams that feed it. Often the hubbub of bird voices could be heard in my camp more than a kilometre away. In several expeditions to the region, when I was able to explore only a minute part of the seemingly unending swampland yet travelled great distances by land and water, I recorded more than sixty kinds of birds associated with water, all but a few being swimming or wading species, and there must have been many I did not see or did not identify.

On this occasion we spent the first day only a few kilometres from Abyei. The Dinka cattle having grazed much of the undulating plain except where the land was under water, the grass was mostly stubble but for the occasional tall patch. Even here, close to Abyei, there came only herdboys, for the hunters and fishermen kept downstream where the fish and game were more plentiful, and there was little to attract the tall, naked tribesmen.

Like all the truly Nilotic peoples, the Dinka (the English name comes from the Arabic, *Denkawi*, but the people call themselves

Jeng) are proud and independent. They have not the cohesion of the Shilluk, united under one king, for they belong to many different tribal branches, nor the truculence of the wild Nuer, although they can be as warlike as any when threatened. Some are miserable, ill-fed and diseased, living in filthy villages in the midst of foul-smelling swamps where they are seldom dry, and fishing is their main occupation, but the great majority of the Dinka clans are cattle-owning and value their herds above all else. They may grow some millet, fish and hunt, but their whole life centres around cattle to a degree that equals, if it does not exceed, that of any other pastoral tribe in Africa. Not only is every calf born named and classified, but several generations of its ancestors will be remembered, and a Dinka will identify with his cattle to an almost pathological extent. But poor bogtrotter or rich cattle-owning marshman, none that I met lacked self-respect, kindliness and natural good manners.

The cattle of the south are great horned descendants of the extinct wild cattle of the Nile Valley, their blood mixed with that of the lateral horned zebu introduced from Asia in very early times.

Amongst the Dinka cattle are found some magnificent beasts weighing seven hundred kilos or even more, with massive horns spanning two and a half metres or so from tip to tip. These southern cattle are very different from the cattle I knew in the Nuba Mountains, where isolation from the rest of the world has led to the development of a distinct breed of dwarf cattle, as unique to the Nuba Mountains as are the human and many of the other animal and plant inhabitants of that ecological island.

But on this day by the Bahr el Arab we met no human and saw no cattle – nor yet any animal other than birds. The first bird I saw in numbers was the crested or crowned crane; in the beginning small flocks of twenty to fifty or sixty and then, still on the flat but dry ground not far from Abyei, a vast single flock that spread to the horizon, more of these striking birds than I ever saw before or since.

The crowned crane is tall, nearly a metre high, and although mostly greyish-black in colour, it has long shaggy neck feathers and a large band of white visible on the folded wings. But the most distinctive feature is the head, for the bare cheeks are coloured red and white and there is a velvety glossy black cap of fine, close fur-like feathers surmounted by a fan of long, stiff and erect bristles. While sometimes killed for food (the flesh, according to the Arabs, is sweet and succulent) it is the striking head-dress that is more often its downfall for man is seldom content to observe beauty without wanting to possess it; and white, brown and black people alike scalp many birds for the sake of the cap and crest to wear as an ornament or shield emblem, while it is used as a badge by the Sudan Camel Corps.

I spent all that day watching the cranes, called *umm gharnuk* in Arabic, despite the temptation to explore further or study the many other birds. At first, as the Land Rover approached, they would take to flight with much to-do and a mournful honking as of marsh spirits, but they did not fly far, circling to land again in a few minutes. In flight the large birds invariably fly in a close formation that sometimes becomes a 'V' over longer distances, the neck and legs outstretched like a flamingo.

Soon I was able to drive closer and stopped to watch, it being much easier and less alarming to the birds for me to stay in the Land Rover than approach on foot. After perhaps twenty minutes, during which time we sat silently, the flock spread all around our vehicle, the nearest birds no more than ten metres away. Crowned cranes feed on almost any animal to the size of a large frog or moderate-sized reptile, as well as grass seeds, cultivated grain and other small seeds. The ones I watched were eating mainly grass seeds, insects and a small snail commonly found on the grass.

As gawky as an egret or heron when chasing an insect or when alarmed, crowned cranes are nevertheless more graceful birds. It was too late in the year to see their display dances, but on other occasions, in September and October, I watched the mating ceremonies when I saw pairs follow their ritual in an increasing frenzy of excitement. The male approached the female on the ground with curious tip-toed movements, the stilt legs long-striding, to begin his dance. With guttural grunts he waltzed round, spreading his wings and giving leaps into the air so that his feet scarcely touched the soil, bowing and discordantly trumpeting until the female was sufficiently impressed to allow him close enough to intertwine his neck with hers, a mating ceremony that is copied in the 'crane dance' of some tribes.

After watching the cranes for a long time it occurred to me that perhaps I could catch one, they seemed so disinterested in us. I slipped out of the Land Rover to hide in ambush amongst some tall grass growing in a clump about a stunted tree. Younis drove off very slowly, the cranes making way for the vehicle but not taking flight. I felt I was being foolish but I had caught a gorged vulture and, by accident, a ground hornbill, by hand, and there was just a faint chance I could catch an unwary crane. After circling round, Younis slowly returned, driving the birds towards my lair. The nearest crane came within about three metres of my hiding place; I rushed out but with a startled honk the bird rose in the air before I could catch it. Obviously, I would never catch one in this way.

It would have been easy to snare a crane, but it might have injured itself and I was not prepared to try. I thought that the next time I came I might net or devise some other safe means of catching one, but there was the possibility of finding a nest.

I knew something of the breeding of cranes. That there was only one family a year, that they undoubtedly bred at this time of the year in this locality where there must be hundreds of nests. I knew also that the nests, flat mounds of dry vegetation built quite openly and readily seen (for the reeds about the nest would be trampled), would be somewhere deep in the swamps, and I did not relish wading into that smelly, uncharted labyrinth of vegetation. Younis and Badr had little hesitation, however, and volunteered to go and look for nests. After telling them on no account to touch a nest if they found any, I watched them go while Ahmed put the kettle on.

Sipping tea, I waited, rather anxiously staring over the marsh from the hump of ground where I had camped. Apart from birds, the tangled rushes and reeds, often intertwined by purple-flowered *Ipomoea* or straggling stems of *Vigna*, desertedly stretched to the heat-hazed horizon. There were no hippo here, the water was too shallow and I could see no indication that they even came here at night to feed; nor did I see any crocodiles, although they occurred not far downstream. But I did not know what the men might find once deep in the swamp where the main channel of the river was hidden. I was thankful to see their return. They had found a few nests on a low island of trampled reeds, but none occupied, they said.

Following the men I was soon wet and muddy to the chest as I floundered along, fighting the reeds and glutinous mud at every step; despite being up to my waist in water, sweat ran down my back and dripped from my nose into the swamp; the torrid air, hanging motionless trapped in the reed-mace above our heads, seemed a miasma devoid of oxygen. Even the mosquitoes were torpid; I saw several hundred just resting on Badr's back in front of me. I could tolerate the discomfort, and had little apprehension of crocodiles, but I did fear the unseen, water-borne diseases readily contracted in such a place.

Our efforts were unsuccessful. We found a few of the large glossy, brown-spotted eggs, but only two chicks, both too young to risk trying to rear, so we returned empty-handed. The cranes take over a month to incubate their eggs (rarely more than three to a nest) and, like other cranes, both sexes take turns to sit. It is probable that the young leave the nest only a few days after hatching for I have seen very young chicks, miniature editions of the parents only brown like the reed stems, and with large, ridiculous looking straw tufts on their heads, following an adult bird. The chicks we left, squawking anxiously, on their nest would be unable to fly before the end of the dry season, and it would not be until after their second rains they would develop adult plumage and breed.

The next three days were a delight as we made our way slowly along by the swamps and open water, never knowing what we would find next. Sometimes the terrain was flat, almost treeless and covered with dry, trampled and windblown grasses and, by the water, new green shoots pushing upwards; sometimes it was more undulating and broken with scattered trees and bushes that frequently formed small copses, and now and again we entered a large area of woodland. There were no villages or communities of any description, and we saw no sign of man anywhere.

The variety of birds seemed endless. Overhead, the bateleur eagle was the commonest bird of prey, soaring, gliding, in patient watchfulness. Towards evening and in the early morning, the sky was often filled with flocking birds. Herons, cranes, egrets, storks and ibises strode amid flocks of smaller birds on the flat, more open land, where we flushed an occasional swamp owl from the grass. Where the woodland reached the water, the tree branches often meeting above a sluggish stream or pool, I heard the cackling laugh of the giant kingfisher and sometimes saw its black and white shape; the largest in Africa, approaching half a metre long, it is much shyer, more wary, than the smaller pied kingfisher that was to be seen everywhere by open water.

In the woods, too, I watched several swallow-tailed bee-eaters, a golden green with bright yellow throat and deep blue belly, birds I never saw again on the Bahr el Arab. Such wooded streams and swamps were the haunt of the prehistoric darter and the mysterious white-backed night heron, while the trees often supported weaver-bird nests that hung down on slender stems like monstrous fuzzy green fruits.

Along the muddy water's edge were stilts, dunlins, sandpipers, greenshanks, ruffs (by the thousand) and, once or twice, a small party of freshly laundered avocets. Usually away from the commonalty, so reminiscent of a crowded holiday beach, were the more furtive birds, such as the black crake with its bright green bill and orange feet, painted snipe and gallinules. Riding the water or standing half hidden in the reeds the squadrons of ducks and geese, pelicans and spoonbills, rested, becoming active in the early morning or evening, or at night, while the jacanas or lily trotters pattered about on the floating weeds.

Aloof in the marsh, or flying with the slow beat of great wings, I watched several grey and rufous goliath herons, the giant of the heron family, a stately bird but not as handsome or as common as the equally dignified jabiru or saddle-bill stork.

Standing about one point two metres (four feet) tall the jabiru, or *abu mairam*, is one of the tallest of African birds and the most striking and colourful of the storks; when seen close to its black and white plumage is iridescent with green, violet and blue gleams, while the black legs are red-jointed and the thirty-centimetre bright red bill is divided in the middle by a black band with a glowing yellow shield or saddle at the base. Later I kept one of these lordly birds but only for a short time. It was commonly seen in all swampy regions, but is a solitary bird that I saw only singly or in pairs, stalking slowly along seemingly disinterested in its surroundings until a lightning strike with the huge coloured bill to catch frog or small fish disclosed a mind concentrating not on the absolute but on food. Like other storks, herons and similar birds, the jabiru seems to eat anything it can swallow.

These few days passed as quickly as any I had known. It was difficult to make up my mind to begin the long journey home, but I could delay no longer. In the course of my entomological research it was sooner or later always possible to spend a few hours exploring and observing in the Nuba Mountains, but the opportunity to visit more distant places like the 'Bog' came seldom.

We did not set out for Kadugli empty-handed. I had caught numbers of insects, several reptiles and a knob-nose goose. We first returned to Abyei for food and petrol, and while waiting for Younis and the others I went to look at a newly-built, half-thatched Dinka hut. After a few moments a tall Dinka appeared, but I could communicate only in mime as he knew no Arabic. I indicated my interest in the hut, and by signs he invited me to see the nearby homestead where he lived; huts built on stilts as the ground was subject to flooding and surrounded by a grass fence. In this compound I found a tame crested crane. The Dinka agreed to sell the bird to me for a trifling sum, so I added the crane to my collection.

It was difficult to fit the big bird into the Land Rover, but finally I was satisfied that it would come to no harm; telling Badr to knock on the cab if the jolting upset the bird we set off for home.

Our return journey was uneventful until we camped for the night at our usual place in a well-watered, densely wooded area east of Muglad on the Wadi el Galla. It had been a long, hot drive and I wanted to start again at dawn, so immediately after supper we all settled down to sleep. Without bothering to put down the tent awnings we slept in the open wrapped in blankets around the fire a short distance from the Land Rover. Before going to bed, after feeding the crane, I tethered it on a short string. I thought it would be much happier in the open than in the back of the Land Rover, but I left the other animals aboard.

The crane stood close to my head while Younis slept on the other side of it and Badr and Ahmed slept close by.

It was only faintly light when we awoke the next morning, but the crane had vanished leaving the broken string and one feather. Carefully we examined the ground, and then looked further afield. Not far away we found a little pile of feathers; it was obvious what had happened. In the night a spotted hyaena, bolder than most, had crept amongst our sleeping bodies to reach the bird, closing its jaws on the crane's head without waking it, and then carrying it off to devour at leisure. The hyaena's spoor was plain on the soil we had swept before lying down to sleep; the beast had stepped over me to reach the tethered crane, one footprint being close to my head, yet it had not awakened me, the men or the crane itself, and by seizing the bird by the head had prevented it from making any sound. Then, scarcely twenty metres away, it had eaten the bird leaving nothing but the few small feathers we had found.

I was upset and annoyed with myself for not taking more precautions to ensure the safety of the bird, but at the same time thankful that the hyaenas – for there had been several, although only the one had come close – had not attacked one of us.

The next year I managed to obtain a pair of crested cranes which I brought back safely, and which lived in my zoo until I left the Sudan, at which time I passed them on to a Sudanese friend who would take good care of them.

In the world of the bog-bird

A couple of months or so after losing the crested crane to the marauding hyaena, I found time to revisit the swamps of the Bahr el Arab. Before I could leave I had first to go to Dilling to examine the results of some experiments there. When my work was completed, I left Dilling for the Nyima Hills, on my way to Muglad and the Bahr el Arab.

I had paid several visits to these hills and learnt a little about the Nuba there. Despite being on the northerly edge of the Nuba Mountains and having strong links with Dilling, the Nyima Nuba had retained their traditions resisting Islamic and other foreign influences unlike some other clans overwhelmed by outside ideas. Their last serious revolt against the ruling power in the Sudan, the British and Egyptians, was in 1917 when they killed a District Commissioner; a disproportionately large, British-officered, army force was sent in November, including cavalry and the Camel Corps, artillery, bombs and machine-guns, that, after losses on both sides, captured *Shirra* (Chief) Agabna and executed him.

The inhabitants of Dar Nuba, collectively known as the Nuba tribes, are far from a homogeneous whole; not only do their languages or dialects, moral codes, laws and general culture often differ, but they may be also physically different, having probably arisen from varying stocks. The tribes may be likened to the clans of Scotland in the Middle Ages, but with the greatest outside pressure being from the Arabs instead of the English. In the townships of Dilling and Kadugli the inhabitants are mostly mixed, and include Arabic, Hamitic and Nilotic strains, as well as some 'pure' Nuba. Despite the differences amongst the Nuba there are also strong similarities, and all clans have a tradition of age-group initiation with emphasis on competitive sports, wrestling, stick-fighting, athletics, and, in some clans, spear-fighting and bracelet-fighting. Strength, skill and courage are primary virtues in all tribes.

The Nyima Nuba, who call themselves the 'People of the seven hills' despite the numerous inhabited and uninhabited hills of their *dar*, were slave-keeping and frequently taken as slaves themselves not long ago; today they supply many recruits for the Sudan Defence Corps, are relatively law-abiding, but still keep themselves to themselves. In general terms, and no doubt differing in detail in various places in the Nyima Hills, their lives follow a similar pattern.

The small boys herd the goats and calves (I saw none of the black pigs that are common further south) until about ten or eleven when they begin to sleep in the cattle camps to look after the cows. During this time they undergo cicatrisation on various parts of the body, especially their necks, and the tribal face marks are cut. Now, too, they begin to learn the tribal sports and practise wrestling and stick-fighting, a duel with staffs of wood about a metre long, each boy trying to beat the other about the head and upper body while protecting himself with a small shield held in his other hand.

The Nyima marry comparatively late in life, in their mid-twenties, although the girls are usually younger than the men. The rites seem to take place whenever there are sufficient candidates and when the community feels rich enough to afford the celebrations, there being considerable expense for the fathers or other relatives of the young men who have to supply *merissa* (beer) and animals for sacrifice, but always in the dry season, about October.

At any time from about sixteen to twenty-two or even older one of the most important ceremonies in a Nyima boy's life takes place, circumcision. The young men make their way in small groups to the uninhabited hills. Here, completely naked, they have to live for about a month. When exploring the hills I once disturbed a small group of eight or nine miserable-looking youths clustered in a hollow at the summit of a *jebel*. Startling me as much as I startled them, they disappeared like so many wild animals down the other side of the *jebel*, for they were supposed to remain unseen, but I never witnessed, nor wished to, the actual circumcision.

While in the mountains the youths are fed by their 'slaves', younger boys and girls, who carry food to them daily in covered containers in the early dawn, or after dusk when they cannot be seen. These same children also tend the youths after circumcision applying oil or other 'medicines' to the wound until it heals.

The circumcision is carried out by a *kujur* (priest). Assisted by his servants, the young man kneels by a flat rock; the foreskin of his penis is stretched out on the rock and cut off by means of a more or less sharp axe wielded by the *kujur*. The youth must not cry out or show any sign of pain. Afterwards he waits another few days for the wound to heal, during which time some foods, such as meat and beer, are taboo as these may 'prevent healing'.

When the *sori*, or young initiates, come back to the village the festivities commence and may continue for weeks. Firstly, a bull is selected and led out to be chased by the newly circumcised *sori* to be beaten to death with clubs and afterwards presented to the *kujur;* each youth, now dressed in all his finery or at least a loin-cloth, is given a new name to commemorate his newly adult status, a name that usually reflects some physical or temperamental characteristic. Next comes the general jubilation, no work being done by anybody, the *sori* visiting everybody, sleeping by day but dancing and drinking by night until most are insensible.

During these weeks many wrestling matches are staged, but the newly circumcised *sori* are not allowed to wrestle one another. The final ceremony, religious in function, seems to be – as are almost all Nuba rites except those concerned with warding off evil spirits – a fertility dance. The sacred musical instruments are brought from hiding, the lyre or *kweedu*, the drums and the kudu horn or *taro*. A goat or ram is sacrificed and the blood is dripped on the sacred lyre before it is hidden again with the other instruments until the next circumcision *sibr* or festival.

The young men are now able to marry and raise a family, sons being more welcome than daughters since they mean more wealth and prestige. They dig the soil and tend their crops in the wet season but still take part in the sporting events of the dry season until they become 'grandfathers' (not necessarily literally). But almost until death they will still undergo tests of endurance and fitness, for the old men have great power and are treated with much reverence, as long as they retain reasonably sound minds and healthy bodies. On entering the 'grandfather' age they will be given new names again that are, to some extent, indicative of their status.

There seem to be no equivalent 'age-grades' for the girls amongst the Nyima; when a girl reaches puberty she has her ear lobes pierced and is cicatrised with designs on belly, buttocks and shoulders, while her hair is dressed in a new fashion, and, after marriage, in a different fashion again.

Like all the Nuba, the Nyima people have a strong belief in magic and they are animists. When a man dies it is believed that his 'shade' travels to the abode of the shades, said to be only a few days' journey from the Nyima Hills, and apparently believed to be an actual place in the Nuba Mountains. As all things also have a shade, food and drink are scattered and spilt at the grave, so that their spirits can go with that of the man to nourish him on his journey. A man is believed to have several souls or shades which, in the form of animals, may leave him when he is asleep – all except one which must remain or the man will die.

The spirit of the dead often returns to the village to haunt people or to commit evil if the dead man had a grievance, and may possess a living person. Such ghosts often possess *kujurs* or spirit-priests, the rainmaker being the most powerful *kujur*. Like the oracles of ancient times in the western world, the *kujur* while in a state of trance or dissociation makes pronouncements that will guide community decisions. Having seen a *kujur* possessed, I have no doubt of the genuineness of the hysteria and final catalepsy, a thanatosis as convincing as that of any spider, weevil or other creature that feigns death to avoid an enemy, self-induced though it might be.

A *kujur* may also be possessed by other spirits, usually but not always, evil ones, of an entirely supernatural origin, and by communicating with such ghosts he is able to discover what they want and how to satisfy their needs. At times, shouting, fires and bull-roarers are used to frighten away evil spirits, but during the maturing of the *dura* heads, noise is frowned upon in case the 'souls' of the plants are frightened away.

My knowledge of the Nyima Nuba, as I saw them only occasionally, is sketchy; much of what I learnt was hearsay, the result of persistent questioning. But I found the Nyima always interesting, and I did obtain fascinating glimpses of their lives and beliefs, sometimes quite by accident.

On this occasion, as I drove through the hills on my way to the Bahr el Arab, we came upon a large gathering of Nyima, and I stopped. It was a *sibr* in celebration of the recent circumcision. The crowd of perhaps three or four hundred was a large one for the region, and had arranged themselves in a rough circle in the centre of which there were several wrestling pairs and the 'referees'. Spirits were high and the *merissa* must have been plentiful. I wanted to take some cine-film but the dust and jostling made it difficult.

The wrestlers, dressed in pantaloons or a rectangle of brightly coloured cloth suspended like a flag from the waist, and often with a strip of cloth round the neck like a broad tie, were in furious action. As I filmed one man lifted his opponent above his head and dashed him to the hard ground with a thud that I could hear even above the shrieking crowd. Another youth rushed out to challenge the victor, but was pushed away by two referees and returned to the crowd. He was a circumcision 'brother' and thus prohibited from wrestling the winner of the fight I had just witnessed. Despite the apparent chaos, there was strict control and the rules were enforced. But I had seen many such wrestling tournaments; what made this *sibr* particularly interesting for me was the appearance of the women. Usually, the women were inconspicuous or kept in the background, but here there were almost as many women as men and never before had I seen such elaborate 'costumes' or such a display of hair arrangements.

On the opposite side of the 'ring' was a line of some fifteen young girls, some almost unrecognisable as Nuba girls and looking like Oriental importations. One girl was dressed in a Victorian style frock that made her look like a red pagoda, there being flounces from top to bottom; her already slit eyes were emphasised by a bright yellow line drawn on her skin at each outer corner; her face and neck were oiled with *simsim* (sesame) oil and then apparently powdered with dry cattle dung that lightened the skin to give her a distinctly yellowish-brown hue. Her greased, straightened and then braided hair, which hung evenly like a fringe of dark ropes all round her head, twinkled with small silver Egyptian coins, the hair threaded through their central holes. She looked rather like a Mandarin doll, and her jerky arm and leg movements, her hands held together or else half extended and the little steps she took as she came forward now and again to dance added to her 'Chinese' look.

Several other girls wore only narrow cotton strips wound like a cummerbund around their loins, or made up into very brief 'shorts' scarcely ten centimetres long. Above these their naked bodies were coloured. One was dusted all over with powdered dung except for purple lips, stained with the juice of some plant, red ochred eyes, and shiny, oiled breasts the nipples of which were coloured bright blue. Several had red or yellow ochre designs of different patterns painted on their naked torsos and feet.

One girl, with a strikingly beautiful figure, wore the pelt of a bushbuck, one hind and one front leg of the buck being tied together around her waist so that the skin fell down one thigh but left all else exposed. Her upper body was shining with oil and painted with bright blue dashes from hips to neck; her breasts were encircled by bands of alternating colours separated by her natural skin colour, while her legs were thickly chalk-white from crotch to ankles, her feet Prussian blue, a beautiful colour derived from mixing *henna* (the orange dye obtained from the leaves of a common plant, *Lawsonia alba*, sometimes called Egyptian privet) with indigo (a bright blue dye probably extracted from one of the several common *Indigofera* spp., papilionaceous plants, of which there are more than fifty kinds in the Sudan).

Only a woman would have been able to describe adequately the elaborately dressed hair of some of the dancing girls and of their numerous sisters crowding round to watch the wrestling. Some of the intricate geometrical designs obtained using strands of hair, coins, shells, beads and *suc-suc* (braidwork), and sometimes employing dyes, glue (gum from trees) and a feather or two (although feathers were mostly worn by the men), must have taken hours, if not days, of preparation. Even so, these coiffures scarcely attained the elaborate artistry sometimes found amongst the Shilluk and some other Nilotic tribes.

On reaching Abyei I found once again that the ferry was unusable. Stopping there for only a short time, I watched a uniformed askari playing *mancala* (an Arab game played with counters and a board – in this case holes in the sand and pebbles – that, in many different forms, is found throughout most of Africa) with his prisoner outside the *merkas* (police-station) while Younis and the others visited the *suq*. Then we drove some twenty or thirty kilometres back towards Muglad where I turned off the road to try and reach the Bahr el Arab further upstream beyond the limit of our previous exploration.

We made slow progress across country for the terrain soon became surprisingly well-wooded and criss-crossed by small gullies and *khors*. Several times we disturbed antelopes, mostly reedbuck, bushbuck, lelwel hartebeeste and tiang, but all in small numbers, and we came upon buffalo tracks but did not see the animals on this occasion. I was surprised to see a troop of patas monkeys which I had not expected to find in this habitat.

Although I have scarcely mentioned this monkey, the patas or red hussar (called *abu lang* by the Baggara and *ko-yu* by the Nuba) is the commonest monkey of the Nuba Mountains, except possibly for the yellow or anubis baboon. Like the baboon it is a ground-dwelling species, but has long, fine sandy fur that appears much redder at a distance, almost white legs, arms and underparts, deep chestnut pate and a blackish line extending back from the eyes on each side of the head. It is a very attractive monkey (although the West African races I have seen for sale in European pet-shops in small cages look miserable and bad-tempered) with a blackish face, white or grey side whiskers, black eyebrows and brown eyes with black pupils. The tail is not prehensile, but like that of a baboon, more or less pointing upwards for the first few centimetres and then drooping. A large male may be almost a metre (head and body) and may weigh twenty-two kilos or so. It is really a West African species, varying a good deal in colour and size over its range. The several in my zoo caused almost as much mischief as Tigl and Umm Chita, the baboons.

It was late afternoon before we reached open water and stopped to make camp. It was impossible to know if we had reached the

Bahr el Arab or if this was just a tributary, but it was unimportant. The water was perhaps five metres wide between low banks, but shallow and with no perceptible current; earlier in the season a much larger area had been waterlogged, but now the ground was crusted over.

Leaving the men to make camp I went to investigate. I strolled along until I came to a bend where a darter was busily fishing. The bird was slowly swimming under water by the far bank, only its long S-neck visible jerking in time with the swimming movements of the invisible legs. The darter is like a cormorant in size and habits but is a more solitary bird; I never saw more than three together. The neck is not only very long but unlike the cormorant has a kink in it that enables the darter to shoot its head and bill forward with great speed, and the stiletto bill is straight and not curved. Like the divers and the grebes, the darter is capable of altering its buoyancy by a shift of internally stored air to enable it to float in the water at various depths, or to sink almost instantaneously below the surface.

As the darter is so often seen swimming with just the slender, white-striped neck, small head and long olive bill visible it is also called the snake-bird, although no snake could swim in this fashion. I spent a long time watching the snake-bird silently hunting, scarcely a ripple caused by his long neck where it broke the water surface. With the speed of a striking viper the head plunged below the water, pointed bill poised like a lance, to reappear almost at once the bill piercing the side of a small fish that it tossed upwards with a violent shake of its head to catch again athwart the now open, serrated bill. With another toss the fish was thrown in line with the bill and convulsively swallowed head first. Then cocking its head sideways the darter regarded me with one bright, yellow-gold eye. Apparently still satisfied that I was no threat (for all along the bird had been aware of my presence), it again began to swim slowly. Darters not only eat fish and frogs, but probably most other aquatic creatures, and I once saw one spear and swallow a small mouse that attempted to swim across a stream in front of the bird.

But I could watch darters closer to home and I wanted to see what else might be around or in the water. I moved more quickly and drew close to the bird which silently submerged, popping up again a good deal further away. A few minutes later I disturbed another darter drying its long pointed wings and stiff tail as it perched with short, webbed feet on a bough. With a croaking quack of alarm it flew away steadily, low over the water, following the winding stream until the trees hid it from sight. Darters often roost at night together with cormorants or other large water birds, and often make their nests in a cormorant colony in a tree or amongst reeds, the nest similar to the cormorant's being made from sticks lined with green plant material. The eggs I have seen were very stained to cover much of their greenish colour.

At an open place on the bank I knelt to watch a number of small fish. The bank was covered by a low-growing sedge and a sticky saxifrage bearing a few yellow flowers, together with other procumbent herbs, while in the dark water I could see the whorled, olive leaves of hornwort about which top-minnows were swimming.

Then I noticed another fish, only slightly larger, several of which had appeared and which seemed to have curious shapes. It was only after staring at one for a few moments that I realised it was swimming upside down! I determined to catch one of these strange fishes.

I am not an ichthyologist, or even a fisherman, but like any naturalist I was curious and interested in anything that seemed unusual. I had a folding insect net with me and using this, eventually I managed to trap two of the little fish. Like so many African river fish they had long barbels, blackish sensory filaments about the mouth. The dorsal fin was particularly large and sharply spiny, but the most remarkable characteristic was that the ventral surface was greyish-brown, the dorsal surface almost silvery, a reversal of the usual coloration and in keeping with the fact that they swam on their backs.

In due course I had the fish identified and they proved to be *Synodontis*, a common genus of river fish in Africa having many species and often known as 'squeakers' from the habit of some kinds of grunting when taken from the water (a sound made not by the mouth but by the movement of the pectoral fin spines). Apparently a few kinds of squeakers normally swim upside down, although most swim in the normal position; I had discovered nothing new for this fact was well known even to the Ancient Egyptians, but such personal triumphs are precious, as exciting and joyous as, for example, a child's first view of tadpoles hatching.

I did not have much opportunity to examine many of the fishes of the Sudan, which I now regret, but I did sometimes see fish caught in the streams of the Nuba Mountains where, apart from common barbel (a largish carp called *el fargo* and most sought after), mudfish (the smaller ones called *belboot;* the larger, *umm kuroo*) and *gurghur* (*Synodontis clarias*, which swims the normal way up), the commonest fish I saw was called *umm lagi* but has no English name.* This is an elongate somewhat eel-like primitive mud-fish with a row of little spined finlets along the back, and found even in small *khors*. Despite its numerous bones and the evil-smelling, greenish slime covering the body scales, it is eaten with relish. A *belboot* of forty to fifty centimetres cost about five piastres (five new pence) while an *umm kuroo* of perhaps eighty centimetres was worth about ten piastres.

Between Kodok and Abyei I was able to examine fish-traps, or fish speared or netted by Dinka, Shilluk or Nuer fishermen. I saw adult squeakers, thirty centimetres long, fish that had to be handled carefully because of their spiny fins which are said to be poisonous; and which, it has been reported, sometimes kill large predatory fish or even crocodiles by sticking in their throats. I saw some of the fierce, carnivorous Nile perch that resemble the

* *Polypterus.*

perch of temperate lands but may grow to almost two metres long and weigh over a hundred and twenty kilogrammes; the unpleasant *tambera*, or swell-fish, that can puff itself full of air to avoid being swallowed by a larger enemy, and which feeds on molluscs, crushing them with large teeth in the form of a beak that can also remove a man's finger.

On the Nile, too, I examined the very handsome tiger-fish that has flashing iridescent scales of rainbow colours and dark, bold stripes, and is the fiercest and most predatory of all with long, fanged teeth that can cut flesh to ribbons. It is called *kelb el bahr*, or dog-of-the-river, by the Arabs.

Once I came upon some Shilluk fishermen treating with some caution a fish caught in a basket-trap. Going closer I saw they were poking with sticks an unpleasant-looking, soft-skinned fish, a dull pinkish-grey creature with amorphous, blackish spots, and about fifty to sixty centimetres long. The fish was wriggling weakly but despite its repulsive appearance it looked harmless enough. I bent to look at it more closely; the Shilluk could speak no Arabic but stood back in naked aloofness making no attempt to interfere. Perhaps they expected me to touch it, but I had no such intention having seen the care they had taken. At the time I had no idea what fish it could be, but later I discovered that it must have been an electric cat-fish, a not uncommon creature that can give a substantial shock if touched.

There were three fishes, however, that I very much wanted to find. Two I never did see alive; one of these was the African relative (or rather relatives) of the Indian climbing-perch called *Ctenopoma* which, within the gill cavities, has accessory respiratory organs of bony plates covered by mucous membranes to enable it to breathe out of water, and little seems to be known of its habits. The other was an even more curious fish said to attain a length of a hundred and fifty centimetres or so and resembling a conger-eel; it has a dorsal fin extending from head to tail, no anal, ventral or caudal fins, a long tail tapering to a point, while the air-bladder is lung-like. What mainly aroused my curiosity was the breeding habits of this fish (*Gymnarchus niloticus*), for it is said to build extraordinary grass nests in the *toich* (annually flooded grasslands by watercourses) in which to lay its large eggs, and to attack human or other potential predators with great ferocity.

Quite by accident, for I was not looking for it, I discovered the third kind of fish, the Sudan lungfish, shortly after returning to camp with the two little upside-down fish. Later I also found the lungfish in the Nuba Mountains. Some distance upstream from our camp the open water vanished in swampy ground, now largely dry, but obviously the shrunken remnant of an extensive swamp. Here the vegetation was dense with tall *Phragmites*, a reed with sharply pointed, sharp-edged, lanceolate leaves, some papyrus islands in the distance where there was probably more open water, zebra grass and a few stands of a *Pennisetum* that, although young, looked very like elephant grass (the tallest grass of Africa that can grow to over six metres tall) but was unlikely to be so so far to the north-west. Hidden amongst the grasses and reeds of the wetter parts were large numbers of whistling teal and probably other ducks. Younis liked shooting and, as we needed a couple of ducks for supper, he took my old twelve-bore and set off with Badr.

I did not care to shoot these beautiful if tasty ducks, but there were so many of them and they were often the most accessible game. We shot only whistling teal, guinea-fowl, spur-fowl or knob-nose, and then only for the pot, no more than two birds at any time, and then only occasionally to vary a monotonous tinned diet. I had a cup of tea and then followed Younis and Badr.

Younis had shot one whistling teal but only winged it and I arrived in time to see Badr plunge into the swamp to try and retrieve it. This had to be done before it died for, according to Muslim belief, its throat had to be cut before or at the moment of death otherwise the men could not eat it.

But the duck was only slightly winged and, after a chase, was

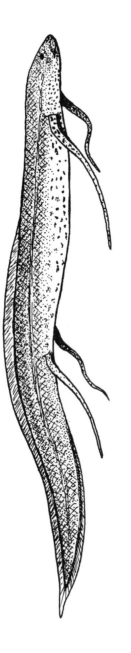

Sudan lungfish, which can reach a size of two metres or more

captured alive. I took it back to my zoo where its wound healed and it lived with another I had obtained some time before.

In captivity the two whistling teal became very tame and lived happily until I left the Sudan; they formed a mixed flock with a pair of spurwings, undisputed leaders, fulvous teal, a couple of knobnose ducks, a mallard pair, egrets and a few other water birds. Whistling teal are compact little birds about forty centimetres in size, the front part of the head and neck being white, the rest of the head and neck black, while the shoulders and chest are glossy chestnut and the rest of the body blackish with barred black and white flanks. It was undoubtedly the commonest duck of the region, with flocks of a thousand or more on the larger swamps. The fulvous teal, very similar in habits and appearance, was less common but often found with the other duck.

The call of both teals is a whistle, and the whistling teal's 'whi-whi-whooo-oo' was easy to imitate, and a flock flying overhead could often be called down by mimicking the whistle. Flights often passed over my zoo, particularly about June or October; the flocks were rarely large and sometimes no more than a pair of ducks.

One day, soon after I caught the second teal, I heard them calling loudly. Looking out of my office window I saw a flight of about a dozen of their relatives circling overhead, attracted by my captive birds. They would have landed had not somebody at that moment begun to cross the compound and the wild ducks flew away. Later on I actually trapped a pair that flew down into the zoo to visit the tame birds, but I set them free again.

Sending Badr back to camp with the live duck, I went with Younis to try and obtain another for supper. Alarmed by the first shot, the ducks had moved further into the swamp after circling around overhead. Soon we came upon a number now feeding on the land. Teal are mainly nocturnal feeders; it was not yet dark, but the light was fading quickly. One duck was closer; from tall grass cover Younis fired. The teal fell dead but a strange shrill scream that certainly did not come from the bird hung for a moment in the air after the sound of the shot died away. I had heard nothing quite like it, but the sound was so evanescent and so rapidly drowned by the alarm calls and whirring wings of many birds that I might have thought it imaginary had not Younis heard it too.

Running forward, Younis knelt down to slit the teal's throat. A movement of the fissured clay just behind the duck caught my attention; something under the surface was moving. With our knives we dug carefully in the ground to unearth a *samarki el tin* (fish-of-the-clay) or lungfish enclosed in its cocoon. Being just behind the shot duck, a pellet or two had hit the fish resting only just below the soil surface, and the shock must have caused it to release air from its air-bladder to cause the very strange scream that we had heard.

The lungfishes belong to an ancient order of bony fishes known as the Dipnoi, or 'double-breathers', thus called as they not only have gills to breathe the air dissolved in water, but also possess an air-bladder that has become a lung, dividing into two lobes with a single opening to the throat. It is believed that lungfishes arose from the same stock as the amphibians, a stock that divided in early times, some branches dying out to leave only two, from one of which developed the primitive amphibians and eventually all land animals, the other represented today by only the lung-fishes.

Only five kinds of lungfishes are known, one in Queensland, one in the Amazon, and the remaining three in Africa; the Sudan lungfish, *Protopterus aethiopicus* (occurring mainly in the Nile system, Lake Chad and the Great Lakes); the Gambian lungfish (of West and Central Africa and the best known species) and the Congo lungfish (mainly of the Congo River). They are all similar in appearance, long, cylindrical and eel-shaped with small cycloid scales embedded in a smooth, slimy skin, and tapering, tentacle-like paired fins that lack fin-rays.

The Sudan lungfish grows to a much larger size than the other African species, as much as two metres or more in length, but I did not discover any of more than about a metre and most were half this size. Its teeth, set in a small mouth, form strong, bony, ridged crushing plates in each jaw, and it seems to be entirely carnivorous eating not only small creatures, such as insects, worms and snails, but also larger molluscs, frogs, crabs and small fish. But like most carnivorous animals it probably eats vegetable matter at times.

The most remarkable feature of the lungfish is its ability to survive for so long out of water. When the dry season comes and the water contracts, many are left high and dry, but then bury themselves in the mud. I have often found other fish, usually dead or dying, trapped on land by receding or evaporated water and while some – such as the mud-fish, *umm lagi* – can live for a few hours or even days, the lungfish can survive if necessary for years.

Having accidentally found one, I searched the ground and soon found others. Two of these I dug up, complete with cocoon, and took back to Kadugli where I kept them on a shelf. At times the air humidity is low with drying winds that seem to extract every last drop of moisture, but when I immersed the fish cocoon in water seventeen months later one of the lungfishes came to life, although the other had shrivelled and was dead. In their natural mud habitat there can be no doubt that survival is almost universal even after the most prolonged drought, and specimens of the Gambian lungfish, taken to England, have revived after four years.

When burying itself in soft mud, slime is discharged by the skin to mix with the mud and form a thin cocoon that soon dries around the curled-up fish to form a hard but brittle shell. The fish, in forming this protective case, wriggles round and round ending up with its mouth at the top opposite a narrow hole in the cocoon through which it can breathe. This hole is too small to allow moisture from within the cocoon to escape, and the layer of mud adhering to the outside is sufficient to prevent the fish becoming overheated no matter how hot the soil surface becomes.

Curled up like an embryo, the fish spends the next few months in its cocoon awaiting the advent of the next rains, breaking out of its self-made prison when the ground again becomes soft and filled with water, the water trickling into the air-breathing hole and into the fish's mouth to awaken it to life. During the time the dormant fish is in the cocoon its metabolic rate slows considerably, it lives on the fat it has accumulated in its kidneys and gonads during the active, feeding season (although it usually loses weight), and only requires to breathe air about once every two hours or so.

With careful observation, once the fish are known to be present, it is not difficult to detect the breathing holes using a straw thrust into any likely crevice. Just as birds and people 'call' up termites and some other creatures by drumming on the surface of the ground or some resonant sounding box, such as a gourd, to imitate the sound of rain, so lungfish can be 'called' towards the end of the dry season; attracted by the apparent and welcome sound of rain, the fish stir or grunt in response and disclose their whereabouts.

Even during the rainy season the fish often needs its air-breathing apparatus, for the swamps where many live may still become very shallow or stagnant. Once during the night when camped in the swamps and all else was quiet, I heard the soft plopping sounds of lungfishes amongst the reeds as they came to the surface to breathe, a sound that I thought was made by frogs until I investigated. The Sudan lungfish seems to lie low during the day and to be active only at night. The breeding sites are found at the edges of the swampy areas, especially where the vegetation is matted and rotting. Here the male prepares a crude nest by scooping out some of the decayed vegetation to make a hole for the female to lay her eggs. The male remains near the nest while the eggs hatch, but to what extent he protects them is difficult to say. When the young hatch they breathe by means of feathery external gills that are gradually lost when the internal gills become functional.

The wounded lungfish, about seventy centimetres long and a mottled greenish-yellow and dark grey colour, soon died. Despite its oily nature and muddy flavour the boys cooked it, eating it together with some of the duck for their supper. I dined on bread and cheese.

Although I spent many days exploring the Bahr el Arab and other marshy rivers, finding much of interest and collecting some of the creatures I found, it was only on my last visit, some two years after finding the lungfish, that I finally managed to cross the Bahr el Arab by the ferry at Abyei to travel in the northern 'Bog'.

On this occasion I mounted quite an expedition; not only did I take a lorry to follow behind the Land Rover and carry extra men. I took also a home-made raft and two collapsible rubber canoes, Some time before I had followed a different route to Abyei, going first to Lake Abyad, south-east to Lake No on the Bahr el Ghazal, to continue to the junction with the Bahr el Arab and so to Abyei. I had taken a native dugout canoe on Lake No, and on the Nile itself, but this was not the same as having my own boat, and now I wanted to explore the Bahr el Arab downstream from Abyei, perhaps as far as the junction with the Bahr el Ghazal some one hundred and thirty kilometres or so by river.

On reaching Abyei the ancient ferry was actually riverworthy at last. The crossing was hazardous, the ferry listing heavily despite the smooth water, two small boys slipping about in the hull as they baled furiously in water to their knees. Still, we reached the other side safely and at least the ferry was not one with a big enough hole in for a boy to be employed to sit in it as was the case with another ferry. This was the first trip the ferry had made in more than two years, yet this was the only link between the 'Bog' and anywhere north for hundreds of miles.

Leaving the lorry and the men to camp by the river, I took the
Land Rover and with Younis and Badr explored parts of the
western 'Bog'; several days later we returned to the ferry. It was
time to try out the raft. Since making it from a wooden framework supported by three big oil drums there had been nowhere to
test it before bringing it all this way. My disappointment was
great to find that no matter how we modified it with our limited
materials and tools, although it floated well we could not stabilise
it; floating high it turned turtle; floating lower in the water it was
too heavy, sluggish and still liable to capsize. After labouring
until nightfall I gave up, for I did not know what hazards we
would encounter and even a strong eddy let alone a surfacing
hippo would have tipped up the raft. Not all the men could swim
and we might easily have been stranded without any possibility
of rescue. With the canoes alone I could make only a very limited
journey, but it would be an experience that could tell me more
about the Sudd than I could learn from Land Rover or on
foot.

Early the next morning we prepared for our canoe journey. I
thought of lashing the boats together to make a kind of catamaran, but this was not feasible. Unfortunately, the canoes were so
small that even with one man aboard each, the freeboard was
only about ten centimetres in the middle; with what *affish*
(luggage) I could take – a mosquito-net, a flask of tea, a blanket,
binoculars, drinking water, some food – this was reduced to only
a few centimetres and I had to paddle very slowly and carefully
to avoid upsetting the boat.

Younis came with me in the other canoe, similarly equipped.
We took only our long knives as weapons, there being no room for
the twelve-bore or for my cameras. The sluggish current carried
us along, and we only had to use the paddles occasionally to keep
in midstream. I had arranged with the lorry driver, a sensible,
trustworthy man, that if we did not return in four days he was to
take the Land Rover across to the east bank to come and look for

us; if due to some mishap or too strong a current we could not return in the canoes I would light a fire; he would look out for the smoke, drive as close to the swamps as he dared and then light a fire himself. We would try and reach him through the swamp, but I did not have much hope that such a rescue plan would succeed.

My chief fear was a puncture in one of the canoes, so we kept a good look-out for submerged snags, often a hazard, but the muddy water remained unbroken by such obstacles. We floated quietly and peacefully on, and while the reeds hid the banks there was always some activity on the river itself; once a shaggy, silky-haired rat swam to the reeds just beside my canoe. It appeared to be a *Dasymys*, although as far as I am aware shaggy rats have been recorded only from Equatoria. I did not see another.

We landed at mid-morning where we found a relatively dry and firm bank. A pair of spur-fowl flew up with indignant clucking and the hoisted tail of a warthog vanished as the snorting pig trotted into the reeds, resentful of our unexpected arrival from the river. Telling Younis we would spend the night here, and leaving him to look after the canoes and unload, I set off to follow the warthog along the nebulous game-path that followed a slight ridge of land.

The ground was little more than a skin able to support a man or animal and in places I sank to my calves in mud or water. This swamp joined up with the main *sudd*, as the permanent papyrus and reed marshes of the Nile and its tributaries are called. Most of the land was *toich*, a Dinka word for seasonally waterlogged ground inhibiting tree growth, but on which grass flourishes in the dry season to form lush meadows. But there were areas of higher ground, seldom flooded, on which trees grew. In this enormous expanse of *sudd* and *toich*, almost entirely deserted by man, there probably gather more kinds and numbers of birds than in any other equivalent area on earth. I walked on, taking good care to leave frequent marks in the mud and to check my

Some birds of the Sudd. *Left to right*: Shoebill, black crake, pied kingfisher, darter and marsh sandpiper. Papyrus in background. *Phragmites* to right of shoebill, sedge in flower to left.

compass bearing. To be lost in the *sudd*, a simple matter, would have only one end, a lingering death.

In this western part centred on the junction of the Lol and Bahr el Arab, and the Bahr el Arab and the Bahr el Ghazal, are such antelopes as the lelwel, tiang, reedbuck, bushbuck, waterbuck and roan. Herds of buffalo are found on the *toich*, and this is the home of the semi-aquatic situtunga that can submerge completely to leave only its nostrils visible above water. The male has twisted, spiral horns and long dark-brown, silky hair, but the female is hornless and reddish. Here, too, occurs the Nile lechwe, often called Mrs Grey's cob, that is found nowhere else in the world, a somewhat smaller animal than the situtunga, about the size of a fallow deer, a beautiful and graceful antelope with long, slender, ridged, double-curved horns, sleek chocolate or blackish coat with cream or yellowish saddle and white facial markings.

A slight rise with a few broad-leaved trees hid the view in front. At the top of this elevated ridge I saw, seeming to stretch to infinity in all directions, a flat plain of waving grasses and glinting water, dotted with the white, grey or black forms of long-legged birds and the larger shapes of antelopes. On the pools and rivulets rode the squadrons of ducks, geese and other birds, umbrageous despite the rainbow gleam of plumage when brought close by the magnifying power of my binoculars – all except the whistling teal whose brilliant white showed like washing spread to dry.

Nearby stood a tall bog-bird, enigmatic and aloof, a stork that more than any other animal is the personification of the spirit of the vast *sudd* of the Sudan, and appropriately the emblem of Bahr el Ghazal Province. Solitary, motionless, mysterious, the bog-bird stood, its great deep bill, nearly as wide as long with a hooked tip, resting on its breast, as though the bird were in deep thought, or as if the bill was too heavy to support. Thus it stood for nearly an hour, only twice in that time giving any indication of life by opening and shutting the huge bill, as if yawning or perhaps laughing silently at its thoughts.

I watched bog-birds, or as they are sometimes called shoebills or whale-headed storks, on several occasions in the swamps where they lived. They stand about a metre tall and, depending on the light, their slaty-grey feathers sometimes have a misty blue or greenish sheen. Day and night they stand with but an occasional sluggish movement, only showing some activity in the early morning or evening when they feed. With gawky steps and awkward stooping they hunt their frog and fish prey, but there is none of the speed and dexterity shown in the rapier strikes of most other storks. Rather the bill is used as a scoop more like that of the pelican. Probably their main food are fishes caught in small pools, where I have watched them hunting, and mudfish, such as *umm lagi*. They are said to feed on small mammals, too, but I never saw one do so except in captivity, and I should imagine they would go very hungry if they had to rely on catching rodents. That such a solitary, sluggish bird summons up enough energy to find a mate and breed may seem surprising, but, of course, it does, and the much stained white eggs are laid in a small area of trampled grass on the *toich* in the dry season.

With an effort I took my attention from the bog-bird from time to time to stare over the swamps, watching first one bird and then another, or following the movements of the buffalo herd not far away or of other antelopes. Above the earth-bound layer of misty bluish-grey haze, the result of moisture rising in perpetual battle with the sun's hot rays, riding the sky like ducks on water, a V-shaped formation of pelicans flew slowly by to settle like flying-boats on invisible water. In the distance I saw skeins of other birds. In a tree nearby a fish-eagle gave forth its unforgettable, piercing cry that was taken up by another further away. Above my head a bateleur eagle ceaselessly patrolled the sky, and far off, swirling like leaves in a dust-devil, vultures kept their eyes on some dying animal. In this primaeval swamp it would have been no surprise, only delight, to see an archosaur lumber into view, or an *Archaeopteryx* glide overhead.

Struck with enchantment, filled with the contentment and sense of well-being that always came to me most strongly at times like this, I became lost to time and discomfort. Only when I was disturbed by Younis, coming to see what had happened to me, did I realise that it was late and I was stiff, tired, hungry and thirsty. Before we returned to the boats, however, I was determined to move the bog-bird, to be able to watch it in flight.

We moved up on it. With a slight movement of the head the bird watched us, opening its beak several times to yawn or laugh at us it seemed, but in reality a form of threatening or warning behaviour. This being of no avail, it clattered its bill. After this its repertoire seemed exhausted and as we came closer still, it launched itself into the air, flying away with great, slow beats of the wings, head held back like that of a heron.

After a frugal meal, we walked downstream squelching through the mud towards a thickly wooded place. A small, glossy, dark-brown spotted-necked otter fled from the bank and into the water with scarcely a ripple, but a moment later showed its flat head as it swam away, not bothering to submerge. This otter is usually shy and wary, but it is probable that this one had never before seen a human-being. It left its prey in the reeds, a bedraggled teal, the only part eaten being the neck which was bare of feathers and flesh for about four centimetres of the length. Whistling teal must have been a common prey for several times before I had found similarly mutilated carcases. Otters move about overland in the rains, and I once found one at Tucma in a temporary pool many kilometres from any known permanent water. The spotted-necked otter seemed to be much commoner than the small-clawed or greater otter; I saw the latter once only in the Sudan. But the marsh or river mongoose was common enough, for I saw many skins, although I seldom glimpsed the living animal.

Amongst the trees, the fairly dense bush had been broken down where the hippo had made paths to reach the grasslands. We stood and watched the open river, active with duck soon to come to the swamp and *toich* to feed. The light was fading quickly. Red-hued in the last rays of the sinking sun, the edge of its huge fiery disc crenellated by the innumerable reed-mace spikes, the dark water broke nearby where a hippo blew before submerging again to leave ever-widening water-flame rings dancing over the surface. Apart from the paths in the undergrowth and reeds, this was the first sign we had seen of the huge animals.

With no warning a large bird, spectral grey in inspissating gloom, flew from a low branch towards us coming so close that we ducked; but it turned with a startled squawk and noisily flapped to rise and vanish. It was a night-heron, seldom seen although common enough, one of the two night-flying herons of the Sudan and about the size of a little egret. The eye is very large as befits a crepuscular bird that hunts after dusk and before dawn, and at the nape of the neck trail two long white plumes, as if the bird was wearing a Glengarry type bonnet.

The mosquitoes were unbelievable in numbers and persistence. The other difficulties of night observations on the marshes were insignificant compared with the torment of mosquitoes; they made it impossible to keep still and even obscured vision like a thick mist. Despite our liberal application of a new repellent I had containing D.M.P. (dimethyl phthalate) that kept most of the ravening hordes at their distance, we were forced to move and decided to return to the canoes and our mosquito-nets. There was no moon, and now the last rays of the sun had died, amongst the trees it was almost too dark to see a man at three paces.

Groping our way, I still kept a look-out for the night-heron; still more I hoped to see the much rarer white-backed night-heron whose habits seemed to be unknown, but neither bird showed. There were mysterious small noises—the plopping of fish and possibly of frogs, although none was calling at this time of the year; rustling in the foliage, normal movements of the night air, and the perpetual whining and pinging of mosquitoes. Once there was a great splash, probably a rodent or monitor lizard since there seemed to be no crocodiles here, and once a small terrapin scuttled to fall into the water.

All at once the earth seemed to shake and the gross grey form of a hippo materialised in front of us, looking as large as a coach as she heaved her bulk along in a panic rush to reach the water. Instinctively, we flung ourselves aside and the massive animal, weighing several tons, rushed past scattering us with bits of stick, mud and leaves kicked up by the huge feet. While we had been further along the bank the animals must have come out of the water to feed.

Half in the mud and half in scratchy shrubbery I listened to the sounds of the blundering beast and heard it fling itself into the river like a landslide; elsewhere amongst the trees were at least two other hippo also rushing for the water, but the awesome sounds soon faded and silence grew again.

That night, muddy and damp, I slept little in the rubber boat drawn up on the reeds, but we both felt better the next morning as soon as the sun had risen to steam our clothes. We determined to go on after all instead of back to Abyei.

Before we started I found an interesting, although not un-common plant, one of the bladderworts (*Utricularia*); bladder-worts are found all over the world, including Britain, mostly in swamps. In Africa they are very widely distributed, there being many different species, some of marshy waters at sea-level, others high on the mountains by mossy streams. They are unusual in that they are carnivorous plants, some of the leaves being highly modified to form traps for small organisms.

The bladderwort I found on this occasion was rootless, floating near the surface of the water. Some of the leaves were in whorls, spongy floats to support the floating plant; others were long and filamentous but otherwise normal; while yet others, the traps, were bladder-like. The plant fed on tiny creatures – small crustacea like *Daphnia*, minute insects, etc. – the bladder being an ingenious device. It had a flexible opening and contained air; any small pressure from an organism swimming in the water forced it open, the ensuing surge of water carrying the prey into the bladder from which it could not escape. Years later, in Mozambique, I found another bladderwort that I had not seen before and never

Sausage tree

saw again. This plant supported itself by twining the flower stalk around grass or reed stems.

An hour or two after re-embarking the sombre river began to widen, the current becoming even more imperceptible: definite banks and all ground, even the mud, vanished under water, the channel limited only by reeds and papyrus, their feet in water. We drifted along very slowly. Weaver-bird nests hung from some of the reeds but did not belong to the vast flock of masked weavers, yellow and black birds with black faces, that lifted in noisy strings as we floated by. A party of dazzling white egrets flew low and quickly above us, veering swiftly to one side as they saw us.

Now we saw the first crocodile, scarcely four feet long, asleep on a flattened reed mass until in alarm it belly-flopped into the water. Several times we attempted to find somewhere to land but there was no solid ground anywhere. There was a sudden disturbance in the water perhaps fifteen metres in front, and the monstrous head of a river-horse materialised, watching us from piggy eyes. Hastily, we paddled to stop the slow drift of the canoes and held on to some reeds. With a yawn cavernous enough to have engulfed one of the small canoes, the hippo disclosed huge yellowing fangs before submerging again leaving ripples that rocked our canoes.

There were few visible crocodiles, but they were there, together with a whole herd of hippo further downstream. With nowhere to land, crocodiles and river-horses liable to upset our fragile craft at any time, few provisions, and at least a hundred kilometres to travel through the swamps before reaching any kind of human settlement, it seemed madness to continue any further. Reluctantly, I told Younis, to his great relief, we would turn back.

Despite the gentle current, paddling was slow progress and we quickly shipped water. The canoes were unsinkable unless punctured, but soon I was sitting in a pool of water. At last, with little light left and the mosquitoes hanging in a huge cloud about us, we found a solid bank, enough to prevent the canoes drifting away. Up to our ankles in water we pulled the canoes into the rank weeds. I spent one of the most uncomfortable nights I remember, the mosquito-net, attached to flimsy reed stems, having fallen down so that I had to wrap it round my body to get some peace from the insects, but many found their way through. Unable to sleep, shivering as if with high fever, we started again long before dawn to drag the canoes back into open water.

It was almost with panic that we found the inflatable side of one of the boats limp and flaccid; it had gone down during the night. Fortunately, each canoe had two separate inflatable rings to support them, and the other ring was still fully blown up. Inflating the flat ring we found the puncture was only small and below water when the canoe was manned, so little air escaped.

When, towards nightfall, we paddled, very stiff and tired, in my case with blistered hands, to the shore at Abyei I felt I never wanted to see a swamp again, but in fact it was an interesting and unforgettable experience that had given me an otherwise unattainable insight into the life of the vast *sudd*.

Darfur journey

The dark form of the animal disappeared amongst the low herbage just beyond the fitful, flickering light of the campfire, and I obtained no more than a glimpse of it. When I reached the spot I found I was amongst a stand of *heskanit*, a widespread spiny grass only about half a metre tall but one of the more unpleasant plants of the Sudan. So, after marking the place, I returned to bed, scratched and temporarily baffled.

We were on our way to Jebel Marra, one of the two highest of Sudan's mountains, in northern Darfur. It was Christmas, 1954, and this was the first of two such journeys I made to the region. We had travelled along a narrow, sandy track through dense and seemingly interminable acacia forest, tangled and leafless trees flanking the roadway like barbed wire defences. The Land Rover, hindered by a laden trailer, its wheels not fitting the deep twin ruts left in the sand by lorries, the only vehicles that occasionally used the track, had lurched from side to side for the last sixty or seventy kilometres to give us a bruising ride, although Ahmed in the middle seat had been cushioned by Younis on one side and me on the other, while Badr had been in the back comfortably ensconced amid the bedding. We had left our camp east of Muglad that morning to travel north-west towards Nyala.

Lying comfortably in bed by the dying fire I thought about our journey. I anticipated a ten-day trek, fourteen days at the most, to travel the thousand kilometres to the mountain range, explore part of it, and return, some two thousand five hundred kilometres in all. That was if nothing went wrong. I knew little about the geography of this part of Darfur, and carried no map (the only maps of this and adjacent parts of the Sudan that were available were hopelessly wrong in detail), but this was unimportant. I knew roughly the position of Jebel Marra and the main townships which was all that was necessary. It was the country I wanted to see, the plants and animals; settlements were to be avoided except to replenish our petrol and water. We could carry enough drinking water for a week, and petrol for five hundred kilometres even over the worst country

Darfur and the 'Bog' are the least known provinces of the Sudan, parts being as unexplored today as when Europeans first invaded Africa. As large as Spain, more than twice the size of Uganda, an area almost equivalent to the states of New York, New Jersey, Maryland, Virginia, North and South Carolina combined, Darfur has a population (or had at that time) of scarcely a million people. I remembered that it was only thirty-eight years ago that the notorious Ali Dinar, Sultan of Darfur, when he threatened to invade Kordofan, had been defeated by Wingate's troops and aeroplanes, and that Darfur still had a certain autonomy. Large areas were uninhabited and as inhospitable as the Sahara, but there was seldom more than a hundred and fifty kilometres between larger settlements.

Before starting the next morning I went to the *heskanit* to see if I could find the animal I had seen the night before; I was sure it had gone to ground there. With a hoe we cleared the grass away and discovered a burrow entrance, a hole about eight centimetres in diameter. Digging up the burrow we caught a giant rat, a common enough animal resembling an ordinary rat apart from its size.

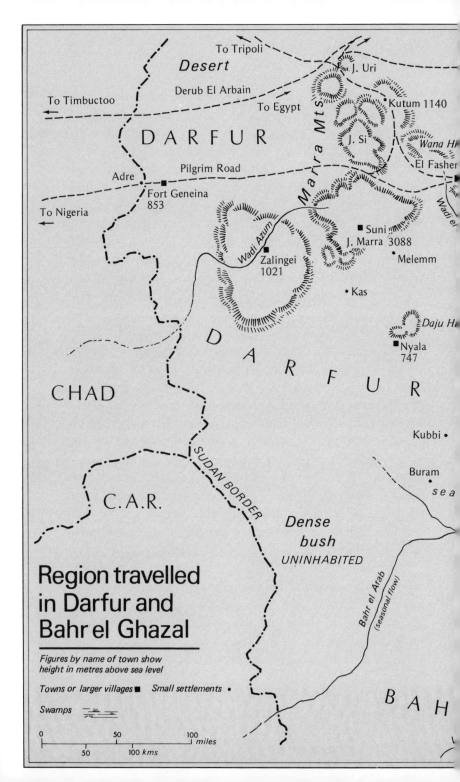

To Tripoli

Desert

J. Uri

Derub El Arbain

To Egypt

Kutum 1140

To Timbuctoo

D A R F U R

Marra Mts.

J. Si

Wana H

Pilgrim Road

El Fasher

Adre

Wadi el

Fort Geneina
853

Wadi Azum

Suni

To Nigeria

Zalingei
1021

J. Marra 3088

Melemm

• Kas

D A R F U R

Daju H

Nyala
747

CHAD

Kubbi •

SUDAN BORDER

Buram

C.A.R.

s e a

*Dense
bush*
UNINHABITED

Region travelled
in Darfur and
Bahr el Ghazal

Bahr el Arab
(seasonal flow)

*Figures by name of town show
height in metres above sea level*

Towns or larger villages ■   Small settlements •

Swamps

B A H

| 0 | 50 | 100 |
miles

50   100 kms

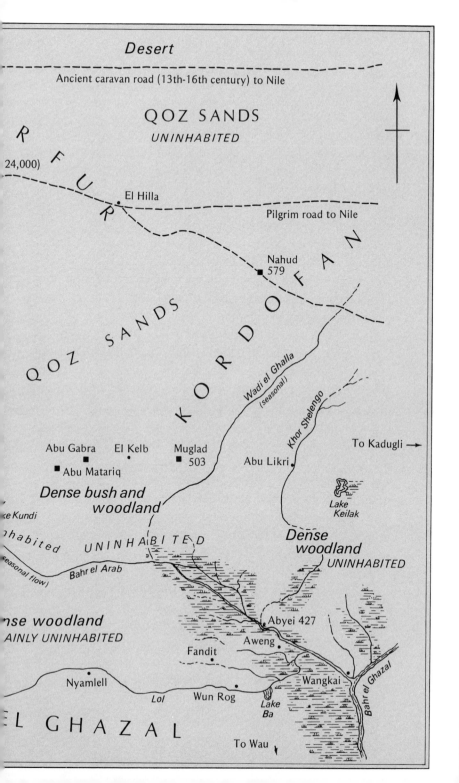

Desert

Ancient caravan road (13th-16th century) to Nile

QOZ SANDS
UNINHABITED

RF UR

(24,000)

El Hilla

Pilgrim road to Nile

Nahud
579

QOZ SANDS

KORDOFAN

Wadi el Ghalla
(seasonal)

Khor Shelengo

To Kadugli →

Abu Gabra   El Kelb   Muglad
                      503

Abu Likri

Abu Matariq

Dense bush and
woodland

Lake Keilak

ke Kundi

Dense
woodland
UNINHABITED

habited

UNINHABITED

seasonal flow)

Bahr el Arab

nse woodland
AINLY UNINHABITED

Abyei 427

Aweng

Fandit

Nyamlell

Wangkai

Bahr el Ghazal

Lol   Wun Rog

Lake Ba

EL GHAZAL

To Wau

Widespread in tropical Africa, the giant rat has been divided into a number of races and is said to grow to a total length of about a hundred and twenty centimetres, although nowhere in any country have I seen one approaching this size. The largest I ever found (in Central Africa) had a total length of eighty-one centimetres, and most adults are about thirty-five centimetres head and body, the tail as long again, with dark furred back, lighter underparts and whitish feet. The long tail is curiously particoloured, the basal part blackish-brown like the body but the end half is greyish-white. Since this rat is normally nocturnal, perhaps the whitish last fifteen centimetres or so of the tail attracts predators to pounce or swoop on the tail instead of the rat, thus enabling the rodent to escape with its life, but I have never found one of these rats minus its tail.

Such a large rat – it weighs about a kilo (average weight of three adult, non-gravid, females was one kilogramme fifty grammes) – might be expected to be a formidable creature, but although it can fight fiercely, it has a much more docile nature than, for example, the brown rat. I kept and bred these rats (in the Nuba Mountains it is called *abunsah-ah* or *kefalou*) and in captivity even adults soon become tame; the young are quite delightful little creatures with outsize heads, large ears and big feet, as confiding and as friendly as any wild mammal can be. This rat, like most, seems to be omnivorous but largely vegetarian. It has enormous cheek-pouches in which it can stuff about a hundred grammes of vegetable food for later consumption, and in captivity they would eat all manner of foods: biscuits, bread, cheese, soup, even sardines.

The giant rat is found normally in woods and lusher regions, but years later I found it in towns in Central Africa where it had adapted to a life in stores and barns and occasionally in houses. Like most rats it is an excellent swimmer, but it does not seem to climb much. Wherever it occurs in populated places in the Sudan it is trapped and eaten, being highly coveted for its sweet flesh.

Putting the giant rat in its cage into the trailer we set off again. Soon we reached a village called El Kelb or Keleb, the Dog, not far from Abu Gabra but a poor place scarcely more than a caravan halt, where we stopped for a few minutes as my men wanted to see if they could buy food and to talk.

Possibly the reason for the curious name of this hamlet was that the area around was a well-known haunt of hunting-dogs, and certainly the thick but broken bush gave indication of plenty of game. *Kelb el wadi* is a name sometimes given to the hunting-dog, but *kelb* usually means the domestic dog, and *simmay* or *awalad ower* are commoner names for the wild beast. Whether or not there was any connection between the name of the village and the hunting-dogs, the Arabs said the dogs were so fierce west of Kelb that nobody dared to travel at night on foot, donkey or camel except in a large, armed party, and that several travellers had been attacked between El Kelb and Abu Gabra or Abu Matariq.

I asked if the dogs had attacked people in the daytime, but they said nobody travelled in the middle hours of the day; people began a journey after sunset unless 'the way was only a few hours' when a before dawn start might be made. Had anybody been attacked recently by the dogs? Yes, I was told, only the month before two travellers, brave but foolish, not wanting to wait until a party gathered to travel together, had risked going alone and both had been killed by the dogs. Now if anybody wanted to take the road he would wait here at El Kelb until there were sufficient numbers going in that direction, and all would go together. The dogs would not attack a large party. He himself had waited three days, but now there were many others to go with him and they would start that evening. Had there always been hunting-dogs in that region? I asked. They were not always seen, I was told, but they were there 'since the days of my father'.

The other Arabs confirmed their spokesman's statements. There were eight or ten spear-armed men, with three camels, a couple of donkeys and two or three women and children, ready to leave at nightfall. As we shook hands and left them there I found it difficult to believe what I had been told. Only once before had I ever heard of hunting-dogs attacking humans.

Travelling on to Nyala we kept a good watch for hunting-dogs or other game, but saw no dogs and little else. I dismissed the Arabs' tales; probably lions or leopards were responsible for their fears. It was not until our return from Jebel Marra that I had cause to remember the Arabs of El Kelb.

At Nyala I slept in a proper bed in civilised surroundings for once, for the Conservator of Forests (D. McC. Ramsey) kindly put me up for the night. It must have been between Nyala and Kas that we saw the cheetah, but I am not sure. All I can recall now is that the plain was vast with only scattered bush, and that there was a large, clay pan in the distance that I thought we must investigate even as I gave chase to the cheetah. Of course, I had no intention of trying to catch the animal, but this was only the third cheetah I had seen and I wanted to get as close as I could.

We roared towards the animal which had stopped to stare, probably never having seen one of these strange, noisy animals ever leave its trail before (lorries, the only vehicles in use, were rare in any case and to date, after four days, we had not met a single vehicle). The Land Rover was scarcely a hundred metres from the cat before it took fright and bounded away. The terrain was flat, but with the trailer bouncing behind, the most speed I could coax from the Land Rover was about seventy kilometres per hour. At first we overhauled the animal, but when within about twenty metres the cat, with incredible ease, sped away to disappear like a hare being chased by an obese but enthusiastic spaniel.

A cheetah can leap four metres in one bound, and is said to be able to attain a speed of about seventy kilometres per hour from a standing start in about three to four seconds, and about a hundred kilometres per hour in five seconds. Having seen this and other feral cheetahs run I can believe it to be the fastest terrestrial sprinter. When running slowly the animal looks quite awkward, but when at full speed it is one of the most beautiful sights I have seen. There is no doubt, however, that a cheetah has little stamina and after scarcely half a kilometre at full stretch is too exhausted to run further. It certainly cannot match the endurance of many antelopes and gazelles, most of which seldom exceed a speed of fifty kilometres per hour.

Cheetahs are almost extinct or becoming increasingly rare everywhere; I saw only five during the whole of my time in the country, including a pair between Kosti and Sennaar in August, 1953, a most unexpected locality; but, outside the game-parks, they are probably still as numerous on the Sudan's vast plains as anywhere in the world. They are unlikely to survive much longer, however, even on the desert fringes.

After Kas we reached the foothills of the Jebel Marra range, and soon drove to Suni at about one thousand eight hundred metres, the most civilised place in the mountains for here were experi- mental plantations of citrus and other crops neatly laid out and eucalyptus and conifer plantations. I had not realised that Jebel Marra was more than an extinct volcanic inselberg; now I could see a seemingly infinite number of peaks and valleys, and appre- ciated that here was a very considerable range dividing the country to the south from the true desert and also forming a watershed between Lake Chad to the west and the Nile to the east.

I climbed to the crater summit of Jebel Marra, about two thou- sand five hundred metres above sea-level, to look at the crater lake. In fact, there were two lakes, one considerably larger than the other in a crater that must have been five kilometres in dia- meter. But although of much interest, the mountain was a dis- appointment for the tufa rock summit was almost completely bare of vegetation, and the lake contained dissolved carbonate of soda or natron giving it a strong salinity. It was very cold and dressed only in shirt, shorts and plimsolls I soon descended to Suni again. On the bracken and heath (*Blaeria*) covered slopes almost the only trees were an occasional clump of pretty, golden-leaved olives, small blackish trees that later would have white flowers and sweet purple fruits, and scattered *haraz* (*Acacia albida*), the largest acacia of the Sudan, but here stunted and sometimes deformed. Many pieces of pumice were lying about and I used one large piece for years afterwards.

Towards dusk we drove from Suni north-east along a good mountain road to try and find a camping site, but it was a couple of hours after nightfall before we found space to leave the track. The only animals I had seen in the mountains to date were several small hares, apparently the same as in the Nuba Mountains, that emerged after nightfall.

The next day I began exploring some of the hills on foot, especially the forested streams. Some of the streams were saline with deposits crystallising on the rocks where the water had evaporated, but in a number of places every drop of water was being used by the Fur, the people who had given their name to the Province.

Although some seventy tribes inhabit Darfur, the Fur – a negro tribe conquered in the past by unknown 'red-skinned' invaders, presumably Hamites, who were absorbed but made the Fur dominant – are the most numerous. The Marra Mountains are the true home of the Fur, who at various times have spread out to conquer surrounding tribes, and indeed towards the end of the seventeenth century are known to have invaded most of Kordofan to reach the Nile. Nominally Moslems, the Fur are still largely animists as well; snake-worship persists and there is a widespread belief in were-animals, many other tribes fearing the Fur for their powers of magic.

Today the hill Fur are rather looked down upon by the lowland Fur who regard them as 'savages', but although I can claim only a slight acquaintance, the highlanders seemed to me far superior, as mountain folk usually are compared with plainsmen in my experience. In some ways the people of the Marra Mountains are similar to the Nuba; they are more sophisticated, more under

Arab influence, live more overcrowded, less hygienic lives and are certainly much dirtier, but like the Nuba they terrace their hills by hand on sound engineering and agricultural principles and value their freedom. They are able to grow many more vegetables than is possible in the Nuba Mountains owing to the perennial streams, and they cultivate tobacco.

I spent some time examining crops. One small valley cultivation with perfect tobacco plants grown in patches here and there where the soil was suitable was irrigated using earthen dams and channels and split bamboo aqueducts. At about one thousand seven hundred to one thousand nine hundred metres' altitude were rain-grown cotton fields ready for picking. Here I collected many insects. The cotton-stainers, when not on cotton, lived almost entirely on a common bushy tree (*Thespesia*), a leathery-leaved relative of cotton with bright yellow flowers each quickly fading to red, and globular fruits four or five centimetres in diameter. The Fur make a good deal of their clothing from their own cotton, it being spun by hand on wooden spindles, and every village seemed to have wooden gins and looms.

After lunch beneath a *safsaf* or willow tree by a deserted up-stream pool, where I had a brief, very cold but extremely refreshing dip in the salty water watched only by two sun-squirrels and a small troop of Patas monkeys, I returned to the Land Rover to drive on north-east. The roadway soon became little more than a footpath, for either the motorable track we had started on petered out or we managed to lose it. For the rest of the day we saw nobody. The scarcely used track, apparently an old camel caravan trail, meandered on, the valleys green but the eroded, volcanic rocks, grey and rugged, devoid of vegetation, rose in fanged peaks to the horizon each time we breasted a rise to obtain a distant view. There was no sign of human habitation or even of ancient terracing.

That night we camped in the wilderness of mountains. It was bitterly cold and difficult to find wood. About midnight, unable to sleep, we set out to search for wood. Earlier hyaenas had been calling and in that strange, wild, deserted country the men were uneasy. I caught a climpse of hyraxes amongst a rock outcrop, and startled a white-tailed mongoose feeding on a bird, apparently a rock pigeon which the mongoose carried off as it fled.

Progress became even more difficult the next day, and frequently we had to move rocks to enable the Land Rover to pass. Once we took two hours to reach the top of a steep, stony gradient about one in three, but from then on the narrow, twisting trail improved. In the late afternoon we came to a settlement at last, a village called Guldo. It seemed to be market day at this thriving village and once the people overcame their surprise at our sudden arrival we soon learnt that there was a road to El Fasher. By evening, however, we were lost again but having descended about a thousand metres I hoped we would have a warmer night, but it proved to be about the coldest night I ever spent in the Sudan, frost whitening the grass soon after nightfall. There was plenty of firewood, and I slept warmly in a complete circle of flames.

In the morning we found the El Fasher road, but instead of journeying to the capital I thought I would first go and see the *darub el arbain* or 'forty day road', a centuries old caravan route across the desert to Egypt and not used as much now as formerly.

We crossed another ancient route, the west to east pilgrim's way from Nigeria to Mecca, which passes through Geneina and El Fasher (both places international airports for a short time in the 1940s so that despite the inaccessibility of the region around both are known to many Europeans), and came eventually to Jebel Orrei or Uri, once perhaps the most important city in Darfur standing as it did near the *darub el arbain* at the crossroads with other centuries old caravan routes to Tripoli and Timbuctoo.

The ruins at Jebel Orrei did not impress me greatly since there was little left but a few piles of stones; nevertheless, even the few ruins showed that considerable feats of engineering and building had been carried out and I wished I had known more of the city's history. At its peak it must have covered several square kilometres and contained quite imposing edifices, one perhaps the royal palace, of fitted and faced stone masonry, and at least one paved roadway. The city had been deserted probably because of lack of water since there has been a gradual desiccation of this southern edge of the Libyan Desert, villages having been abandoned very recently owing to the drying up of the wells.

Thirteen days after leaving Nyala we returned there by way of El Fasher. Already I had been away from Kadugli longer than I had intended. Near Nyala I spent an hour or two exploring a marsh, but there were too many people, the birds shy and I do not remember seeing any mammals. However, just before leaving, Younis, who had been talking to some locals, brought news that an Arab living nearby had a leopard and I went to see if I could buy it.

The Arab, Mustapha El Khalil, lived in the usual square mud and wattle house surrounded by a tall reed fence enclosing a compound. Half the local population seemed to be with me when I was admitted by the gate-keeper, a ragged urchin.

I learnt from El Khalil that his leopard had been found as a cub but was now too fierce to handle and he intended to destroy it. Beyond its reach, we looked at the animal tethered by a collar and chain (used normally for horses and camels) to a large tree in the yard. It lay as though asleep. El Khalil moved closer and called; only a baleful stare from the greenish-yellow eyes showed that the cat was aware of our presence. I moved closer, too, and behind me the crowd of onlookers pressed forward. Without warning, the leopard exploded into life, snarling as it charged to be brought up short in a shower of sand at the limit of the chain. Everybody tumbled back as the cat, with lashing tail, bared teeth and deep growls, sank down to stare at the scoffing people from eyes that seemed to glow with fierce hatred. Yet I think it was more frightened than savage.

A bargain was soon made; Younis went to the *suq* to see if he could find some Arab to make a crate big enough for the animal. The problem now was that of the mice in the fable, who was going to bell the cat? It was one thing being the owner of the leopard, but first I had to get it into the crate. I had no anaesthetic; we would have to use force and trickery. The first thing to do was to rid ourselves of the foolish crowd of Arab onlookers who were frightening and exciting the animal. The mob reluctantly departed and El Khalil tried to calm the cat.

At last Younis returned with a strong, slatted crate of stout board and a handful of nails which cost me as much as the leopard. Several times we managed to persuade the animal into the crate, which was about one and a half metres long, a metre tall and about sixty centimetres wide, but each time it clawed out again before we could fasten the lid. Finally, however, with the aid of stout sticks and by unfastening the chain from the tree to pull it through between two slats, we managed to imprison the leopard without any hurt other than injured feelings, but I suffered a long scratch, luckily not deep, and Younis miraculously escaped injury when a sweep of a massive paw ripped his fluttering *gibba* from top to bottom.

The crate took up most of the back of the Land Rover, but with difficulty we loaded up again without smothering the cat. Besides the leopard and the giant rat we had quite a collection of other live animals gathered during our journey; several snakes, including a two-metre-long python, an egg-eater and a Moila snake; a rock monitor, about a metre long, caught in the mountains; an Abdim's stork, sixty centimetres tall, a black (really glossy greenish-purple) and white bird, the commonest stork of the Sudan, that had been injured when found but recovered in my zoo, and lastly a pair of jerboas caught in the desert.

We had caught the three-toed jerboas, a common desert animal although seemingly less universally distributed than gerbils, in the Libyan Desert. I had stopped the Land Rover to watch a desert fox, an animal I had never seen in the Nuba Mountains although frequent enough on the *qoz* sands of Kordofan further north, as it trotted over the darker yellow sand, the fox an almost silvery colour in the moonlight with a distinctly black-tipped tail. As we watched the fox disappear, a small movement on the sand attracted my attention. For several silent minutes I saw nothing more; then a small shape hopped into full view on a ridge of sand and I realised it was a jerboa, an animal I had seldom seen before.

We camped then and there and I went to watch for the appearance of more of the little animals. I saw several hopping about on

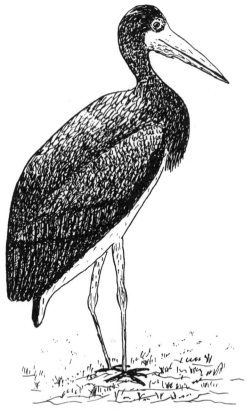

Abdim's stork

their greatly exaggerated hind-limbs, like miniature kangaroos with an attenuated tail almost twice the length of the body, but even in the bright moonlight it was difficult to see one plainly for they took advantage of every small shadow, stopping in the the shade of a stone, small weed or sand ridge. When we tried to catch one, it hopped away in great half-metre-long leaps using the black-tipped tail as a stabiliser and displaying great agility in evading us. As they were not only able to turn suddenly at right-angles, but could jump as fast, if not faster, than we could run on the loose sand, we had no hope of catching one, and soon they all disappeared from sight.

Later, however, we trapped one crouching in a form-like hollow below a stone, and another with my insect net. Once caught, the little creatures made no attempt to bite. The hind feet were enormous, half the length of the ten-centimetre body, and each equipped with three claws. The fur was a light sandy colour liberally speckled with black-tipped hairs, the underparts a fluffy white. As befits a nocturnal animal, the eyes were very large and somewhat protuberant, while the ears were enormous and quite out of proportion.

The three-toed jerboa feeds largely on grass and other small seeds, and in captivity I found that it would eat most small soft or immature seeds, including those of cotton, hibiscus, tomato and other cultivated plants, but seemed to find difficulty masticating any with a hard shell. I was interested that they ate winged termites with gusto, so that these supposedly herbivorous animals, like so many others, are partly carnivorous. When feeding, the jerboa often employs all four feet to walk about, in a distinctly ungainly fashion, as it looks for seeds, and uses its front feet not only to scrape for seeds and perhaps for insects, but also to hold the food like a squirrel. When moving at speed the front legs are tucked away and only the powerful hind legs are used as it hops along. Although it moves awkwardly, it can climb vertical wire or rough bark.

By the time we had loaded, and I had made sure Badr was unlikely to fall off the trailer, it was quite dark. I was anxious to reach home. We still had seven hundred and fifty kilometres to travel, I was days behind schedule. That night we travelled fifty or sixty kilometres before camping. The next day we reached Abu Matariq by nightfall, only just over two hundred kilometres from Nyala, for not only did the sand hold down the speed of our heavily laden vehicle and I did not want Badr to be thrown off the bucking trailer, but we made several halts.

I decided to drive on through the night; it was cooler then and there was more chance of seeing animals. Younis travelled on the trailer for a while to give Badr, choked with dust and a reddish-brown shade from the sand adhering to his normally chocolate-coloured body, a respite in the cab. The python, monitor, stork and leopard needed frequent attention, and we stopped every hour or so to tend their needs, dusting them down and giving them water if need be. The stork was the worst off since he had to keep his footing in an ever-moving world, but he had found a perch in one corner where the canvas hood supported his back and side.

We passed through Abu Gabra, distinguished from the sur-rounding bush by a row of shadowy, flat-roofed buildings, a few twinkling oil-lamps, the smell and glow of wood fires, a solitary, burnouse-hidden sexless figure rising to watch us, and the high-pitched yelping of a cur or two. The moon was just rising.

A zorilla ran along in front for a few moments before turning aside, but I did not stop. Two or three times a gazelle or antelope fled, a brief, amorphous shadow, and sometimes hares bounded off the track.

I was tired, almost dozing. I told Ahmed to splash water on my face. I calculated we were about three-quarters of the way to El Kelb and thought we would camp as soon as that hamlet was passed. From El Kelb to Muglad was about sixty-five kilometres;

from Muglad to Kadugli nearly three hundred kilometres, so we should be home in another two days all being well.

At that moment my thoughts ceased and I became wide awake; running just a short distance from the off-side front wheel was an animal that I imagined for a moment to be a hyaena. I slowed to bring the headlights to bear on it, and saw the irregularly blotched black, buff and yellowish-brown coat, and bushy grey-tipped tail of a hunting-dog. The large erect ears and somewhat sloping quarters had given me the impression it was a hyaena.

'There's a *simmay* here, too, Doktor,' Younis said. I saw two more, fleeting shadows leaping to look over the bushes at the side of the track. I stopped the Land Rover to make sure Badr was all right, banging my hands on the side of the Land Rover in the hope of scaring the dogs off. Thinking of what the Arabs at El Kelb had told me, I crunched back over the cooling sand. Badr said he was all right and, perched high on the trailer, he seemed in no danger. All the same, I gave him the end of a rope, the other end held by Younis in the cab, telling him to pull it if he felt in any trouble and I would stop. Looking about, I could not see any of the dogs. It was still only about nine to ten p.m., but now the moon's full radiance bathed the wooded landscape with a waxen light.

The hunting-dog was at one time called a 'hyaena-dog' because of the hyaena resemblance, but the name 'hunting-dog' is also misleading since although superficially dog-like, this animal is unique and not nearly as closely related to the true dogs as the wolf or jackal. Yet the hunting-dog has round eye-pupils as in the true dogs unlike the vertically elliptic pupils of the wolf and jackal.

We had not driven far before we saw the dogs as before loping along parallel with or behind us. I remembered an occasion in Kenya, between Mombasa and the Tanganyika border, travelling at night when a pack of spotted hyaenas ran along beside the car for a time, but they had kept at a much greater distance. Hunting-dogs always show some curiosity towards vehicles and little fear

Bateleur eagle

Sacred ibis

Crocodile (*above left*)
Hippotamus (*centre left*)
Pangolins, Samsim and her
son, Sam (*below left*)

Striped hyaena

Spotted hyaena

Nuba stick-fighters

Bracelet fight in progress at Jebel Kau

of men, but never before had they taken as much interest in us; this pursuit was quite different. They were behaving as a pack of hungry wolves is reputed to do.

I told Younis to fire the twelve-bore into the air out of the window. The fastest speed I could coax from the Land Rover on the deep sand was scarcely twenty kilometres per hour, but in fact I was not particularly interested in leaving the dogs behind; I wanted to see how bold they would become. I did not seriously consider that they would try to attack Badr.

Younis fired the gun; the hunting-dogs we could see seemed to withdraw and I thought they had left us. But a few moments later Younis told me Badr was signalling. I stopped in a hurry. Taking the gun from Younis I stepped down and walked back to the trailer. The dogs were still with us; I could see several. The nearest, looking as big as the leopard in the crate, stood silently, tongue hanging out, scarcely fifteen metres away in the middle of the track.

Badr said that the animals had been running very close to the trailer and he was scared for the nearest ones had been jumping as though trying to reach him. The dogs, mostly half hidden, stood all around, perhaps a dozen or fifteen of them. There were probably others on the far side of the Land Rover. Shepherding Badr, I made him squeeze into the cab beside the others. There was not much room when I took my place at the wheel again; leaving the door open I waited to see what the dogs would do.

Soon, almost imperceptibly, they drew closer but avoiding the headlight glow. Younis swung the spotlight, but each time the light illuminated one of the dogs it backed away into darkness. The animals varied considerably in size and markings, some being heavily blotched, others with smaller spots, some with a great deal of black, others lighter in colour. They had no intention of leaving, it seemed, but whether simply from curiosity or whether they really wanted to attack I could not determine. But I was not surprised that Badr was still shaken. The deserted, lonely bush in the mysterious moonlight even without the reality of our savage, silent followers, was an alien world always ready to shatter rational thought into fragments of primitive fear; no wonder the bush, full of strange sounds, is populated in the imagination of all aborigines, black and brown alike, with djinns and mythical monsters. I decided to break my rule and shoot one of the beasts. It would prove to my men that the animals were real flesh and blood and I would be able to examine one properly for the first time.

Selecting the largest I could see, only a few metres away, I fired, and at that range should have killed the dog almost immediately. There was the heartrending whimper of a dog in pain, the first sound any had made, but a cry that stopped almost at once. Despite the almost pointblank range I knew I had not killed it, and to my surprise, the other dogs, instead of running away, hardly retreated at all and in seconds had closed with the car again.

Younis focused the spotlight on the wounded animal as it stumbled away and I drove after it. It was difficult for Younis, who now had the gun, to obtain another shot at it as I had to turn the Land Rover to avoid trees, but at last we came closer. The second discharge toppled the hunting-dog over, but it stumbled to its feet again and made off. It fell over several times, staggering several hundred metres before it finally collapsed.

The other dogs, or some of them, had followed us, but I was scarcely aware of them so intent was I in trying to end the life of the wounded beast. We stopped close to the prone animal, the other dogs furtive in the shadows. I was not sure what they would do, so different was their present behaviour to any I had experienced or heard about before, and the men were very reluctant to leave the safety of the car. Younis and I cautiously walked to the wounded animal, however, Younis with the double-barrelled shot-gun ready and cocked, while I took my single-shot .22 pistol (the only other gun I had). The dog was still alive but could not rise and I put two .22 bullets through its head.

While Younis kept guard, I examined the dog. Even Ahmed and Badr came to look. The dog measured a hundred and fifty centimetres of which the tail was about thirty centimetres, a particularly large specimen for few attain this size. One back leg was broken in two places, a front foot was damaged, and there was a large wound in the shoulder, while most of the body was peppered with shot. It says a great deal for the toughness and vitality of these animals that this one had been able to drag itself so far. The short, coarse, rather woolly fur was mostly pale, ranging from white to buff and yellowish-brown, but the patches of different colours were quite irregular and blackish blotches of varying shapes and sizes gave a skewbald effect.

The hair of the neck was long, forming quite a strong ruff, while the backs of the ears were black, the tail very bushy with long greyish-white hairs towards the end. Despite its size and the deep chest, the legs, with their four-toed feet, were long and slender. The head was short-muzzled with large teeth, and a hunting-dog's jaws must be nearly as powerful as a hyaena's. It seemed to be in good condition, although the coat was very dirty and full of burrs and ticks.

Called *ka-wili* by the Kadugli Nuba, *nawo* or *nawa* by those at Miri, the hunting-dog is uncommonly seen in the Nuba Mountains where there is little game, certainly not enough to sustain even a small pack for long. But I did see the dogs once in *El Liri* district, near Terter, and between Talodi and Kalogi, and, I was told, they had been seen that year to the west of Lagowa, between Lagowa and Dar Kebir. But they were more commonly seen to the west and south of the Nuba Mountains, especially north-west and west of Muglad. Apparently only in the neighbourhood of El Kelb did thay have a reputation for attacking travellers, such behaviour being quite abnormal despite their fierce, predatory habits.

Most reports I have seen say that the hunting-dog is diurnal, but in the Sudan I saw the dogs active only at night or at dusk.

Normally they lie up in the daytime amongst dense grasses or thickets, perhaps sometimes in burrows, but usually only the young and breeding females live underground. I think that normally a pack may be active at any time of the day or night, depending on circumstances, but that the animal is intrinsically crepuscular, their activity periods being around dawn and dusk. Thus when the moon is full or hunger prevails they may hunt for most of the night, but in cool, cloudy weather or in the season of antelope births hunting may be mainly during daylight hours, but other factors undoubtedly influence the periodicity of a pack.

In general it seems unlikely that the dogs often hunt large, adult ungulates, but the helpless calves of such animals are often destroyed. Their main food consists of smaller animals, even lizards and rodents, besides duikers and such antelope; but, unlike hyaenas and lions, they very rarely eat carrion and never return to their prey (there is seldom anything left, however). Nevertheless, there are records of hunting-dogs chasing and killing the largest antelopes, such as roan, sable and eland; even more unusual must be an attack on a lion, hippo, buffalo or elephant. Only when driven by extreme hunger would the dogs attack an animal even as big as, say, a wildebeest.

The hunting-dog, widely distributed in Africa (but seldom common), an intelligent and resourceful social hunter, certainly adapts to local conditions so it would be unwise to be too assertive about any of its habits. In some habitats, where large herds of antelopes still exist in savanna country, bigger animals may be killed, but still it is the smaller species, the calves, weakly or isolated beasts, that are their target.

In the El Liri forest one night a small party of tiang, a reddish coloured bastard hartebeest with a black face, burst from dense bush close to me; considerably startled by their sudden appearance and the interruption of my peaceful stalking of a striped mouse (*Lemniscomys*), I cowered behind a tree. Closely behind the tiang appeared a single hunting-dog, running but not unduly quickly,

Hunting-dogs and duikers, Darfur

that disappeared after the antelope, and a minute or two later three more dogs crossed the clearing. Although I did not move for some minutes more I saw no more of the animals, nor was there any sound other than the first crepitations of the tiang for the dogs had quite silently appeared in the moonlight and as quietly vanished again. This was one of the very few occasions I saw *abu bareiga* or tiang (a Nuer word) in the Nuba Mountains region. The striped mice, startled, had rapidly vanished and I saw no more of them that night.

On a few other occasions I saw or heard hunting-dogs between about seven p.m. and midnight. Often they seemed to haunt man-made paths or roads; but such tracks were often used by animals of all kinds in preference to the dense bush, and probably the dogs found it easier to ambush their prey. Capable of out-staying even the most enduring antelope, since one or two dogs usually made the running and when tired fell back to allow fresher dogs to take their places, hunting-dogs in the Muglad region anyway seemed to be lazy, preferring to catch their prey with as little effort as possible.

The hunting-dog is regarded as a nomadic animal, the sugges-tion being that as they are such ruthless hunters all game flies at a whiff of their scent (which is, in fact, pungent). But this is untrue, at least for the pack or packs in the Muglad area. No doubt the dogs hunt widely, but they seem invariably to be present there. Nor does the game always disappear when dogs are present; in fact, herbivores seem to take no more notice of them than of other predators in the region.

On the El Kelb road the hunting system seemed to be that one dog stationed itself in one place, hidden from the road; another watched half a kilometre or so further along the track, while the main body of dogs remained hidden between these two scouts. It seemed to me, although it was impossible to be certain, that the scouts gave warning when an animal or man approached. It may have been that the dogs simply spread out near the roadway.

Contrary to the experiences of others, I never heard the dogs make any audible sound on these occasions or when chasing prey. The only communication as far as I could make out was by leaping; a dog, finding quarry, by jumping up and down could be seen at a fair distance in bright moonlight. Yet, infrequently, at other times I have heard the dogs utter short, sharp barks like those of a baboon, and they sometimes growl at each other or whine excitedly when meeting or feeding. In fact, their silence lends an added eeriness to these strange animals. In Mozambique, I later heard a scattered party of hunting-dogs baying to one another, a curiously soft, eerie call carrying a long way as described by many hunters, but I never heard this call in the Sudan. Also in Mozambique I once saw the dogs chasing an unseen animal and yapping as they ran, but I think only two or three half-grown pups were calling.

Night observations of this animal were extremely difficult, and it was only more or less by accident that I ever caught a glimpse of them even in the dry season. To approach them unseen was out of the question; they were always aware of my presence. The only time I saw an antelope killed was when they pulled down one of a pair of duikers; the other escaped. But late one day, near Muglad, I did discover a small pack lying up in the tall grasses growing round a termitary, itself at the base of a leafy *sahab* tree, and I was able to watch them for a time through my binoculars from the cover of trees, I think without detection, the animals being downwind.

I did not learn a great deal, however, for almost the whole time – over an hour and a half until it grew too dark to see – the dogs lolled about with little movement. All the same towards dusk I had some reward for my patience. One dog chased, apparently a lizard (perhaps a small rodent) that misguidedly attracted its attention, bounding about in the grass like a puppy playing with a ball as it used its feet to stamp on its prey. It caught the lizard (or rodent) gulping it down whole. I saw another dog eating grass, just as a domestic cat or dog will, but most cat- or doglike predators in Africa eat grass at times.

The largest pack I saw was on the El Kelb road, and numbered between fifteen and twenty animals; no other pack I saw seemed to be of more than six or eight, possibly ten, individuals. Hunting-dogs cannot be said to have any predaceous enemies (excepting man who has virtually eradicated them in many more populated parts), but their numbers are never great. Rarely there are conflicts with leopards, some are killed in the chase but, as I have said, in this region where they usually hunt smaller, defenceless animals, the number of dogs so killed or wounded must be very few. Why, then, do they not multiply and destroy all game and finally themselves? Different packs seldom attack each other, and squabbles with serious injury within a pack seem to be very rare.

I think, as is the case with most gregarious animals, the weaker members of the pack rarely obtain a fair share of food and thus die. An injury to a paw, such as a festering thorn, probably means death. The hazards of the bush are many, but the most important limiting factor is probably disease, particularly intestinal parasites and endemic diseases such as rabies. It seemed unlikely that more than two packs lived in the vast region enclosed by Abu Matariq to the west, Abu Likri to the east, the Bahr el Arab in the south and near Nahud to the north, but this was by no means certain.

In southern Kordofan and southern Darfur, hunting-dogs normally breed towards the end of the dry season before the start of the rains. As many as ten or twelve to a litter is possible, but more than seven is rare and from two to six is normal. The gestation period is about two and a half months, and the puppies are normally born in a burrow, mostly made by the dogs themselves in this region but sometimes an enlargement of that of another animal such as an aardvark, pangolin or warthog. Usually an earth has more than one entrance, and is sometimes shared by several mothers. Long before weaning (at about two and a half to three months), as well as after weaning, the pups are fed on regurgitated food supplied by the mother, and often by the father as well; indeed, I think it possible that adults other than the parents will regurgitate to a hungry puppy, and often the meat is devoured and regurgitated by several adults before it reaches the pup.

When about three months old the puppies often leave the burrow for I have seen them with older dogs, but they do not seem to go hunting with the pack for several more months. Occasionally, I saw much younger puppies near a burrow entrance, especially in the evening. The young were never left deserted by all the dogs even when a hunt was on.

I have kept only one whelp, which was, unfortunately, weakly and did not live for long, but other people have kept tame hunting-dogs. Some reports suggest that such pets remain wild and undisciplined, but other people have found them responsive to good treatment, showing as much intelligence and affection as most domestic sporting dogs.

After examining the dog we had shot we returned to the Land Rover. The other hunting-dogs were still lurking nearby but made no attempt to attack us. Having made sure our leopard and other animals were secure, I drove away but stopped again where I could still see the dead dog. I wanted to see if the other dogs would devour it. After a few moments one and then others approached and almost at once began to tear up the carcass. This was interesting for accounts I had read suggested that they never attack a fallen comrade. With their sharp teeth and powerful jaws there was soon little left of the corpse; the animals ignored the Land Rover now, and even at that distance I could hear the crunching of bones.

Leaving them to their grisly feast, we continued our journey and saw no more of the dogs.

Back at Kadugli I lost no time in seeing to the animals we had carried such a long distance. Despite the dust, heat and bumping they all seemed in good condition, although the leopard was particularly bad-tempered. It still retained its collar, however, so

I was able temporarily to tether it on a long horse chain to a tree in my garden until a new home in the zoo could be prepared. After some days of peace, it seemed to be settling down, allowing me fairly close, although still I did not dare touch the animal. Once in the zoo I was sure it would become more friendly.

Alas, just as the new quarters were ready, the leopard broke free during the night, still with some centimetres of chain dangling from its collar. Having been away for so long, there was a lot of work for me to deal with and it was impossible to find time to go and look for the animal, but I sent a search party immediately. Two or three days later Younis, in charge of the searchers, came to tell me they had found tracks and caught a glimpse of the animal in the hills behind my house. Had the length of chain not been round its neck I would probably have left the leopard to fend for itself, but I knew it would be lucky to find any prey for wherever it went the rattling chain would go too. Taking nets and ropes, I went with the searchers to where they had seen the animal, a region of chaotic boulders, tree-strewn hillsides and water gullies. Not surprisingly we could not find it. All the same I kept scouts out to try and keep track of the beast.

After about two weeks I began to think that the leopard, which had been seen once or twice more, would survive fending for itself. Then a few days later two goatherds came to me complaining that my leopard (everybody knew he was mine despite the fact there were other leopards about) had attacked them. In proof, one exhibited his ragged shorts which he said had been ripped by the leopard – fortunately, I saw, without even scratching his own skin. Then came a report that it had killed a goat. I was pleased the leopard was finding food, and not sorry that one of the pestiferous goats had been its prey, although I felt sympathetic towards the goat-owner and wished the leopard would move away from the villages.

Not long after this, when the leopard entered the nearby village of Semma, the villagers set upon it, notwithstanding the reward I had offered, and killed it. The length of chain was still around its neck. I blamed myself for not taking greater care to prevent the escape of the animal; the villagers were only protecting their own. It was a sad end for the leopard after I had rescued it from death only a few weeks before, transported it so far and prepared comfortable quarters for it. When I heard of its death I wished I had released the animal in the deserted countryside near Muglad.

Leopards at large

There seemed to be any number of dead or dying trees in this part of the woods. Presumably, some disease had decimated them since no fire had passed that way for a long time and the other bushes, saplings and creepers were quite healthy. I stopped the Land Rover and went to examine some of the small trees, many of which were rotten and full of holes, hoping to find they harboured animals.

A grey-cheeked woodpecker flew off uttering its excitable, chattering cry interspersed with metallic chinks, but otherwise the wood seemed deserted and silent. I was alone, on my way back to Kadugli having been to inspect the work of some of my staff who were enumerating the stainer-bugs on numbered *tebeldi* trees a few miles away. For an hour or so I poked into all the holes and peered into the hollow trunks, but I found only some insects and disturbed a few lizards. There were not even any galagos. I had wandered from my car and now began to work my way back towards it, searching likely trees. At last, arm deep in a rotting trunk, I felt something move; I pulled away the punky wood to disclose a nest of grasses mixed with a few leaves, and in the nest was a dormouse which merely blinked at me before, twittering at the disturbance, it burrowed down again into the ball of grass. I was able to remove nest complete with dormouse and slip it into a bag.

The shadows had lengthened and I began to hurry. With relief, just after the sun had slipped behind the distant *jebels*, I saw the Land Rover. Urgency gone, I stopped to watch a late-flying spider-hunting wasp, whose large, black shape strained to lift a spider on the ground almost as big and certainly as heavy as itself. A wandering velvet-ant, red and white, diverted my attention and then, a moment later, as I bent to catch the insect, a tiny rodent ran across the ground to take refuge below a leaf where I caught it. It was a pigmy mouse. I discovered that I was almost standing on the burrow, the entrance little larger than that of a cricket's and blocked with a pebble. Putting down the dormouse and my belongings, I placed a big stone over a second exit to the burrow before digging carefully with my sheath-knife to disclose a slanting tunnel where I finally caught two more adult pigmy mice.

The dormouse and the pigmy mice lived for a long time in my zoo. Called *mallo* by the Nuba (but apparently unknown to the Arabs since they had no name for it), Butler's dormouse* is a soft furry little creature scarcely nine centimetres long with a silky-haired squirrel-like tail almost as long again. Ashy-grey in colour, it has small rounded ears, large dark eyes and surprisingly long hind feet. Essentially arboreal, it feeds on seeds, young buds, shoots, gum and insects, but at night it often descends to the ground to feed on grass seeds and insects, sleeping by day in a tree hole or sometimes a bird's nest. The gestation period is about three weeks, and two or three tiny, naked, blind and help-less babies occur in a litter. The young grow quickly, however, and in a short time are able to support themselves. Some months later I caught another adult that raided my insect-breeding cages before I discovered it nesting in a filing cabinet in the laboratory.

Butler's dormouse has a twittering cry not unlike that of a

* *Claviglis butleri.*

ground-squirrel; it gives the impression that it is swearing under its breath, but at the same time appears quite unafraid. By day my dormouse was quite lethargic but at night was very active and wide-awake, continually on the move, exploring every inch of its outside quarters, leaping short distances, poking about on the ground and climbing plants. It slept by day in a box affixed to the trunk of a small tree about two metres from the ground. From the entrance to this box a wire-enclosed passage led to a large, naturally vegetated enclosure were it could roam at will.

I was surprised that neither of my dormice showed any fear of humans even at the time of their capture. The one from my laboratory escaped from a small cage into my living room on the day it had been caught. In trying to recapture it my servant and I chased it round the furniture, but the little creature did not seem at all perturbed. It began unconcernedly to nibble a dead insect discovered on the floor, eating like a squirrel, sitting up to hold the insect between the front paws, and made no move even as I went to grasp it; then, with a flick of the tail and an exasperated twitter, it moved a few centimetres before resuming its meal.

In the Nuba Mountains Butler's dormouse does not seem to aestivate or hibernate but remains active all the year round. In captivity, at any rate, it sleeps rolling itself into a ball with the tail wrapped round the body, head and legs well tucked in, but not as a rule on its side, as might be expected, but on its back.

The little pigmy mouse,* about five centimetres long plus a tail of three centimetres, was the smallest mammal except for shrews that I recorded in the Nuba Mountains. Called *koko hagirat* by the Arabs (presumably in reference to the stones used to block up the tunnel entrance), *tay-fay* or *te-fay* by the Nuba, the pigmy mouse has soft, dark-brown or greyish-brown fur with whitish underparts, large rounded, upright ears and a naked tail. It produces two to six young to a litter (rarely two) which are born in a grass nest at the end of a small burrow, or in a side tunnel off the main

* *Mus matschiei.*

shaft. Naked and blind at birth, the young mouse grows chestnut hair on the flanks but is blackish on the back, with the underparts white as in the adult. The hair is very soft and silky. The mice, which are nocturnal and, as a rule, gregarious, usually have a burrow with two entrances but sometimes live below a rock or amongst tree roots.

These little creatures are very active in the evening or at night, seeming to skim over the ground and obstacles with great ease and agility; they are excellent climbers and swimmers. When chased they often take refuge under the nearest cover. The entrance to the burrow is normally closed in the daytime with soil or stones; if soil is used it is usually scraped to the entrance, the mouse using its front feet and entering the burrow backwards pulling the soil after it; at other times tiny pebbles are pushed or carried in the mouth for this purpose.

My mice lived for at least twenty-one months in captivity in a large, outside cage, and were very easy to keep and breed. I say 'at least twenty-one months', but they may have been with me much longer since after a time they were able to come and go as they pleased. Originally, they had been put in their cage against the outer fence of the zoo where they thrived and bred until I had about a dozen of the mice. I rarely disturbed them, but fed them regularly and occasionally watched them at night, so I never knew exactly how many there were. Eventually, the wire of the cage rotted at one corner and I found that the little animals were running in and out of the zoo fence; but they did not desert their cage or the burrows they had made until a long time afterwards.

It was while I was kneeling down in the dusky woodland to excavate the pigmy mouse burrow with my sheath knife that I became aware again of the silence. I glanced up and standing watching, scarcely ten metres away, was a leopard.

For a moment I thought it was an hallucination since in the gloom the shape was indistinct and the outline broken by the shady foliage, but it was real enough. The animal did not move and neither did I, although I gripped my long knife ready to defend myself should it decide to attack. A tribesman armed only with a knife or spear has occasionally won a battle with a leopard, but a severe mauling or death is more likely and I had no desire for combat. I hoped the leopard felt the same.

Long minutes seemed to pass as we stared at each other without movement. After my first shocked surprise at the silent, unexpected materialisation of the big cat, I felt no fear, only thrilled wonderment that chance had given me the opportunity to look long at such a beautiful beast that until now, except for fleeting glimpses, I had never seen in its natural habitat. Then the Land Rover took a hand; it had been standing in the sun since I left it, but with the cooling of the night air the metal began to contract and suddenly gave out a crack as loud as a distant rifle shot. Hardly had the sound died than the leopard vanished as mysteriously as it had appeared. I stood up and watched for a minute or two, but the cat had obviously made off, so I knelt down again to finish digging out the mouse's burrow.

Leopards, the most secretive, the most cunning and the most formidable of the big cats of Africa, were found throughout the Nuba Mountains. That they are common there can be no doubt, for this cat is normally seldom seen and can live in an area for years without people being aware of the fact, yet every year there were reports of them, sometimes from a dozen different places. Generally, leopards of the arid scrub of desert margins further north are much paler, while those of montane forest or humid regions tend to be dark. Ranging today from the Caucasus to Manchuria and Java, and throughout most of Africa, the leopard varies surprisingly little except in size and small differences in markings and coloration; in fact the pelt pattern of no two is quite alike. Truly melanic but not truly albino animals are known.

In the Nuba Mountains, except in the extreme south perhaps, leopards tended to be small and rarely exceeded two metres in total length and seldom more than about forty-five kilos in weight.

There were exceptions, of course, but the largest I saw, a male killed in a village in the Korongo Jebels in the south, measured a hundred and thirty-one centimetres head and body with a seventy-three point five centimetre tail. Females are smaller and lighter than males.

The monthly diaries of Kordofan Province record numerous references to attacks by leopards upon people. For example, in March, 1947, the diary mentions a Messaria who went to wash in a pool near Lagowa and saw a leopard behind him. He flung his spear and wounded the animal, which then charged and savaged both his arms before it clambered up a tree. The Nazir's brother shot it. In August, 1948, a leopard attacked a young Korongo at dusk near Dimadonga; another Nuba youth went to his aid. Both were injured before a third Korongo speared and killed the animal. The skin is said to have measured eight feet two and a half inches (two hundred and forty-six point twenty-five centimetres) from nose to tip of tail. In October, 1949, leopards were reported as being 'troublesome at Kadugli'. Often, in fact, conflicts were not reported.

In 1953, some thirty kilometres from Kadugli, I met a small party of Nuba carrying a man tied to a wooden plank bed; with severe lacerations on his head and chest, and with limb wounds as well, his injuries seemed mortal. He had been mauled by a leopard when out hunting, but it was not clear if he had been hunting the leopard or another animal. I turned about and took him to Kadugli hospital in my Land Rover and, although crippled for life, he eventually recovered. Another man was mauled near Kadugli when a leopard attacked his dog and he tried to drive it off; the cat knocked the man down, killed the dog and carried it away. Several other Nuba I met had lost a limb or its use after being mauled, and two or three had severe facial injuries, one having lost an eye and part of his nose. Such cases were commonplace enough.

Despite its considerably smaller size and less formidable appearance, in my view the leopard is a much more dangerous adversary than a lion. It is less predictable, of more cryptic habits, and often more familiar with man, since it survives in many places where the lion cannot. Such familiarity with man can breed contempt rather than fear, and most Africans in contact with both big cats respect and fear the leopard more than the lion. For its size the leopard is astonishingly powerful. It can leap almost vertically three metres in the air, clear a two-metre-tall thorn fence carrying a goat, and can haul a dead animal of equal weight to itself twenty-five metres high up a tree. While a leopard will usually retreat given the opportunity, at bay or when wounded there is probably no more belligerent, agile or ferocious carnivore in Africa except the ratel.

The common Nuba name for the leopard is *terigo*, but unlike the lion which is said to have three hundred or so names in Arabic, the leopard seems to have few Arabic names. In Africa, animals are often miscalled by natives and foreigners alike. For example, in Afrikaans the Boers call a leopard a 'tiger'; a hyaena a 'wolf'; a giraffe a 'camel'; a bustard a 'peacock'. The English often call a francolin or spur-fowl a 'partridge', the French a monitor lizard an 'iguana', while names in negro languages are frequently confused. The common Sudan Arabic name for leopard is *nimir*, which is really the Arabic for tiger, *fahad* being used loosely for smaller cats.

In Dar Nuba leopards find refuge and cover in the wild *jebels*, particularly those that are uninhabited where, for the most part, they are safe from man. They feed on monkeys, duikers, harte- beests and other antelopes; sometimes they kill jackals, a favourite prey, and other small carnivores. No sizable animal or carrion comes amiss, but larger rodents, particularly hares and porcupines, hyraces and ground birds or any bird roosting at night from the size of doves upwards probably constitute the main prey, since only these are common in most areas. In parts of the Nuba Mountains leaopards would often go very hungry or move else- where were it not for the domestic animals, particularly goats and

domestic birds. A leopard will return to its own kill, no matter
how putrid, until it is all devoured but often at irregular intervals,
sometimes not returning to a carcass for several nights.

Unless the villagers are lucky enough to destroy it quickly or
frighten it away before it learns too much, a leopard may plague a
village for years and the cubs may follow the parent's example. By
nature unsociable, a solitary hunter (although a mother teaches her
cubs to hunt and almost full-grown young are sometimes seen
with their parent) the nocturnal leopard, one of the most resourceful and the most tenacious of hunters in pursuit of its prey, is a
stealthy foe feared more than any other animal especially by the
more sophisticated, more effete, culturally mixed villagers of the
plains who are neither Arab nor Nuba and in some ways more
degenerate than either. The pagan Nuba clans, better able to look
after themselves, may even welcome the attentions of such an
intruder as it gives them a better chance of killing it, almost every
part of the animal being of value. The pelt, teeth and claws are
used for ornament or barter, while the liver, heart and much of
the flesh is eaten (unless the leopard happens to be a taboo animal)
not only to fill a meat-starved belly but in the belief that the
prowess of the leopard will be passed to the consumers.

There is no doubt that leopards attack men more frequently
than do any other of the big cats, and possibly more often become
man-eaters. But true man-eaters are much less common in Africa
than is often believed despite a few sensational, well-authenticated
accounts. Men hunting or trapping leopards are often injured or
killed, since a leopard cornered or confused, disturbed at or balked
of its prey will frequently attack a man. This does not make it an
habitual man-eater, however.

Other than fear there is no reason, of course, why any leopard
should not prey upon human-beings. Baboons and other monkeys
are a favourite food, and even baboons can drive off a leopard at
times. When man fails to protect himself a leopard may soon take
advantage and begin to kill the terrified people. For example,

there are often cases when the leopard is regarded as supernatural and therefore indestructible, the people making no effort to kill it or drive it away, only to hide from it. The old habit of abandoning dead and dying people in the bush in the belief that they were bewitched and better out of the village, a custom common to many tribes, was also a cause of attacks by leopards.

Other factors, of course, may induce a leopard to become a man-eater. When it becomes old and less capable of catching prey, a lone woman or child gathering sticks or herbs becomes a tempting target, a prey that is easy to catch and presenting little opposition. Famine amongst the human population may be a major cause since weak, starving people provide ready prey. The worst and most persistent cases of man-eating leopards are known from India with its much higher density human population and near-famine or famine conditions in many places. No leopard became a man-eater in the Nuba Mountains, however, during my residence there, nor was there any record of there ever having been one.

It was impossible to spend much time observing other animals without coming upon traces of a leopard or seeing one occasionally. In *The Scurrying Bush* I mentioned how the agitated behaviour of birds led me to startle a leopard in a covert, and once in El Liri forest I saw the hind leg of an antelope, the rest of the carcass invisible, dangling from the leafy top of a tall *dom* palm, a common tree, where only a leopard could have placed it. Having killed prey larger than it can devour at one time a leopard will attempt to conceal the carcass from other predators either by hauling it up a tree or hiding it below a bush or in a thicket and partly covering it with leaves. This was the only time I saw such a cache in the Sudan, but, of course, in the game reserves of East and South Africa, where larger animals are commoner, such a sight is not infrequent. Apart from these instances, the leopard that watched me find the pigmy mice, frequent discovery of droppings or spoor, and a rare and fleeting sighting, I had had no experience of leopards and I had found no cubs.

Soon after the death of the Darfur leopard, however, there were
many reports of leopards in Kadugli District for the next year or
two. That same year leopards were reported to me from Hagir el
Mek, about one and a half kilometres from Kadugli, from Kulba
and Semma, villages about five kilometres away, and from other
hamlets. I saw one myself in the western hills overshadowing
Kadugli no more than a few hundred metres from my house. To
trap one alive or find cubs was another matter.

Until now I had given no thought to trapping an adult alive
and I had made no special search to try and find a cub. But after
the disappointing escape of my Darfur leopard, and the news of
village marauding leopards so close by, it seemed a good time to
try and construct a trap.

My first trap was built at Hagir el Mek, constructed on the
classic lines probably first devised by Colonel Patterson, who
describes his trap for lions in *The Man-Eaters of Tsavo* (1907). My
traps did not require to be as massive as his, and were baited with
goats not with coolies, although some villagers at Hagir el Mek
suggested a girl-child would make a better bait than a goat, as
she would make more cries and was less valuable, an idea that was
firmly vetoed by the majority and the headman who said, 'The
Hakuma would not approve.'

There was no doubt that the leopard plaguing Hagir el Mek
was very bold and the people were terrified of it. It was easy to
reconstruct what had happened. The leopard, a female with cubs
to feed, lived somewhere in the wild, uninhabited *jebels* that
overshadowed the hamlet of Hagir el Mek. It had made its first
tentative nocturnal attack some weeks before, no doubt taking
advantage of every scrap of cover when it scented the sleeping
goats in a small herd left loose and unguarded on the village out-
skirts, furtively stalking its prey, mistrustful of every sound. At
this time it might easily have been frightened away by any noise of
movement of people, although it would probably have returned,
for a leopard, especially with cubs to feed, will often persist,

taking most of the night if necessary, before it finally, silently and efficiently kills by severing the jugular vein or breaking the neck of its prey and carrying it off.

As it was, nothing disturbed it and the first knowledge the villagers had of its presence was the absence of a goat. It was not until days later, after the disappearance of more domestic animals, that the leopard was seen and the people knew for certain what was responsible for the thefts. The few traces left by the intruder would have been plain only to the skilled eye.

The leopard, after its first success, returned again and again with every raid becoming more daring and audacious, until at the time we erected the trap sometimes it was raiding before dark, entering the village and even the huts in its search for food. Naturally, after their first loss, the villagers kept a closer watch on their animals but to little avail. By now the leopard had lost its fear of man, since the people had not attacked it because they were afraid and because they seemed to regard the intruder as supernatural, or at least sent by some evil agency to destroy them.

The villagers were voluble about their troubles, yet apathetic and fatalistic, unwilling even to help me construct the trap, or supply a goat to bait it with. They had not, as far as I knew, approached the *merkaz* (authorities) for help. Although nobody had yet been injured by the cat it seemed only a matter of time. Only one man – when the leopard was on the roof of his hut in which he, his family, several goats and hens were sleeping – had made any attempt at self-defence. He had fired his muzzle-loader at the roof, frightening away the leopard but apparently not injuring it. There were several old guns in the village and all had spears, of course, but no attempt had been made to track and try and kill their foe. As the guns, if fired, would probably have been almost as dangerous to themselves as to the leopard, with little likelihood of doing more than annoying the beast, it was perhaps as well the people were not more aggressive.

The most difficult part of the trap to construct was the guillotine door, but after several tests I was satisfied that no more than a touch would be needed to release the string holding it up; the other end of the string was attached to a twig on which was smeared blood and scraps of meat. The kid was enclosed in a separate wigwam-shaped cage at the far end of the trap and the whole was enclosed by the thorniest brushwood we could find, except, of course, for the doorway.

Normally, goats never seem to stop eating and grunt, cough, wheeze and sneeze all day and night; the kid that was the bait (which, of course, the leopard could not reach) protested vigorously and noisily until in the wigwam, but once there made no more sounds and appeared to go to sleep. Agog with anticipation, we retired some way off where the headman had made a kind of redoubt of boulders. It was late afternoon; the headman said that the leopard might come at any moment, its usual appearance being any time between about four p.m. and midnight. 'We should see it, *Jenabak*, as it comes down there. It always comes that way to the village.' He waved his arm towards the open slope sparsely studded with large boulders and a few trees and bushes about two hundred metres away. If it came before dark we should certainly obtain a glimpse, but I waited until well after nightfall, the mosquitoes a torment, although it was the dry season, without the animal appearing.

I had not the time or the inclination to watch for the animal night after night, but between us the headman and I arranged a rota of watchmen. They seemed reasonably safe within the redoubt for the boulders had been arranged around an isolated hut in which the men could take refuge.

Two or three days later one of my men, who had been on watch, reported great excitement, as it was thought the leopard had been caught. They had not gone near the trap during the night being too fearful, but they had heard the wooden guillotine door fall and movements inside. The next morning, when they cautiously approached, all they found was one of the village curs which had been attracted by the meaty smell.

We reset the trap and changed the goat, now so used to being put daily into the wigwam that it went in of its own accord. The new goat kid was full of bleats so I was hopeful.

Late that afternoon, from the redoubt, I saw the leopard for the first time. Just as the headman had said, it came down the slope from the *jebel* heading towards the village. At that distance it looked scarcely bigger than a civet-cat. A moment later, however, it vanished behind rising ground and I did not see it again. I expected to hear noises from the village but nothing happened and apparently the leopard took no prey there that night, for no domestic animal was missed. This was the last time I watched for it.

The next day I was told the leopard had taken a dog in the village, being seen by several people who ran away and barricaded themselves in their huts. After the dog's disappearance I told the villagers to make certain that all their animals were in safety by the afternoon; they had been keeping their goats shut up but had not bothered too much about their hens or dogs. I hoped if the leopard could find nothing else it would be more likely to attempt to reach the kid in the trap.

Again nothing happened for a couple of days, but several nights later the leopard went to the trap. Nobody saw or heard it for we had dropped the idea of keeping regular watch, but it had obviously tried to reach the goat by tearing down the thorns around the wigwam instead of entering the trap. In its efforts to reach the goat the leopard must have caught the string supporting the guillotine door which closed with a bang, frightening the animal, which made off.

After this I did not expect that it would return again to the village, but in fact it did, taking another goat a day or two later; but as far as I knew it never went near the trap again. In the meantime I made an unsuccessful search for the leopard's lair in the hills, hoping to find the cubs while the parent was away hunting. The animal probably lived in a glen near the top of one *jebel* but we could not find the lair; to search the tumbled rocks and caves would have taken weeks and the leopard left no trace on the dry, barren ground. A few weeks later I passed through the village and asked about the leopard, having had no word from the headman for some time. The villagers had almost forgotten about their enemy; it had not been seen nor had it worried them for some time and they presumed it had left the area. 'Now,' said the head-man, 'we are plagued with bees and with rats eating our grain.' Bees had settled in a tree near the headman's hut and were keeping him out, as well as attacking people entering nearby houses. I removed the bees for them, but I told them to seek advice about the rats from the *merkas*.

Almost as soon as the trap at Hagir el Mek had been completed, I heard that a leopard had been killed near Umm Dorein, another female probably with cubs. I visited the area and offered a reward for the cubs alive and unharmed. By good luck one of the Nuba discovered them in a rock cleft and they came into my hands. There were three about six or eight weeks old and they quite soon developed very different personalities. One I called Juan (pro-nounced *jarn*, meaning hunger), as it came first to every meal; the second, with a particularly dark and close spotted coat, was called Dool (meaning shadow) and the third, the most timorous and cautious, always coming to food or for a drink after the other two, I called Bardi Bukra (the day after tomorrow).

The gestation of a leopard is about three months, and although cubs are usually found towards the end of the rains from about August to October, young could be born at almost any time. In the Nuba Mountains and northwards there seemed on the avail-able evidence to be a fairly definite breeding season, but further south occasionally cubs were recorded late in the dry season and in the early rains. Juan, Dool and Bardi Bukra must have been born in November or December.

In most cases there are two to four cubs in a litter, very rarely only one or five or six, and when only one is present it seems likely that the others have died. In a large litter it seems to be rare for more than two of the infants to survive to adulthood; at least I did not hear or see a mother accompanied by more than two cubs, and in most parts it would be a great struggle for the parent to feed even two offspring.

A baby leopard is blind at birth and only fifteen to sixteen centi-metres long, but it grows rapidly if well fed. The eyes are a faded blue, the colour of a dying forget-me-not flower; the fur is strangely dulled without the gloss of an older animal, and the spots more solid, only spreading with growth. By the time the animal is about six months, the eyes have changed to become nearer to the greenish-yellow of the adult's eyes, while the coat has become glossier and the white of the large, rounded ears (which in the small cub have distinctly white apices like the serval) has faded.

A leopard family will remain together usually for about the first two years of the cub's life; or at least the mother and her cubs will, the father often taking himself off, for by nature he favours a solitary life only seeking companionship when the mating urge is on him and he takes little interest in his offspring once they begin to leave the lair. By the time the cub is a year old it is usually well over half-grown, and becomes fully grown when between two and three years, probably capable of breeding before it is two. But growth varies and, of course, depends on locality and the availability of food although a mature leopard can survive for weeks with very little or no food.

Juan, Dool and Bardi Bukra lived together in a large cage made from lengths of expanded metal like massive wire netting of the type used for reinforcing concrete structures, metal that I had scrounged from the source of most of my materials, the cotton ginnery. This cage, two metres tall, had a door for easy access and had been built for my Darfur leopard. The three cubs were lost in it and it was weeks before they explored its confines. However, they had a den at one end made from a large packing case and immediately made themselves at home in this.

Juan was not only the hungriest but the most adventurous. He was the initiator of every private activity, but never became friendly with humans despite my efforts. For some time all three leopards had to be handfed by Abdulla or myself, and Dool and Bardi Bukra came to respond to caresses and even to play after the first few weeks when their only desire after food had been to crawl on their swollen bellies back to their den to sleep until the next meal. Juan, on the other hand, never failed to spit and snarl his distrust to the time when we finally parted company. He would tolerate handling, but I felt only because I was bigger and stronger than he was. He gave the impression of only waiting until he was old enough before rending me tooth and claw.

As the cubs grew rapidly in size, strength and courage, Juan was the first voluntarily to leave the den to explore the rest of the large cage, sinuously slinking belly flat on the sandy ground, pausing suspiciously at every sound, ready to show a snarling face to the world.

One night, a few months after the cubs arrived, the cage door was left open by accident. Juan, now twice his original size, wandered through into the zoo enclosure as silent as a passing cloud. Fortunately, one or some of the other animals saw or sensed him in the moonlight, and soon there was an uproar of shrieks, whistles, barks, groans and chattering as most of the zoo inhabitants, led by the particularly vocal baboons, patas and verve monkeys, joined in a concert of disapproval.

The noise even awakened the *ghaffir* (watchman) and the old man cautiously opened the narrow gate a crack to see the cause of the alarm. He saw nothing, but sensibly despatched a *walad* (small boy) to fetch me. When I arrived the hullabaloo had died somewhat. Inside the zoo compound I found Juan, who might easily have escaped, cowering in a corner; he seemed so completely demoralised by the noisy condemnation of the rest of the zoo that he did not even snarl when I put him back into his cage, where Dool and Bardi Bukra were unconcernedly asleep.

Bardi Bukra, and to some extent Dool, finding more confidence in us as time passed, became not only less fearful but, in the case of B.B., even friendly in the rather aloof manner common to cats. As the leopards grew from cubs into young cats B.B., a female, was the only one that could be handled by Abdulla, but Dool would only tolerate me. But no leopard I ever kept showed the trust and affection of Dindi or other servals, of other smaller wild cats, or of hyaenas, mongooses and similar animals, nor could I be certain of their behaviour. B.B. was the only one I could allow out of the cage (except at the beginning when they were very young) and then only when she was carefully watched.

Perhaps had I kept them longer, or if they had had more individual attention from me (much of the time I had to leave them to Abdulla and I could not visit them as often as I wished), they might have responded more favourably. They were scarcely more than half-grown when I had to leave Kadugli. I presented the leopards and other animals to Khartoum zoo.

After I obtained the three cubs I received some disturbing news. Soon after building the leopard trap at Hagir el Mek I had constructed a similar trap at another village. Early one morning I heard a leopard had been caught in it the night before. If I had not obtained Juan, Dool and Bardi Bukra I would have been delighted, of course; but with three leopards already I did not want a fourth. However, I had to collect this one and I hurried to the village.

The leopard was young, about three-quarters grown, perhaps eighteen months or two years old. The villagers were highly pleased to have caught this marauder and had probably been tormenting the animal, only leaving it alone when it clawed and snarled so ferociously they grew afraid that it would free itself from the trap. It was small enough to turn round in the trap but only with difficulty.

As I approached the animal growled and snarled in welcome, showing its large canines and glaring an almost tangible hate from glittering eyes. During the night it had made savage attacks with its knife-edged, curved claws and fearsome teeth on the imprisoning log bars, so that slivers of wood had been torn off the green wood and its mouth was bloody. If it had turned its attentions to the sliding door, made merely of thin plank, it would have escaped before now.

Feeling sorry for it, my inclination was to free it then and there, but, of course, this was impossible. I was not going to let the villagers kill it, however, so I would have to take it away. The problem was to get it into the slatted crate previously occupied by the Darfur leopard.

Putting the open end of the crate by the guillotine door of the trap, I lifted the door to allow the animal to move from trap to crate. It took a long time to persuade it to do so, but eventually, with the encouragement of poles, it left the trap and, enclosed in the crate, was ready to take away.

Having decided not to let the villagers kill it, I now had to decide where to release it. I took the Land Rover by myself to uninhabited country south-west of Lake Keilak where the leopard would be unlikely to encounter men, except perhaps a few nomads passing through with their herds. A leopard often ranges widely and its territory may cover seventy or eighty kilometres in any direction from its lair so it was impossible to ensure, unless I took it to the waterless desert, that it would never trouble men again. The other possibility was that, as leopards have strong territorial instincts, a young, incursive leopard released in the area might receive a very hostile reception from an incumbent; but it seemed to me that the odds were favourable and the animal would have a good opportunity to live to an old age here.

Letting it go was not too easy. I had to pull out the nails and cut the ropes holding one side of the crate, hoping as I did so that the leopard would not try to assist me before I could take refuge in the Land Rover's cab. But the animal, despite throaty, defiant growls and occasional strikes of its great paws, drew as far away from me as possible within the confinement of its prison. Finally, with only a single nail holding the slatted side in place, I ran to jump quickly into the cab. Opening the sliding perspex window at the rear of the cab, I pushed a stick through into the crate, trying to persuade the leopard to leave, but the animal only turned in fury to attack the stick.

Fortunately, just as I could see no way of removing the leopard short of driving up a very steep incline (there was none) to tip out the crate, the animal's furious movements at last knocked out the loose side and it was free. For a moment it persisted in facing me to attack the stick, then suddenly with a leap it was out and on the ground.

Crouching it eyed the Land Rover, long tail furiously beating the dusty ground into a cloud above it, and I thought it was about to spring at the vehicle. I put my head out of the side window and shouted, beating on the side of the car. With a harsh grunt in reply the leopard raced off towards some trees, its flashing brilliance blurred with speed, and in a second or two had merged with the brown grass stubble where I lost sight of it.

I waited a short time, but I did not see the leopard again.

The haunted jebel

While camped in the Moro Hills I went to watch a Nuba harvest festival, a *Sibr el Ma'rad*, that culminated in one of the big wrestling matches of the year with spectators gathering from miles around. The village was perched high on the *jebel*, each homestead built on a base of massive rocks carried and levered into position. Stone walls and terraces kept the thin soil from sliding down into the valley.

The *sibr* was a serious religious ceremony of considerable importance having many complicated observances of which I was ignorant, and the tribesmen were at first none too pleased at our arrival. However, we were recognised by one or two of the Nuba and no serious objection was made to our presence, nor did the *kujur* disapprove of my cine-camera, but we were warned not to smoke.

Tired from our climb Younis, Badr and I sat in the shade, for, as usual on these occasions, nothing happened for a while. At first I watched the colourful crowd. The wrestlers were simply dressed, their naked bodies with no more ornament than a collar of fibre, a goat's hair or leather belt sometimes sporting a kudu's or bull's tail or a bunch of feathers, or ivory or silver nose or earrings, but the majority of the crowd were armed with long throwing spears and often rectangular, square or round shields. I even saw one with a round, iron-embossed centre that if I had seen it in a museum I would have thought to be of Viking origin.

Many of the shields were constructed of wickerwork, however, with a metre-long bamboo thrust through the centre so that the complete shield resembled the paper sail and matchstick mast of a child's boat; others were of giraffe or cowhide, while one or two were made of *tebeldi* tree fibre plaited into a thick rope and then bound into a flat coil. Strangely, the Nuba have no knowledge of the bow, and I never saw a Nuba with a throwing stick (a kind of primitive boomerang called a *trombash* by the Arabs), although one visitor to my zoo had one, and this weapon is found in the Ingassana Hills and amongst the Fur. The Nuba's weapons include long throwing spears, shorter stabbing spears, clubs, sticks, knives, swords and guns, ancient matchlocks or early rifles obtained from the Arabs.

When the first Sudanese Governor of Kordofan visited the Nuba Mountains and I went with him to film some of the Independence celebrations, I was surprised at the number of guns produced in the Moslem villages. He visited Miri, which lies on a small flat plain surrounded by a circle of *jebels* like the walls of a fortress, where the villagers had waited since before dawn to greet him. Almost every male possessed a gun and during the march past an improvised dais, on which stood the Governor, the *Mek* and a few other officials, the people fired their guns into the air, or tried to since many refused to go off at the first attempt. Dressed in white *gibbas* reaching their ankles, waving flags, shouting greetings, the local sheiks and other richer, more important persons riding tiny Sudanese donkeys (an averaged sized man's feet trail in the dust) at the head of each detachment, the small army marched round in a continuous circle to make it appear to have unending numbers. Although the guns were presumably only primed with gunpowder and without bullets, they were fired so wildly and with such enthusiasm that a pall of

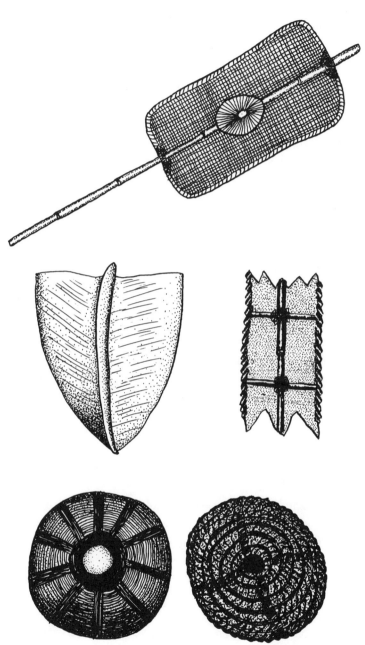

Types of Nuba shields

grey-blue smoke obscured the Governor and he seemed to be in imminent danger, until the circling white snake was persuaded to move to a safer distance. More intriguing, however, is the antique chain-mail still possessed by a few Baggara which is produced on such occasions. Presumably, this ancient armour is centuries old, perhaps originally worn by Crusaders.

The guns that the Arabs bartered with the Nuba, however, were seldom more than ornaments. I borrowed one from a nearby Nuba while waiting for the festival to start. Reluctant to part with it, he let me look while he hung on to the barrel. It had a chased silver butt and breech, now black, but was so rusted and pitted that it would have been impossible to fire.

After nearly two hours of waiting I grew tired of watching the crowd and wandered away to search some nearby bushes where I found a chamaeleon that suspiciously eyed me with one glinting eye as it swayed, tiptoeing with infinite slowness along a branch. The other eye swivelled in the hooded socket to look at a small brown-bordered, orange butterfly that weakly fluttered by before alighting on a leaf close by, but the left eye, like a drop of dark honey in a wrinkled acorn cup, remained pointed at me.

The butterfly, *Acraea terpischore*, by far the commonest of the genus in the Nuba Mountains (the yellowish-green larvae were often abundant feeding on the leaves of Sterculiaceae), shivered its wings without altering position, grateful for the warm heat of the sun that until now had been shielded by misty cloud. For long moments the brownish-green chamaeleon watched me with one eye and the butterfly with the other. But it must have been hungry, the dull weather having inhibited its heliolatrous insect prey and now, as I showed no threat, its left eye slowly swivelled to regard the butterfly; with two eyes on the insect it could judge both distance and direction.

The butterfly was just out of range. With painful slowness the chamaeleon lifted first one front foot, then one hind foot, both eyes in their cone sockets swivelling with little jerks, wary of danger. Its thin body having moved a few centimetres along the branch both eyes once more turned towards its prey. Slowly the thick grey tip of its tongue pushed open the jaws, as though blowing a bubble of chewing gum. Then as quickly as a taut piece of elastic suddenly released, twelve or thirteen centimetres of tongue shot forward to be as rapidly withdrawn, the hapless butterfly glued to the bulbous end. The weight and snap of the retracting tongue nearly rocked the chamaeleon from its perch, but the opposable fingers and toes had a firm grip, and the reptile's jaws started to champ.

As I watched, despite the seeming impossibility of expression on that reptilian face, somehow the chamaeleon conveyed to me its disgust. With rolling eyes and working jaws it gradually pushed the mangled butterfly forward until it was able to drop it to the ground. The butterfly was still alive but too injured to survive. Usually chamaeleons ignore Acraeid butterflies and similarly unpalatable insects, recognising that they are distasteful or poisonous, but this one, hungry and inexperienced or just foolish, was now suffering for its mistake. Even minutes later it still mumbled and rubbed its foreleg across its mouth, trying to be rid of the unpleasant taste.

I did not want to catch another of these chamaeleons since I had two already that I had kept for a year. As I walked away the reptile was swaying back and forth on the branch in further frustration, for a fly had settled on the end of its nose out of reach, yet presumably just visible to its upturned eyes.

Chamaeleons, called *herboyia* by the Baggara, *balo* by the Nuba, were not at all abundant in the Nuba Mountains, and I came upon one only occasionally. This kind, *Chamaeleo senegalensis laevigatus*, was in fact the only species I found in the Nuba Mountains proper, but another, *C. africanus*, was quite plentiful north of Dilling where it inhabited drier, less humid – indeed often very arid – regions. I took several *C. africanus* to Kadugli, but the climate seemed unsuitable for them there.

Younis called me, and we returned to the village in time to see a small group of tribesmen moving in a huddle across the plateau that was the village 'sportsfield'. Apart from the man I took to be the rain-maker or *kujur* only one other wore any clothing, a dirty stained *gibba* similar to that of the rain-maker. The naked tribesmen, all wrestlers, carried a huge clod of clay soil in the middle of which stood a single stem of *dura* or sorghum heavy with seed.

In the centre of the wrestling arena, an area of about a hectare, a large hole had been dug. Intact in the great lump of soil, the *dura* was carefully lowered by four or five men into this hole and ceremonially 'planted' as I filmed the process. The rain-maker muttered what were presumably prayers, to which the seven or eight naked wrestlers grunted a response. They ignored me entirely. Several of the men, including the rain-maker, carried gourds filled with wood-ash, and the ash was liberally sprinkled over the *dura* to lie thickly on and around it on the transported soil.

This ash represented rain and the rites, taken extremely seriously by the participants, although no other Nuba came near the lone group, lasted five minutes or more. The ceremony was a thanksgiving for the past harvest but also, more important, a prayer for rain and fertility the next year. A ring of similarly sized, whitened stones were placed in a circle around the plant and the rites were concluded. Before moving off, however, the wrestlers crouched to enable the robed men to sprinkle them liberally with the remainder of the wood-ash until the gourds were empty. With his hands each wrestler rubbed the grey powder over his own body until his gleaming black skin took on an unhealthy-looking, leprous appearance. The 'rain' would ensure his strength and fertility as for the crops.

Most Nuba religious rites are connected with fertility and strength, and the more important all involve tribal sporting events, usually wrestling or stick-fighting. It was the time for celebration, drinking, dancing and sports, the dry-season relaxation after harvest and before the soil must be prepared once again. The growing season, especially after sowing and before the setting of the crops, was a time of quiet, for then no singing or dancing, not even loud voices, must disturb the spirit of the grain in case the souls of the plants deserted or caused ill to fall on the people.

In many clans even the women wrestle, including those who have children, although pregnant women are barred and women wrestle only with each other, never with men. Only once did I witness women wrestling and then for a short time, since as the Nuba men are not supposed to watch women's sports I felt it was discourteous to do so. All the same I did see various youths at a distance pretending to be engaged in their own concerns but close enough covertly to watch their womenfolk.

Like the men, the women wrestlers were almost completely naked, but while there was no lack of enthusiasm the wrestling seemed to me to be altogether of a milder nature. Each combatant gripped the other round the waist, straining to throw her on the ground, or trying to catch one leg or trip her so that she would fall, but if a throw did not take place within a minute or so, the girls were separated by the closely observant referees.

After the planting of the magic *dura* there was another long hiatus, but at length a look-out posted on the hilltop signalled to the waiting tribesmen that the opposing team was coming. An imposing figure – the *mek* or chief – strode alone across the open arena wearing a decorated, red fez surmounted by a tall crane's feather. His waist was encircled by a variety of skins and even at that distance I could recognise colobus monkey fur, an animal unknown in the Nuba Mountains.

This was the signal for the tribesmen to surge forward in a body of several hundred, waving spears, shields and guns, to meet the newcomers, now within sight. The visitors were also armed and bunched together like an attacking force. As the two factions reached each other I almost expected a great clash of arms, but with only warlike shouting and strutting, the home tribesmen escorted the newcomers back towards the arena in a cloud of dust.

The visitors looked not only warlike but impressive as they marched to the beat of several drums and the wild, deep, eerie notes of the *toros,* or kudu horn trumpets. In the van loped four massively muscular, naked wrestlers with a peculiar dancing hop; behind them the *mek* and *kujur,* more wrestlers and the rabble of spearsmen, while the reddening rays of the sun, beginning to sink towards distant ragged *jebel* peaks, glinted on the rifles and spears and ringed the black bodies with fire.

But my eyes were held by the startling colossus who elephantinely pranced in front of the wrestling champions, his cicatrised body exceptionally large even for a Nuba. Cicatrisation marks, made by carefully nicking the skin, rubbing ash into the wounds or inserting small pebbles, are not simply for ornamentation. It is true that amongst women there is a belief that the scars enhance their beauty, but they are part of initiation ceremonies, an indication to the world that their owner has passed the physical ordeals demanded by society. In some clans, a certain pattern of cicatrisation indicates that the warrior has killed a leopard.

The brobdingnagian figure that now threatened to shake the earth as he led the visiting tribesmen to the wrestling ground looked powerful enough to make short work of any leopard even if he had not so far done so. However, he was not wrestling on this occasion despite the fact that he was one of the great champions. His role was simply to be the *tor,* or bull; like the *dura* that had been so carefully planted, he was a symbol of fertility, and while his body was partly clothed his genitals were deliberately exposed. His hugeness was further emphasised by the slit sheepskin over his shoulders, the coveted prize of a champion wrestler, and by the spreading ostrich feathers extending from the skins he wore. His legs were chalked with geometric designs and zebra stripes while his face was a startling mask of colours with fiery, inflamed eyes (whether from drink or purposely made sore I could not tell).

The wrestling began, the audience spreading itself in a large circle to limit the arena where the *tor* strode or leapt. In the middle the magic dura head stood, avoided by the stumbling wrestlers and the wild, spear-throwing onlookers who rushed to the centre to salute the victors.

In wrestling contests a great deal goes on at once; there are always several pairs wrestling, marshals using sticks or whips to keep the crowd at bay, other wrestlers, prancing, boasting of their skill and strength, while various non-participants wander about in the arena. One Homeric struggle took place just in front of me. It started with the two wrestlers, hands on knees, staring at each other implacably face to face. Suddenly one grabbed the other and they locked together, staggering this way and that. They fell amongst the people near me who pushed them back into the ring. Breaking loose, they furiously began to slap each other with open palms. Blows with fists, or grips on salient features such as the ears or nose, gouging and so on are fouls and I did not see any such behaviour. Coming to grips again, one wrestler attacked with such fury that he drove the other back, obtained a hold on one leg, hoisted his rival into the air almost at full arm's stretch, and then hurled him to the ground.

I expected the fallen youth at best to be stunned on the hard, beaten earth. There was a rush forward of tribesmen around me as they saluted the victor, hurling their spears into the ground dangerously near the prone wrestler. But the boy rose, seemingly none the worse, and, crestfallen, walked away. I saw an evenly matched pair separated by a referee, and one wrestler challenging another who danced slowly backwards, indicating refusal. The youth who had been challenged was a novice, so no stigma was attached to the refusal.

A whirlwind fight took place near me; for some minutes the wrestling pair staggered about until by mutual agreement, they separated to wipe their sweating palms on the sand before closing again. One was thrown over backwards to land on neck and shoulders. The victor, triumphant, threw up his arms, springing in the air to the plaudits of the section of the crowd near him. A thin man came up and without warning lashed the exultant wrestler twice across the chest with his whip, causing him to wince but not cry out. Unexpected blows after victory were made not in anger, but deliberately, to 'give strength'.

Such wrestling tournaments are tough, but Nuba boys begin to learn to wrestle almost from the time they can walk. Wrestling

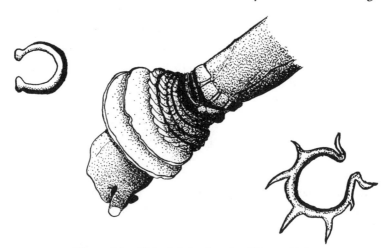

Silver anklet; Nuba fighting bracelet, Wetu spiked fighting bracelet, Bahr el Ghazal

is a childish activity compared with the contests with quarter-staves, used like sabres, and spear fighting; but the toughest and bloodiest sport is undoubtedly bracelet fighting.

Fighting bracelets are found amongst other tribes; the now extinct or near extinct Mittu (Wetu) of the Bahr el Ghazal have or had an iron wrist bracelet with projecting spikes. The Mittu is only one of many tribes in the southern Sudan destroyed or absorbed, or reduced to a few hundred, crushed between the slave-making Arabs to the north and the invading Azande to the south. Only about a quarter of the Azande, a Bantu tribe of short, squat people with broad noses and thick lips, live in the Sudan, the rest dwelling across the borders. As unlike the Nilotic people in physique and habits as hyaenas are to cheetahs, the Azande are called Nyam-nyam by the Arabs, an expressive onomatopoeic name for these cannibals who undoubtedly ate hundreds of defeated Mittu. The Acholi, still numerous in the Sudan, and another Nilotic tribe, the Lango of Uganda, are other tribes that have fighting bracelets, but I have only seen the Nuba use them.

Amongst the Nuba, bracelet fighting is found only in the Fungor, Niaro and Kau Hills, an isolated group of *jebels* situated in a vast grass plain about thirty kilometres due west of Kaka on the Nile. The Nuba here are primitive, adhering to their own customs and eschewing the Moslem faith despite being in the midst of Arab country and under the nominal rule of the Awlad Hemeid Baggara tribe, itself part of Tegele. I twice witnessed the annual bracelet fighting festival.

Like other contests, bracelet fighting is a graduation ceremony, and it is necessary for a young man to prove himself as a *suar*, or bracelet fighter, before he can marry. The bracelet itself is a heavy, solid brass, three-quarter circle clipped loosely on one wrist. Two flanges, sharp, rough-edged and about five centimetres deep, run round the base to project from it. The weapon resembles a miniature motor-car wheel with a section cut from it and without a tyre. Such a bracelet, used with skill and force, can kill a man at a blow, and the 'sport' is an all-male affair, no woman being allowed to watch.

The future of the young men depends on their behaviour and courage at the festival. Winning is not important, although naturally a victorious *suar* is highly regarded. Living for this moment during the first seventeen or twenty years of their lives, an event on which their status and marriage depends, it is little wonder that a would-be *suar* is as nervous of his honour and as captious as any French duellist of the seventeenth century. It surprises me that tempers are not lost more often; only a few years before I saw this event fighting broke out leading to open warfare between two of the settlements and resulting in some twenty deaths.

Nuba ceremonies, like most affairs in Africa, are not absolute fixtures, but are variable; they may not even occur in the same month each year. They depend on the moon, the omens, the *kujur,* the state of the crops and other imponderables; it is by no means easy for a stranger to know when the festival is going to take place, but on this occasion I arrived on the right day. The Nuba were in no hurry, however, and it was two or three hours before the first fight began.

Perhaps two to three hundred men were present, including Arab representatives of the Sheik of Tegele. Many of the fiercest and most savage-looking youths were not due to fight that day; their time was to come next year or the year after, but as we waited I studied them.

Many had painted their bodies with stripes, bars and spots of white clay usually in a chevron or angular pattern. Painted faces lent many a sinister air. One, for example, had a painted black and white symmetrical design converging on his nose and mouth which were left unadorned, while a fringe of buff-coloured goat's hair stretched as a false beard from ear to ear and on his head he wore the black, velvety pompom (the soft, pubescent, fur-like scalp feathers) taken from a crested crane. Such pompoms were worn by many. Another youth was noticeable for his face that had been first whitened and then carefully painted with black ladders of varying lengths like those of a snakes and ladders board. Yet another possessed a fine brass bell of the sort used to call servants to the dinner table, the top fastened to and hidden in his ball of black hair, the base rim and clapper exposed at the back of his head, the rest of his hair shaven to leave only this topknot. Like many others he wore a dagger or ceremonial throwing knife, called an *arnger,* probably made by an Arab smith, in a skin sheath strapped just above the elbow. The *arnger* is very popular and conveniently carried where it can be drawn by the right hand.

I was interested to see that several youths displayed old coins. One boy, startlingly blackened from scalp to toes with charcoal and sporting a small mirror on his buttocks, wore a necklace of blue beads from which was suspended a square leather holder containing a large silver rupee which, in cash value, must have been worth more than all his possessions put together. I saw several ancient silver coins displayed, even one gold one, but so rubbed that I had no idea what they represented. One silver coin must have measured about seven centimetres in diameter.

Unlike many other clans equally primitive, or more so, which have adopted the custom from the Arabs, the Nuba of the hills were uncircumcised, yet almost all of them wore Arabic charms. While still holding to their own beliefs, like most peoples con-

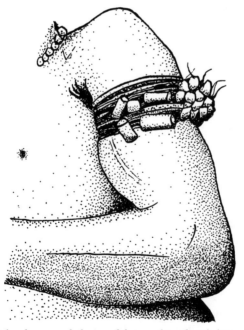

Nuba charms and cluster of *dom* nut kernels, Jebel Fungor

fronted by a more powerful, more sophisticated and in some respects more civilised race, they saw no harm in propitiating the powerful spirits of the Arabs. Several Nuba wore clusters of square or barrel-shaped leather charm-holders often together with a bunch of *dom* nut kernels fastened to arms that then resembled black branches covered with oak-apple galls. The kernel of the *dom* nut is so hard that it can be carved like ivory, but it is not as good as ivory from the true ivory nuts, *Phytelephas*, a genus of central American palms, and naturally no vegetable ivory compares with animal ivory.

The nails of some youths were reddened with *henna*, also an Arab custom, while several smoked wooden or clay pipes, similar to those used by the Nilotics of the great river.

The bracelet fighting arena lay near the rocky feet of the *jebels* where grew a tangle of *dom* palm and *tebeldi* dominated vegetation; close to the arena grew more leafless baobabs, great trunks that loomed in groups from the level, sandy ground, an impressive setting for the gladiatorial contests about to begin on the sun-bleached ground beyond.

The charcoaled or zebra-striped tribesmen, who were not potential *suar* this season, gave way to a number arriving from another settlement in the hills and to their own candidates. Men from the same village were not usually matched, so the youths from the nearby hamlet had one longitudinal half of the body yellowed with a paste made from dry cow's dung to distinguish them. It gave the effect of a Red Indian cleft down the middle and joined to half a black man similarly split. The local competitors retained their own skin colour but were heavily oiled.

The contestants had been chosen a year previously when a marathon had been run, a course of some fifteen kilometres up and down the wild hillsides, only the firstcomers qualifying as undergraduate *suar*. A few days after the day's bracelet contests another marathon would be run to choose the contestants for next year. At the time of this marathon the youths usually know the

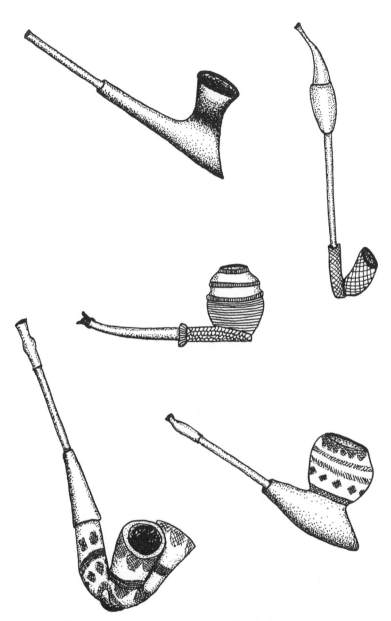

Some tobacco pipes seen in the region. *Top left:* Kau Nuba wooden pipe smoked by men and women; *bottom left:* Shilluk double pipe of clay with brass and bamboo stem; *others:* Nuer and Dinka pipes

girls they will marry, so the 'choosing' of a virgin by the *suar* at the feast that takes place after the bracelet contests are over is preordained, and Nuba people of all clans seldom marry except by parental consent and for mutual love.

The first pair of naked fighters went into the arena together with two referees, similarly unclad, each holding two sticks. The two contestants began their fight with metre-long poles, as for a normal stick-fight, but their sabre-like blows were not fierce, simply a warming up before the real duel. Soon the quarter-staves were tossed aside. Each faced the other, right arm with the bracelet raised but bent at the elbow, left arm outstretched as in a Fascist salute, the palm flat.

The blows from the bracelet have to be downwards or swinging, directed at the head, shoulders or chest but not lower; the flat-palmed hand is used to try and shield the head from a bracelet cut. The youths circled, looking for an opening, then one leant forward, knocking the braceleted arm of his opponent to one side with his free hand while aiming a downward blow with his bracelet. The other, dodging back, received the knock on his chest, severe enough to make the blood flow. But he recovered and struck back hitting the first man in the mouth to cut lip and chin and, as I saw afterwards, to dislodge three teeth. The first man, in pain and fury, attacked to kill, but the referees both caught him, dragging him away after an argument that took them dancing and hopping around the arena.

This was the only serious display of temper I saw. The other fights took place and some severe wounds were inflicted, but no fighter received any crippling injury. In a week or two the hurts would be forgotten. One fighter I noticed was left-handed, but I did not see how he managed against his right-handed opponent, since at the crucial time I became fascinated by a *suar* with startlingly red hair and a necklace of hippo teeth; his tight curls presented such a smooth appearance that I thought at first he was wearing a cap, but then I realised his hair had been dyed.

The fighting over, a feast and celebration followed that night in the nearby *jebel* village, and from my camp where I had retired for a meal I could hear the occasional awe-inspiring howl of one of the *suar*, a long-drawn-out cry that reverberated through the hills and would have put any wolf to shame, being unlike any human sound that I had ever heard. This call, made by the *suar* as he arches his back and holds one hand before his mouth before howling with all the force of powerful lungs while swinging his tensed body around on his toes, is a triumphant mating cry expressing his very soul.

I climbed to the settlement in the *jebel* above the arena and my camp in time to see the virgins arrive, giggling and herded together, their naked bodies glistening with oil. They wore silver anklets, silver rings on wrist or arm, and sometimes beads or a small square of *suc-suc*, parts of their bodies painted in bright blue, yellow, red or crimson patterns, and looked most alluring in the light of flickering fire-flames under the cold starlight. Soon the *suar* of the day gathered with more ear-piercing yells and boastful strutting, impetuously leaping in front of the girls to fling spears into the ground at their feet and fire rifles in the air over their heads, raising fearful screams from their prospective brides, as in mock horror they cowered before their tempestuous suitors. Despite every appearance of an orgy of rape and pillage, however, these were simply ritual courtship manners, as meaningful but almost as seemly as the bestowing of a ring in European society, if a good deal noisier. There was no contact between youth and maiden until a *suar* took the girl of his choice by the hand to lead her away.

Some time after my second visit to the Nuba of Fungor I passed through their hills again for the last time on my way from Kaka to Jebel Eliri. Had I not seen the tribesmen previously and watched their savage fighting I would have thought the silent hills deserted, for their villages cannot be seen from the motor track and only baboons occupied the *tebeldi* studded foothills. Heading almost due west through the Tira Hills we came to Jebel Gedir, where we camped for the night.

Jebel Gedir, where the Mahdi retired after his first victory on Aba Island in the Nile in 1881 when his motley supporters decimated some two hundred soldiers from the steamer sent to capture him, is remote and almost inaccessible, about a hundred and thirty kilometres almost due west of Kaka and a hundred kilometres north-east of Eliri.

Ahmed had prepared an evening meal. I sat down to eat and read my book by the light of the electric lamp powered by the car battery. Then, like a rising wind, came a sound that I had never heard by night before; the strange, dry rattling of a million insect wings.

I went outside my tent and looked up. Flying over the pale face of the moon, almost obscuring it, moved an unending stream of small, elongate shapes. It was exactly forty-seven minutes before the last stragglers of the locust swarm passed and their sounds died away.

As locust swarms occur, when a swarm means fifty to a hundred million and a plague consists of hundreds of such swarms, this was not even a crowd. Nobody who has not been in an upsurge of flying locusts or a swarm of dioch birds can have any conception of these most extreme examples of nature's fecundity. Other animals sometimes multiply as greatly, but on land or in water there is not the same encompassing visual impact, and locusts have the same inevitability, and almost as great a power and devastation potential as an errupting volcano. But unlike a volcano, locusts may spread over two thousand kilometres.

Fortunately today organisations, often international in concept, efficiently control the major locusts (the desert, the migratory, the red and the brown locusts) of Africa, but the power of the locust is still latent, still potentially as awesome as at the time of the plagues of Egypt.

For a few moments I stared up at the mass of insects all flying from east to west, and then I fetched my twelve-bore. I wanted to obtain some specimens to discover what kind they were. Pointing the gun straight upwards I pulled the trigger; immediately I was showered by locusts, each six or seven centimetres in length, in such numbers that I picked up fifteen or twenty from my clothing or at my feet, feeling amazed at the result of shot intended to kill a large bird.

It was the tree-locust, *Anacridium wernerellum*, passing overhead, a large grasshopper with migratory tendencies (which is all any 'locust' is). Normally, the tree-locust does not form very large swarms, and this was certainly the biggest I had ever experienced. The Arabs call this locust 'the night wanderer' (*dar el lel*) because of its nocturnal habits. It breeds in the rainy season, producing a single generation a year, and feeds mainly on small trees such as *Acacia*, *Zizyphus*, etc, hence the English name. It does sometimes attack grain crops and cotton, however. The female lays her eggs in the ground, the pod containing, according to my counts, between one and two hundred eggs, and three such pods may be laid by each fertile female.

The next morning I went with Younis to look at the Mahdi's hideout, a small cave where he spent about a year. It was easily found for it was still a place of pilgrimage for the few who passed that way. The cave was but a cleft in the rocks high on the *jebel*, but it gave an uninterrupted view of the surrounding countryside. In front of the cave was a rock with two rounded impressions, said to be left by the Mahdi's knees where he habitually knelt to pray, but when I looked elsewhere I found similar moulds, the result, of course, of water erosion. On the way down I saw several trees, each with a stone in its first fork, a common sight in the Nuba Mountains where it is a custom to put a stone in such a position for luck when on a journey. I added my own stone.

After spending a day examining cotton plants in the neighbour-hood of Eliri, the main purpose of my visit, I returned to the village the next morning. Before returning to Kadugli via Talodi, I wanted to fulfil an ambition to climb the *jebel* that towers above the village, a small community with a police-post and a medical dispensary. The settlement is an Arabicised one, the people are largely a mixture of Eliri, Lafofa and Arab elements, although other villages in the extensive hill ranges of the immediate area remain essentially Nuba.

I begun my preparations for the ascent. I hoped to obtain bats, so I took my .22 pistol and bat-net. It was one of the few areas where I believed green mambas to exist, since I had glimpsed one some time before on the thickly wooded slopes, so I carried a couple of cotton bags with drawstring openings. Insect tubes, knife, pooter, trowel, large water thermos and some food com-pleted our equipment.

Full of curiosity, a small crowd had gathered around our vehicle. When they heard we intended to climb Jebel Eliri the people were suddenly silent, some of them hurrying away, but a few men began to talk to Younis shaking their heads and gesticulating towards the mountain. Two approached me, the sheik and the medical assistant, the latter a Sudani from the north who spoke good English. 'If you were to climb that *jebel*,' he said, 'it would be too dangerous; nobody can climb it.'

I looked at the grave faces of the two men, obviously sincere and perturbed. 'It does not look difficult,' I said. 'Anyway, I do not need to climb to the top; I am going to look for animals and there must be paths on the hills.'

'There is a path, but it is easy to be lost. Do not go, *Jenabak*. It is an evil place.'

Asking me to drink coffee, the medical assistant, the sheik and one or two others continued to try and persuade me not to venture up the *jebel*. I was puzzled by their insistence; almost any large uninhabited *jebel* is believed to have guardian spirits jealous to keep people away. Local people, however, while they might not dream of going near themselves, usually paid little heed to crazy foreigners who had special protection anyway.

One lofty *jebel* near Kadugli, for example, was said to possess *djinns* in the form of great eagles that attacked any human trespassers. Legend had it there was a cave near the summit; if a man escaped the eagles and entered the cave there was a narrow passage inside leading to a marvellous land of lush meadows and fat cattle, a Shangri-la.

It was said that only one or two men had ever found the way into this cave and the land beyond, and they had never returned. I explored this *jebel* several times, and was surprised to find at the summit signs of past habitation, so it had not always been deserted; I was just as interested to find a huge cliff face falling almost sheer for some hundreds of feet in which, about halfway down, was apparently a cave opening just as described. Twice I tried to reach this cave, but being no mountaineer and without long enough ropes I failed. Fan-tailed ravens and the red-tailed buzzard, sometimes called the jackal or augur buzzard, nested on the cliff, some birds always present, and occasionally the great black shape of an eagle circled overhead with a gull-like yelping cry, a bird I also saw once or twice darkly brooding on a spur of rock. This was Verreaux's eagle, very much of flesh and blood, but no doubt at least partly responsible for the legend. If anybody really had reached this cave and failed to return, their bones probably lay hidden in the dense vegetation in the inaccessible valley below the cliff.

I drank the muddy coffee, treacly with coarse, sandy sugar, as quickly as possible for I wanted to start the climb while the morning was still young. But the villagers were reluctant to let me go.

'There are evil spirits on the *jebel, Jenabak*, very jealous ones. Not even we can go there, and they hate all foreigners. If you were to go, you would die. Once, long ago, came two officer soldiers and wanted to climb the mountain, taking guns. Before they had gone far one was shot dead by accident. The other brought him down, but became sick and died too. They are both buried here. Other people have died too. A missionary from Tonga came. He climbed, but when he returned to his horse to ride away a *majnun* [madman] killed him with a spear.'

Another man said, 'These are not the only ones to die. There was a snake killed one, a leopard another. All die who trespass on the *jebel*.'

'Well,' I said, 'we are going now and we will take care. *Inshalla*, we shall not die.'

'Let us show you the graves of the dead soldiers, then you will believe,' said the medical assistant. I was curious enough to go with them to look at the graves which were there without doubt, but, of course, I did not change my mind.

'At least leave all guns behind, *Jenabak*,' pleaded the sheik. I told him I was taking only my pistol. After these stories, Badr and Ahmed had no desire to come, so I left them with the Land Rover; Younis went with me, reluctantly, more worried for me than for himself, for the spirits of the mountains hated foreigners much more than Sudanis.

The climb was easy enough, the path at first distinct. 'Plenty of people come here, Younis, despite what they say,' I said as we paused for breath. 'Yes, Doktor. But this is the path to other villages.' He waved his hand. 'They do not go up further.'

Below I could see Eliri settlement with a small crowd of tiny figures staring up. Ahead, forbiddingly, rose the great slabs of granite clothed with vegetation at lower levels, but nearer the summit they were bare and grey-glinting in the sunlight. I thought perhaps people did not want us to climb the mountain because of the *kujur* or rain-maker; perhaps there was a sacred shrine here or some taboo place. There were many such in the Nuba Mountains, ground strictly forbidden to all but the *kujur* and his assistants. But I thought of the medical assistant; he was not a Nuba and the other men I had spoken to were all Muslims not

likely to be in particular awe of a Nuba *kujur*. Then I forgot about
the people below as we climbed again and I began to look about
me. It was true about the paths; they crossed the side of the *jebel*
but did not ascend far.

Making our own path upwards, climbing became steadily
steeper. After about three-quarters of an hour we almost reached
what appeared to be the summit. To our left were huge, bare rock
faces and the entrance to a cave. Edging our way across we
reached the cave. I sat for a moment on a rock, precipitous
ground at my feet, while above me Younis sat on another boulder
outside the cave. There were bound to be bats, and I took my
pistol from my belt to load it.

This single-shot pistol had been given to me by J. S. Owen,
once District Commissioner, Torit; where he had obtained it I
do not know, but it was an ancient firearm with a long barrel and
no safety-catch. In theory it had to be cocked before it could be
fired but in practice, if it were loaded, a jolt could set it off. For
this reason I kept it unloaded until it was actually required, which
was very seldom. I had a few solid .22 bullets but most of those I
had were 'dust-shot', a few hundred small pieces of lead in the
nose designed to spread after firing and used to shoot such
creatures as bats and rodents, so that they could be collected
without serious damage.

Just after I loaded the pistol, somehow it slipped from my
grasp to bounce down the rocks in front of me. As it struck the
first rock the gun went off. I had taken off my shirt to let the sun
dry the perspiration after our climb; the bullet, at close range,
entered my stomach on the right-hand side just below my ribs,
and the blood began to pour out of the inch-long wound. Younis
slithered down to me.

'*Wallahi*, are you hurt, Doktor?' he said. I had not felt much
pain, but the blood flowed so copiously that already it had turned
a slab of rock bright red and was beginning to drip to the next.
'I don't think it's serious, Younis,' I said hopefully, trying to stem

the blood flow with my hand. 'Tear up my shirt, will you, and tie it round the wound.'

Younis had retrieved the pistol. Now he tore my shirt to strips and bound it tightly round my waist. It rapidly turned red, but little more blood dropped. I could not believe that the small pellets had penetrated far and thought only a bit of skin and muscle had been torn. In fact, as I discovered later, the discharge at such short range had had considerable velocity; the lead shot had entered almost as one solid bullet and penetrated six centimetres or so. Fortunately for me, however, the gun had been pointing upwards and not inwards, so the pellets had not damaged my stomach or lungs. Naturally, I did not know this, but as I did not think the wound was critical, I still wanted to explore the cave having come so far.

Younis was horrified, and insisted that we go down the mountain at once. On reflection, I knew he was right. As it was, it took us much longer to return than to reach the cave, for the blood began to spurt again and Younis had to help me over the rougher slopes.

At the settlement again the people said, 'We told you so, *Jenabak*. but, *al hamdu li-llahi* [Praise to God] you are still alive.' The medical assistant was extremely competent, but worried. I told him I had no intention of staying but would drive back to Kadugli, a hundred and seventy kilometres, that day.

'Go only to Talodi, sir. Do not go all the way to Kadugli.'

'You were fortunate, *Jenabak*,' said an old man, 'the spirits were kind to you; you must like our country or they would not have been so kind.'

'I may stop in Talodi,' I told the medical assistant, but I knew I would not. There was a hospital there but no doctor, while at Kadugli a Sudanese doctor had recently arrived after the township had been without one for months. In any case I wanted to get home.

Younis wanted to drive, but I felt more secure holding the

steering wheel. The medical assistant had disinfected and tightly bound my wound. With cries of '*Allah yusallim-ak*' and '*Ibshir bil kheir*' (God keep you), we set off. Six hours later, well after dark, we arrived back in Kadugli. Faint and exhausted, I went to bed.

When I woke the next morning Younis was waiting with Ahmed and Badr. 'You must go to the *hakim* at once,' they said severely, and so to the doctor I went. With a local anaesthetic, that wore off halfway through, the doctor probed and probed my wound with a pair of forceps for an hour or more, searching for every small fragment of lead. Finally, he was satisfied. 'You're very lucky to be alive,' he said, 'a slightly different angle with infected lead rupturing the peritoneum and I could have done nothing.' The wound healed cleanly and he removed the stitches some weeks later.

I was very anxious to return to Jebel Eliri again, not only to look for bats and snakes, but to show the people that there was no truth in their legend. However, there was no opportunity and a few months later I left the Sudan. I could have stayed to work in the Gezira, but the authorities would not let me return to the *jebels* for after independence the policy was not to allow expatriates to return to their old stations. But I did not want to stay in the Gezira or the north, so much less interesting than the south, so instead I decided to find a job elsewhere in Africa. No doubt Jebel Eliri is still as haunted as ever.

I was very sad to leave the Sudan; despite the few difficulties of one sort of another, it was and still is my favourite African country, and the Sudanese the people I like the best. When I left the *jebels*, the townsfolk held a farewell party. I was the last Britisher to go. Although there were many flattering speeches and presents, I valued most the presents left anonymously in my car not for the nature of the gifts, but because they had been put there (as I learnt accidentally) by a Sudanese with whom I had a serious dispute about the price of bricks I had bought from him; a man who had refused to speak to me for months but who, when he heard I was leaving, came and wished me God Speed before secretly leaving his gifts.

Almost nine months later I was in the Sudan again, but only stopping over at Khartoum before flying on to Nairobi and Nyasaland where I had been sent by the Colonial Research Service. I took the opportunity of visiting Khartoum zoo. All the senior staff had changed; I could not recognise any of the animals I had sent them except one. Perhaps they had been exchanged with other zoos. I thought the big python was probably one of mine, but I could not be sure. But Tik, the hyaena, was there, grown bigger and heavier. I called him, and as he came immediately to be stroked and petted, I would like to think he remembered me.